Praise for *10 Virtues of Outstanding Lea*

"*10 Virtues of Outstanding Leaders* is an extraordinarily insightful, compelling, and timely discussion of the very foundation of leadership – the character of leaders. Al Gini and Ronald Green powerfully and persuasively make the case that it's imperative for leaders to be attuned to their ethical responsibility to others. And they are right. All the programs to develop leaders, all the courses and classes, all the books and tapes, all the blogs and websites offering tips and techniques are meaningless unless the people who are supposed to follow believe in the person who's supposed to lead. In an era in which it often seems that anything goes, it's vital that every leader and every leadership educator take Gini's and Green's message to heart. It's vital not only for their personal success, it's vital for the long-term viability of our society. *10 Virtues of Outstanding Leaders* is a must read, and I urge you to get started immediately."

—**Jim Kouzes**, coauthor of the bestselling *The Leadership Challenge* and Dean's Executive Fellow of Leadership, Leavey School of Business, Santa Clara University

"*10 Virtues of Outstanding Leaders* is a thoughtful and thorough exploration of that knottiest of all leadership questions – what constitutes 'good' leadership? Gini and Green have been wrestling with related issues for years, and it shows. The book is a valuable contribution to the never-ending discussion of what it takes to lead wisely and well."

—**Barbara Kellerman**, Harvard Kennedy School, and author and editor of many books on leadership and followership including, most recently, *The End of Leadership* and *Leadership: Essential Selections on Power, Authority, and Influence*

"Few leadership books mine the field of philosophy for its practical knowledge. Few use the treasury of insights available in the writings of philosophers that speak to issues of character and ethics, ones that are critical for successful leadership. Fewer still apply those insights to living examples of leadership: Abraham Lincoln, Winston Churchill, and Steve Jobs. In their new book, *10 Virtues of Outstanding Leaders*, the philosophers Gini and Green do all this, and more."

—**Thomas Donaldson, Mark O. Winkelman Professor**, The Wharton School of the University of Pennsylvania, Director of the Zicklin Center for Business Ethics Research, and coauthor of *Ties that Bind: A Social Contracts Approach to Business Ethics*

Foundations of Business Ethics
Series editors: W. Michael Hoffman and Robert E. Frederick

Written by an assembly of the most distinguished figures in business ethics, the Foundations of Business Ethics series aims to explain and assess the fundamental issues that motivate interest in each of the main subjects of contemporary research. In addition to a general introduction to business ethics, individual volumes cover key ethical issues in management, marketing, finance, accounting, and computing. The books, which are complementary yet complete in themselves, allow instructors maximum flexibility in the design and presentation of course materials without sacrificing either depth of coverage or the discipline-based focus of many business courses. The volumes can be used separately or in combination with anthologies and case studies, depending on the needs and interests of the instructors and students.

1 John R. Boatright, *Ethics in Finance*, second edition
2 Ronald Duska, Brenda Shay Duska, and Julie Ragatz,
   Accounting Ethics, second edition
3 Richard T. De George, *The Ethics of Information Technology and Business*
4 Patricia H. Werhane and Tara J. Radin with Norman E. Bowie,
   Employment and Employee Rights
5 Norman E. Bowie with Patricia H. Werhane, *Management Ethics*
6 Lisa H. Newton, *Business Ethics and the Natural Environment*
7 Kenneth E. Goodpaster, *Conscience and Corporate Culture*
8 George G. Brenkert, *Marketing Ethics*
9 Al Gini and Ronald M. Green,
   10 Virtues of Outstanding Leaders: Leadership and Character

Forthcoming

Denis Arnold, *Ethics of Global Business*

AL GINI AND RONALD M. GREEN

10
VIRTUES OF
OUTSTANDING
LEADERS

LEADERSHIP & CHARACTER

WILEY-BLACKWELL

A John Wiley & Sons, Ltd., Publication

This edition first published 2013
© 2013 John Wiley & Sons, Inc.

Wiley-Blackwell is an imprint of John Wiley & Sons, formed by the merger of Wiley's global Scientific, Technical and Medical business with Blackwell Publishing.

Registered Office
John Wiley & Sons Ltd, The Atrium, Southern Gate, Chichester, West Sussex, PO19 8SQ, UK

Editorial Offices
350 Main Street, Malden, MA 02148-5020, USA
9600 Garsington Road, Oxford, OX4 2DQ, UK
The Atrium, Southern Gate, Chichester, West Sussex, PO19 8SQ, UK

For details of our global editorial offices, for customer services, and for information about how to apply for permission to reuse the copyright material in this book please see our website at www.wiley.com/wiley-blackwell.

The right of Al Gini and Ronald M. Green to be identified as the authors of this work has been asserted in accordance with the UK Copyright, Designs and Patents Act 1988.

Library of Congress Cataloging-in-Publication Data
Gini, Al, 1944–
　10 virtues of outstanding leaders : leadership and character / Al Gini, Ronald M. Green.
　　　pages cm. – (Foundations of business ethics)
　Includes bibliographical references and index.
　ISBN 978-0-470-67231-0 (pbk. : alk. paper) – ISBN 978-0-470-67230-3 (cloth : alk. paper)
1. Leadership. 2. Character. 3. Business ethics. I. Green, Ronald Michael. II. Title.
　HD57.7.G555　2013
　658.4'092–dc23

2012050365

A catalogue record for this book is available from the British Library.

Cover design by www.simonlevyassociates.co.uk

Set in 10.5/12.5 pt Minion by Toppan Best-set Premedia Limited
Printed in Malaysia by Ho Printing (M) Sdn Bhd

1　2013

To our supportive wives:
Sherry L. Gini
Mary Jean Green

CONTENTS

ABOUT THE AUTHORS

Al Gini is Professor of Business Ethics at Loyola University Chicago, USA, where he is also Chair of the Department of Management in the Quinlan School of Business. A co-founder and long-time associate editor of *Business Ethics Quarterly*, the journal of the Society for Business Ethics, Professor Gini has for 25 years been the resident philosopher on the NPR affiliate in Chicago, WBEZ-FM, and is a regular speaker on the public lecture circuit. His books include *The Ethics of Business* (2012), which he coauthored with Alexei Marcoux; *Seeking the Truth of Things* (2010); *Why It's Hard to Be Good* (2006); and *The Importance of Being Lazy: In Praise of Play, Leisure, and Vacation* (2003).

Ronald M. Green is Eunice & Julian Cohen Professor for the Study of Ethics and Human Values at Dartmouth College, USA. He served as the director of Dartmouth's Ethics Institute from 1992 until 2011. Professor Green is actively involved in numerous fields of applied ethics, particularly bioethics and business ethics, and is a consultant to a number of leading corporations including Ogilvy & Mather. A former director of the National Institutes of Health's National Human Genome Research Institute, Professor Green has also been a member of the NIH's Human Embryo Research Panel. He was awarded a Guggenheim Fellowship in 2005. Professor Green's many publications include *The Ethical Manager* (1993) and *Babies by Design* (2007).

PROLOGUE

We need heroes (leaders), people who can inspire us, help shape us morally, spur us on to purposeful action . . .

Robert Coles[1]

As a species we are fascinated and often preoccupied by the concept of leadership and the conduct of individual leaders. But, while leaders enthrall us, we are uneasy in regard to our relationship to them. We alternately love them, hate them, like them, loathe them, desire them, despise them, seek them out, and shun them. Yet, despite our confusion, our desire for leaders is unending. Like in the pursuit of the Holy Grail, we are ineluctably drawn to them. We are constantly in search of the latest candidate for fame, the newest model off the assembly line, the next great hope.

Anthropologist Joseph Campbell argues that all cultures, all societies, and, by extension, all organizations (political or otherwise) are engaged in a "hero quest." All cultures search for a unique, larger-than-life, gifted person or for a singular idea, belief, or iconic symbol that helps to organize, explain, and give meaning, purpose, and direction to life. Campbell believes that the "hero quest" is in effect a "leadership quest." The hero, like the leader, imposes order, offers a moral compass, and defines and directs the geography of life for everyone. For Campbell, leadership and the quest for a leader are anthropological constants, necessary conditions for collective/communal existence.[2] According to Barbara Kellerman of the Center for Public Leadership at Harvard's Kennedy School of Government, putting aside the notion of type (democratic or despotic) and effectiveness (successful or unsuccessful) of a particular leader, our collective fascination with and pursuit of a champion on a white horse are part of who we are.[3] We want, need, and seek out leadership.

The last twenty years have seen the emergence of new, empirically based studies of leadership that make a powerful contribution to our understanding of the role that ethics plays in organizational life. These studies seek to document the relationship between "stated ethical values," "specific leader conduct and behavior," the "specific leader-level outcomes" of that behavior, and its "long and short term impact" on leaders and followers alike.[4] Perhaps the most influential and highly acclaimed example of this genre is James M. Kouzes and Barry Z. Posner's bestseller *The Leadership Challenge* (over 1.8 million copies sold). The authors are committed to the proposition that leadership is not primarily about personality but about specific kinds of behavior.[5] Although each leader is a unique individual, Kouzes and Posner are convinced that there are shared patterns to the practice of leadership and that these practices can be learned.[6] Since 1983, the authors have conducted a series of surveys with over seventy-five thousand business and government workers and executives and asked them: "What specific values, personal traits, or characteristics do you look for and admire in a leader?" and "What do you most look for and admire in a leader, someone whose direction you would willingly follow?"[7]

The authors claim that the results of these surveys have been constant over time and consistent across countries, cultures, ethnicities, industries, and organizations, as well as across gender, education, and age groups. The vast majority of the individuals surveyed believe that, to create a following, the leader must be honest, forward-looking, inspiring, and competent.[8] The essence of their argument is straightforward and quantitatively supported. In all forms of organized life, in order for leaders to get extraordinary things done, they "must act," and they "ought to act" in an "exemplary" way, which in turn elicits and inspires "exemplary" behavior from those whom they lead.

Kouzes and Posner's studies show that much can be learned from continuing empirical research in leadership studies. But we believe that more needs to be done philosophically as well. It is not enough to identify the values that people say they admire. It is also crucial to understand the moral basis of these values and the role that particular moral excellences (virtues) play in organizational life. This is the traditional task of philosophy. Thus students of leadership need to meditate on Socrates as well as on statistics. Quantitative work on leadership needs a kind of guidance and interpretation that is informed by a philosophical analysis of human values.

This book is a meant as a contribution to the literature on leadership. We come to the issue not from the perspective of social science, management, political theory, or organizational development. We are students of philosophy, and our primary area of interest is ethics. We are convinced that leadership is an ethical enterprise. We believe that leadership is a duty, an obligation, and a service to others. We believe that the ethics of leaders establishes the ethics, vision, and mission of those being led. We believe that leadership must also focus on the character of those who are being led and on others whom they affect. We agree with former CEO and author Max DePree: "The signs of outstanding leadership appear primarily among the followers. Are the followers reaching their potential?"[9]

Drawing on the research and writing of thinkers like James MacGregor Burns, Joseph Rost, Warren Bennis, Peter Drucker, Dietrich Bonhoeffer, and many others, we believe that the central working theses of this text can be expressed in the following manner.

- Ethical leadership is character driven. Character is about integrity, duty, and a social sense of responsibility.
- Ethical leaders exercise leadership in the interest of the common good.
- Ethical leaders put followers' needs before their own.
- Ethical leaders exemplify a set of moral virtues and related personal excellences.
- The greatest leaders are those whose lives display one or more of the key moral virtues.

In what follows we identify, ground, and illustrate in action what we believe are the chief virtues of leadership. While we recognize that there are many other excellences that can contribute to outstanding leadership, we offer 10 virtues that we feel are among the most important. These virtues are:

- deep honesty;
- moral courage;
- moral vision;
- compassion and care;
- fairness;
- intellectual excellence;
- creative thinking;
- aesthetic sensitivity;
- good timing;
- deep selflessness.

Leadership is one of the most written about topics, both in the professional literature (management studies, organizational development, political theory) and in the popular press in the twentieth century. According to Ralph Stogdill and Bernard Bass, there were more than 4,725 studies of leadership prior to 1981.[10] Recently, a staggering and almost unbelievable statistic generated by Amazon.com suggests that since 1989 more than twenty thousand books have been published with the word "leadership" in the title. Why, then, are we offering yet another book on the topic?

We believe we have two things to help refocus the leadership debate. The first is our insistence that ethics, character, and virtue are essential to real leadership; we call leadership without ethics *misleadership*. Valuable qualities like intelligence, charisma, charm, or influence, though good in themselves, can undermine organizational vitality and survival if they are employed without a foundation in ethical integrity and concern for others. This does not mean that outstanding leaders flaunt their commitment to ethics. Nor is ethical leadership the same thing as being "nice." Ethical leaders may sometimes have to exercise stern discipline and to subordinate some people's interests to the common good. But such leaders always act on principle, not on expediency, and their goal is one of common benefit.

Our second contribution is a focus on exemplary leaders who model the virtues of leadership. Aristotle, a founding figure of the discipline of ethics, argued that one does not learn ethics merely by reading a treatise on moral principles. Virtue is learned by witnessing the deeds of others. If character is essential to leadership, the best way to learn leadership is to study character. For Aristotle, the paragons of virtue are "excellent" persons who consistently conduct themselves with dignity and honor.

Hence, this is a book about characters *with character*. After several chapters that ground the importance of ethics in business and present the key virtues of outstanding leaders, we turn to those leaders themselves. As Aristotle argued, we need examples, the testimony of others, to understand how to form ourselves as leaders. In what follows, chapter by chapter, we depict individuals who in real-life situations act out the virtues that marked them as great leaders. Learning virtues is very much a matter of habit and imitation. By holding up these paragons of virtue, we aim to provide a useful tool for enhancing excellence in organizations.

Notes to Prologue

1   Robert Coles, *Lives of Moral Leadership: Men and Women Who Have Made a Difference*. New York: Random House, 2001, p. 1.
2   Joseph Campbell, *The Hero with a Thousand Faces*. Novato, CA: New World Library, 2008; Joseph Campbell and Bill Moyers, *The Power of Myth*. Harpswell, ME: Anchor Publishing, 1991.
3   Barbara Kellerman, *Bad Leadership*. Boston, MA: Harvard Business School Press, 2004, p. xiv.
4   For some of the leading empirical studies, see: Jim Collins, *Good to Great*. New York: HarperBusiness, 2001; Daniel Goleman, "Leadership That Gets Results." *Harvard Business Review*, March–April 2000: 78–90; N. M. Ashkanasy, C. A. Windsor, and L. K. Treviño, "Bad Apples in Bad Barrels Revisited: Cognitive Moral

Development, Just World Beliefs, Rewards, and Ethical Decision-Making." *Business Ethics Quarterly*, 16, 2006: 449–473; W. H. Bommer, R. S. Rubin, and T. T. Baldwin, "Setting the Stage for Effective Leadership: Antecedents of Transformational Leadership Behavior." *The Leadership Quarterly*, 15, 2004: 195–210; M. E. Brown, L. K. Treviño, and D. Harrison, "Ethical Leadership: A Social Learning Perspective for Construct Development and Testing." *Organizational Behavior and Human Decision Processes*, 97, 2005: 117–134; J. R. Detert, L. K. Treviño, E. R. Burris, and M. Andiappan, "Managerial Modes of Influence and Counterproductivity in Organizations: A Longitudinal Business-Unit-Level Investigation." *Journal of Applied Psychology* 92, 2007: 993–1005; E. C. Dierdorff and R. S. Rubin, "Carelessness and Discriminability in Work Role Requirement Judgments: Influences of Role Ambiguity and Cognitive Complexity." *Personnel Psychology*, 60, 2007: 597–625; E. C. Dierdorff, R. S. Rubin, and F. P. Morgeson, "The Milieu of Management: Exploring the Context of Managerial World Role Requirements." *Journal of Applied Psychology*, 94, 2009: 972–988; L. K. Treviño, "A Cultural Perspective on Changing and Developing Organizational Ethics." *Research in Organizational Change and Development*, 4, 1990: 195–230; L. K. Treviño, M. E. Brown, and L. P. Hartman, "A Qualitative Investigation of Perceived Executive Ethical Leadership: Perceptions from Inside and Outside the Executive Suite." *Human Relations*, 55, 2003: 5–37; L. K. Treviño, K. D. Butterfield, and D. L. McCabe, "The Ethical Context in Organizations: Influences on Employee Attitudes and Behaviors." *Business Ethics Quarterly*, 8, 1998: 447–476; L. K. Treviño, G. R. Weaver, and M. E. Brown, "It's Lovely at the Top: Hierarchical Levels, Identities, and Perceptions of Organizational Ethics." *Business Ethics Quarterly*, 18, 2008: 233–253; L. K. Treviño, G. R. Weaver, D. Gibson, and B. Toffler, "Managing Ethics and Legal Compliance: What Works and What Hurts." *California Management Review*, 41, 1999: 131–150; L. K. Treviño, G. R. Weaver, and S. J. Reynolds, "Behavioral Ethics in Organizations: A Review." *Journal of Management*, 32, 2006: 951–990; L. K. Treviño and S. A. Youngblood, "Bad Apples in Bad Barrels: A Causal Analysis of Ethical Decision-Making Behavior." *Journal of Applied Psychology*, 75, 1990: 378–385; Van Velsor, E. Leslie, and J. B. Leslie, "Why Executives Derail: Perspectives across Time and Cultures." *Academy of Management Executive*, 9, 1995: 62–72; J. F. Veiga, T. D. Golden, and K. Dechant, "Why Managers Bend Company Rules." *Academy of Management Executive*, 18, 2004: 84–91; G. R. Weaver, L. K. Treviño, and P. L. Cochran, "Corporate Ethics Programs as Control Systems: Influences of Executive Commitment and Environmental Factors." *Academy of Management Journal* 42, 1999: 41–57.

5   James M. Kouzes and Barry Z. Pozner, *The Leadership Challenge*. San Francisco, CA: Jossey-Bass, 2007, p. 15.

6   Ibid., p. xiii.

7   Ibid., pp. 28–29.

8   Ibid.

9   Max DePree, *Leadership Is an Art*. New York: Doubleday, 1989, p. 12.

10 Joseph C. Rost, *Leadership for the Twenty-First Century*. Westpoint, CT: Praeger, 1993, 69.

PART I

CHARACTER LEADERSHIP

WHAT IS LEADERSHIP?

Twixt kings and tyrants there's this difference known:
kings seek their subjects' good, tyrants their own.

Robert Herrick[1]

We began by observing that leadership is a necessary requirement of life. French President and Second World War hero Charles de Gaulle once observed that human beings can no more survive without direction than they can without eating, drinking, or sleeping. Putting aside the fact that de Gaulle exemplified "the one great person theory" of leadership and that he was most probably talking about himself, his larger point is true.

Today we accord movie star status to many of our leaders. Some of them become cultural icons and cultural role models. For example, the president of the United States is, arguably, the most photographed person in the world. Barack Obama's first inauguration was the most reported event of its time. Former President Bill Clinton is a celebrity. The media have tracked every turn in the life of business leaders like Bill Gates or Steve Jobs. Where once saints dominated our imagination and were looked to for guidance, political and business leaders now play that role.

Why is leadership such a fascinating topic? Why are we so enthralled by leadership and curious about the private and public lives of leaders? According to military historian John Keegan, we are intrigued, inspired, and intimidated by those who wear the "mask of command."[2] We are mesmerized both by the successful exploits and by the front-page failures of individual leaders. We love them, we hate them. We shun them, and yet we seek them out. Many of us

10 Virtues of Outstanding Leaders: Leadership and Character, First Edition.
Al Gini and Ronald M. Green.
© 2013 John Wiley & Sons, Inc. Published 2013 by John Wiley & Sons, Inc.

think that leadership is a magical amulet. If we can just get the right person, the right leader, in the right job, success will naturally and necessarily follow. Leadership seems crucial for personal and organization success.

But how do we define what seems to be a critical and necessary ingredient for success? Unfortunately, although many of us can recognize leaders and leadership, few can give these terms an exact definition. Even when we can describe the concepts denoted by the words we employ, we find ourselves unable to reduce that concept to a few words: we all agree that leadership is important, but we disagree in stating what it is. W. B. Gallie refers to these kinds of words as "essentially contested concepts" and argues that they are a regular part of our lives and vocabulary.[3] The challenge is to go beyond points of disagreement and discover the ideas that are essential to all our understandings of the concept.

Above all, it is important to begin by noting what leadership is *not*. According to John Gardner, leadership should never be confused or directly equated with social status, power, position, rank, or title.

> Even in large corporations and government agencies, the top-ranking person may simply be bureaucrat number one. We have all occasionally encountered top persons who couldn't lead a squad of seven year olds to the ice cream counter.[4]

Perhaps business ethicist Price Pritchett puts it even more exactly when he says: "Putting a man in charge and calling him a leader is like giving a man a Bible and calling him a preacher. Bestowing the title doesn't bestow the talent."[5] The simple fact is, an appropriate label for any person giving orders, monitoring compliance, and administering performance-based rewards and punishments could be "supervisor" or "manager," but not necessarily "leader."[6]

A Reflection

But if the term "leadership" does not apply to all people within organizations who exercise responsibility, nor does it mean that only the "top dog" of an organization exercises leadership. Leadership can (and *should*) arise at all levels of an organization when challenges must be faced and important tasks accomplished. A primary duty of all leaders is to inspire and empower each member of the organization to be a leader within his/her own area of responsibility. At the close of the Second World War, General Dwight Eisenhower put this well when he wrote in his war biography:

In the end, the success of D-Day wasn't superior generalship or years of careful planning. Nor was it our superiority in numbers and supplies. Rather it was the initiative and leadership of countless individual GIs that won the battle for us. It was the courage of men who took charge of the situations they found themselves in and their private determination to prevail.[7]

In their influential book *The Leadership Challenge*, Kouzes and Posner argue that, while there are a multitude of leadership definitions, they all share a common focus or a central theme. Leadership, of every kind and at every level, is about offering others an "action guide," a plan, a challenge, a goal, a purpose that they are willing to embrace and carry on. Leadership is about motivating and mobilizing people to get "something" done, be that extraordinary or otherwise. Leadership is a catalyst for action. Of course, whether that action is moral or immoral, good or bad, positive or negative has to be determined through normative analysis and debate. But the conclusion is the same: all forms of leadership are action-based and action-driven. Although we agree with Kouzes and Posner that leadership is essentially about deliberate and concerted effort and action, we would argue that leadership is also about the personality and character – the ethical substance – of a particular leader. We believe that ethics is what defines leadership.

Bernard Bass, leadership historian and scholar, has observed: "There are almost as many different definitions of leadership as there are persons who have attempted to define the concept."[8] He is right. Having said this, the following definition encapsulates our most basic and shared convictions about leadership:

Leadership is a power-laden, value-based and ethically driven relationship between leaders and followers who share a common vision and accomplish real changes that reflect their mutual purpose and goals.

This definition has five basic components. Let's look at them in the ascending order of their importance to the concept:

1 power-laden;
2 relationship between leaders and followers;
3 common vision;
4 accomplish real changes;
5 value-based and ethically driven.[9]

Power-laden All forms of leadership make use of power. The term comes (indirectly) from the Latin adjective *potis* ("powerful, capable") and verb *posse* ("to be able to"). Power is about control. To have power is to possess the capacity to control change or to direct it. Power need not be coercive, dictatorial, or punitive. It can be used in a non-coercive manner, for instance to orchestrate, mobilize, direct, and guide members of an institution or organization in the pursuit of a goal or series of objectives. The central issue of power in leadership is not "Will it be used?" but rather "Will it be used wisely and well?" In the best of all possible worlds, leaders who seek power should do so out of a sense of service, not for the purposes of personal aggrandizement and career advancement.

Relationship between leaders and followers   One of the most common errors in thinking about leadership is to focus on single individuals. But leadership does not reside exclusively in a single person. Rather it is a dynamic relationship, between leaders and followers alike. Leadership is always plural; it always occurs within the context of others. E. P. Hollander argues that, while the leader is the central and often the most vital part of the phenomenon of leadership, followers are necessary factors in the equation and often have an almost equal importance.

> Without responsive followers there is no leadership . . . [Leadership] involves someone who exerts influence, and those who are influenced . . . The real "power" of a leader lies in his or her ability to influence followers.[10]

Leadership does not take place in a vacuum. Whether passively or actively, leaders cannot lead unless followers follow. "Leaders and followers," James MacGregor Burns writes, "are engaged in a common enterprise; they are dependent on each other, their fortunes rise and fall together."[11]

Directly connected to the issue of followers is the time-honored question: Are leaders born or made? We believe that leaders, good or bad, great or small, arise from the needs and opportunities of a specific time and place. Great leaders require great causes, great issues, and, most importantly, a hungry and willing constituency. If this were not true, would there have been a Lech Walesa, a Martin Luther King, Jr., or a Nelson Mandela?

Common vision   The first job of leadership is to define reality. Leaders reach their goals by identifying, shaping, and representing the shared ideas and values of their organization. This constitutes the leader's vision. Leadership is always ideologically driven and motivated by a philosophical perspective on the challenges facing the community. All leaders have an agenda – a series of beliefs, proposals, values, ideas, and issues they wish to put on the table. In fact, as Burns has suggested, leadership only asserts itself, and followers only become evident, when there is something at stake – ideas to be clarified, issues to be determined, values to be adjudicated.[12] President Franklin D. Roosevelt understood this when he said: "All our great Presidents were leaders of thought at times when certain historic ideas in the life of the nation had to be clarified."[13] What is true of the presidency is true at every level of organizational life and leadership.

Accomplish real changes   All forms of leadership are about transformation. Leadership is not about maintaining the status quo; it is about initiating change in an organization. Simply sustaining the status quo is equivalent to institutional stagnation. "The leadership process," says Burns, "must be defined . . . as carrying through from decision-making stages to the point of concrete changes in people's lives, attitudes, behaviors [and] institutions."[14]

This emphasis on change suggests the following formula for the emergence of leadership:

$$\textbf{leadership} = \textbf{talent} + \textbf{challenge} + \textbf{timing} + \textbf{results}$$

Although we are attempting to describe and define our ideal of leadership, all forms of leadership seek to accomplish results. To adapt the words of Vince Lombardi, when all is said and done, more *should* be done than said![15] Peter Drucker argued throughout his long career that leadership was all about performance and results. Effective leadership is not about making speeches or being liked; leadership is defined by results, not by attributes.[16] Leadership comes to be *so that* something gets accomplished, something gets changed for the better. Simply put, leaders who aren't getting results aren't truly leading. Or, more specifically, leaders who aren't getting the desired results aren't fulfilling their mandate.[17]

In their book *Results-Based Leadership*, Dave Ulrich, Jack Zenger, and Norm Smallwood convincingly argue that, while it is faddish in leadership literature to talk about leaders as people who master competencies and emanate character, neither of these accomplishments is enough. The authors argue that, although organizational capabilities such as agility, adaptability, or mission directedness and personal attributes like character, virtue, or ethics are vital, it is not enough simply to possess these qualities. Although skills and attributes constitute the DNA of leadership, effective leaders must connect them to results. The authors' formula is simple: *Effective leadership = skills and attributes × results*. Results are a leader's brand, a leader's signature. Ulrich, Zenger, and Smallwood argue that a leader's job requires more than skills, character, knowledge, and action; it also demands the capacity to foster positive change:

Leaders exhibiting attributes without results have ideas without substance. They teach what they have not learned. They can talk a good scenario and even act on sound general principles, but they fail to deliver. The means – attributes – have become their end. Often popular because of their charm or charisma, they are not long remembered because their leadership depended more on who they are and how they behave than on what they accomplish.[18]

With regard to the character, attributes, and skills of a leader versus the real achievement of intended results, one can ask: How do we look at leaders who fail to produce results, or produce only negative ones? How would history evaluate an Abraham Lincoln if, during the presidential election campaign of 1864, William Tecumseh Sherman had not taken Atlanta Georgia? How would we look at Lincoln if General George B. McClellan had won the election, sued for peace, and allowed the Confederacy to continue to exist as an independent nation and to maintain the legal status of slavery? How would history look at and evaluate the leadership ability of Mahatma Gandhi if India were still the crown jewel of the British colonial empire? How would history judge the efforts of Martin Luther King, Jr., if his 13 years of public ministry and leadership in the Civil Rights Movement had not resulted in significant legal and cultural changes regarding the rights and dignity of African American citizens? If they had all failed, if these iconic leaders had not produced results, would we revere them as we do? Would we honor them for their intentions and efforts? Probably. Would we respect them for their commitment? Certainly. But would we hold them up as role models to aspire to? No. Would we refer to them as successful? Again, no.

But not all change is good. Leaders can effect change that takes organizations in negative directions. As we will see in the next chapter, destructive change does not qualify as the ideal goal of leadership. Furthermore, change can also be of short duration. Beneficial changes that fail to endure or to take root in organizational life also miss the leadership test.

Value-based and ethically driven   Leadership aims at positive change in the life of an organization or community. This means that leadership is always an ethical enterprise. Peter Drucker, one of the most skilled observers of organizational life, concludes, on the basis of more than 65 years of studying management, that the primary purpose of all business organizations and the grounds and rationale for all forms of managerial authority is to make the human condition more secure, more satisfactory, and more productive.[19] More colloquially, Tony Dungy, former NFL coach, said: "It is not about you . . . Your only job [as a coach, as a leader] is to help your team be better."[20] Centuries before Drucker or Dungy, St. Augustine, himself a formative leader of early Christianity, clearly suggested in the *City of God* that the first and final job of leaders is to attempt to serve the needs and wellbeing of the people they lead.[21]

Ethics, Virtue, and Character

The moral quality of leadership is summed up in the understanding that real leaders are ethical and possess both virtue and character. "Ethics," "virtue," and "character" are all classical Greek concepts. In antiquity, ethics, *ēthikē* (ἠθική), started off as the study of human behavior or custom. It was used to identify the distinguishing values of a civilization, a community, or a person. The corresponding Latin word, *mos* ("custom"), lives on in English words like "mores," "moral(ity)," and "morals." While many people believe that "moral-ity" and "ethics" have different meanings, we will use them interchangeably. An ethical person is someone of moral integrity. A moral philosopher is also called an ethicist.

Since the time of the Greeks, the discipline of ethics – morality – has focused on the question: "What ought I to do with others?" In private con-versations with one of the authors, business ethicist Ed Freeman and theolo-gian Frank Griswald emphasize this understanding. "Ethics," says Freeman, "is how we treat people face to face, person to person, day in and day out over a prolonged period of time." In Griswald's view, "ethics is about the rules we choose to live by once we decide we want to live together." To say, therefore, that leadership is *value-based and ethically driven* and that real leaders are ethical is to say that leaders are always concerned with the question "What ought I to do?" They take seriously their responsibility toward *all* the people impacted by their decisions.

In the Greek world of Plato and Aristotle, *aretē* (ἀρετή) – "virtue" – meant something that is more appropriately translated as "excellence." For the Greeks there were non-ethical, non-moral virtues. Beauty, martial skills, or athletic prowess were all excellences, virtues. But, when we speak of virtue, it is pri-marily the moral excellences we have in mind. What are the qualities of a person that lead to that person's flourishing and to the flourishing of those around him/her? Honesty and fairness are among the crucial virtues for organizational leadership and success. In the chapters ahead we explore these and other moral virtues that are essential to leadership.

Greek philosophers insisted that virtue is a habit. By this they meant that it is not a one-time deed, but a skill or a disposition to act in a certain way, which must be acquired through repetition and exercise. To remain in force and grow, virtue must be practiced again and again, and demonstrated across a range of life choices. Here virtue's wider meaning as "excellence" is helpful. Can we achieve high degrees of athletic performance without training? Can we develop musical skills without practice? The same reasoning applies to the moral virtues. Greek philosophers emphasized this when they said: "Do not judge a person until (s)he is dead." In part they believed this because only a completed life can stand as evidence to the full achievement of one's virtue.

The word "character" comes from a Greek noun meaning "etching" or "engraving": *charaktēr* (χαρακτήρ), itself derived from the verb *charassein* ("to engrave"). Originally *charaktēr* designated the marks impressed on a coin. Applied to human beings, *charaktēr* refers to the enduring marks or etched-in factors that have been impressed on a person's mind (*psuchē*, "soul"). These consist in the person's inborn talents as well as in the learned traits – those acquired through education and experience. These "engravings" set us apart, define us, and motivate our behavior.

Although much of character is impressed on us by the environment, the vagaries of time and place, and the biological (genetic) or behavioral influences of our parents, moral character is about what a person chooses to hold dear, to value, and to believe in. If you want to know about a person's moral character, check their values. People of character value honesty, integrity, and fairness. They value loyalty and, in consistency with the needs of organizational functioning, they are compassionate. They care about other people. In our view, character in precisely this sense is the foundation of leadership.

Gail Sheehy, in her book *Character: America's Search for Leadership*, argues that, while character is the most crucial element of leadership, it is also the most elusive one. In regard to leadership, says Sheehy, character is fundamental and prophetic. "The issues [of leadership]," she claims, "are of today and will change in time. Character is what was yesterday and will be tomorrow." Character establishes both our day-to-day demeanor and our destiny. Therefore it is not only useful but also essential to examine the character of those who wish to lead us. As a journalist and longtime observer of the political scene, Sheehy contends that the Watergate affair of the early 1970s serves as a perfect example of the links between character and leadership. As Richard Nixon demonstrated so well, "[t]he Presidency is not the place to work out one's personal pathology."[22] Leaders rule us, run things, and wield power. Therefore, her argument runs, we must be careful about whom we choose to lead us. Because whom we choose is what we will be. If character is destiny, the destiny our leaders forge will be our own.

Notes to Chapter One

1   Robert Herrick, *Hesperides: Or, the Works Both Humane and Divine of Robert Herrick Esq*. London: Printed for John Williams and Francis Eglesfield, 1648, p. 289.

2   John Keegan, *The Mask of Command*. New York: Penguin Group, 1988.

3   W. B. Gallie, "Essentially Contested Concepts." *Aristotelian Society*, 56, 1956: 167–198.

4   John Gardner, *On Leadership*. New York: The Free Press, 1990, p. 2.

5   Price Pritchett, Chairman & CEO of PRITCHETT, LP. Dallas, TX. Reproduced with permission from Sandi Lindstendt, Permission editor.

6   J. W. Graham, "Transformational Leadership: Fostering Follower Autonomy, not Automatic Followership." In J. G. Hunt, B. R. Baglia, H. P. Crachler, and C. A. Schriescheim (eds.), *Emerging Leadership Vistas*. Lexington, MA: Lexington Books, 1988, p. 74.

7   A CBS Broadcast of June 6, 1964, titled *CBS Reports: D-Day Plus 20 Years: Eisenhower Returns to Normandy* and reported by Walter Cronkite: Walter Cronkite in the Dwight D. Eisenhower Presidential Library and Museum. Archivist, Herb Pankratz.

8   Bernard Bass, *Stogdill's Handbook of Leadership: A Survey of Theory and Research*. New York: Free Press, 1981, p. 7.

9   Al Gini, "Moral Leadership: An Overview." *Journal of Business Ethics*, 16, 1997: 323–330.

10 E. P. Hollander, *Leadership Dynamics*. New York: The Free Press, 1978, pp. 4, 7.

11 James MacGregor Burns, *Leadership*. New York: Harper Torchbooks, 1979, p. 426.

12 Ibid., Chapters 2 and 5.

13 Anne O'Hare McCormick, "Roosevelt's View of the Big Job." *New York Times Magazine*, September 11, 1932, p. SM1.

14 Burns, *Leadership*, p. 414.

15 Vince Lombardi, "When All Is Said and Done, More Is Said Than Done." In Dave Ulrich, Jack Zenger, and Norm Smallwood, *Results-Based Leadership*. Boston, MA: Harvard Business School Press, 1999, p. vii.

16 Peter Drucker, *The Effective Executive*. New York: Collins Business, 2006, pp. ix–xxii.

17 Dave Ulrich, Jack Zenger, and Norm Smallwood, *Results-Based Leadership*. Boston, MA: Harvard Business School Press, 1999, pp. viii, 27.

18 Ibid., p. 20.

19 Peter F. Drucker with J. P. Maciarriello, *The Daily Drucker: 366 Days of Insight and Motivation for Getting the Right Things Done*. New York: Harper Business, 2004, pp. 105, 195.

20 Tony Dungy with Nathan Whitaker, *The Mentor Leader*. Carol Stream, IL: Tyndale House Publishers, 2010.

21 Saint Augustine, *Basic Writings of Saint Augustine*, vol. 5.2: *The City of God*, edited by Whitney J. Ontes. New York: Random House, 1948, pp. 490–491

(=Book XIX, Chapter 14): "those who rule serve those whom they seem to command; for they rule not from the love of power, but from a sense of the duty they owe to others."

22   Gail Sheehy, *Character: America's Search for Leadership*. New York: Bantam Books, 1990, p. 66.

MISLEADERSHIP

There is a lure in power. It can get into a man's blood just like gambling and lust for money have been known to do.

President Harry S. Truman[1]

Barbara Kellerman, in her important book *Bad Leadership*, makes a strong case for depicting and studying both sides of the leadership equation. She suggests that, although most students of leadership are drawn to the "good guy scenarios," if we do not also seriously address the "worst-case scenarios," we remain among those to whom George Santayana's famous warning applies: "Those who cannot remember the past are condemned to repeat it."

Unfortunately, says Kellerman, history has shown us again and again that people can achieve and maintain power and control while being utterly unethical and narcissistically self-serving. Not to understand how and why this happens, not to study and carefully dissect bad leadership is to impair our ability to struggle against it. Kellerman argues that "bad leaders" need to be studied too. For they, too, offer lessons, albeit negative ones, on the use and abuse of power:

> [I]f we pretend that . . . bad leadership is unrelated to good leadership, if we pretend to know the one without knowing the other, we will in the end distort the enterprise. We cannot distance ourselves from even the most extreme example – Hitler . . . Not only was his impact on the twentieth-century history arguably greater than anyone else's, but also he was brilliantly skilled at inspiring, mobilizing, and directing followers. His use of coercion notwithstanding, if this is not leadership, what is?[2]

10 Virtues of Outstanding Leaders: Leadership and Character, First Edition.
Al Gini and Ronald M. Green.
© 2013 John Wiley & Sons, Inc. Published 2013 by John Wiley & Sons, Inc.

In opposition to Kellerman, we believe – and we will argue – that bad leadership is not leadership at all, but "misleadership." Thus we reply to Kellerman's question here by saying that Hitler was not a leader, but a "misleader." Nevertheless, Kellerman's point about the need to consider and study bad leadership along with good is a cogent one. To deny bad leadership, not to take it somehow into account, not to recognize it, not to name it and study it would be analogous to the case of a medical school that might try to teach health while totally ignoring disease. The study of medicine requires the study of both health and illness. The study of disease – of the cause(s) (or etiology), of the origin(s), and of the consequences of a disease – will hopefully lead to diagnosis, cure, and prevention. The same can be said of the "disease" of bad leadership. We need to study it so as to diagnose and possibly prevent and/or cure it.[3] At the same time, however, we should not confuse a state of disease with health, any more than we should judge a misleader to be a leader.

What Is Bad Leadership?

Kellerman argues that the reasons for bad leadership are many and varied. Leaders can simply be guilty of making an honest mistake. Or they can be lazy, maladroit, sleazy, or ignoble. They can also be tyrannical megalomaniacs. They can lack cognitive intelligence, emotional intelligence, or practical intelligence. Worse, they can be malignant narcissists who are sadistically aggressive and sociopathic in their relations with all others: friends, foes, family, and followers.

For Kellerman, bad leadership falls into two basic categories: bad as in ineffective and bad as in unethical. Simply put, ineffective leadership falls short of its intention because of the means leaders employ – or fail to employ. According to Kellerman, unethical leadership acts in a way that may appear to achieve a desired result or outcome but fails to distinguish between right and wrong in achieving these goals. In Kellerman's accounting, these two basic categories can, in turn, be subdivided into seven groups:

1 *Incompetent leadership* The leader lacks the will or skill (or both) to sustain effective action. He or she does not create positive change.
2 *Rigid leadership* The leader is stiff and unyielding. Although competent, he or she is unable or unwilling to adapt to new ideas, new information, or changing times.
3 *Intemperate leadership* The leader lacks self-control and is unwilling or unable to self-correct.

4   *Callous leadership* The leader is uncaring or unkind. The needs, wants, and wishes of most members of the group or organization, especially subordinates, are ignored or discounted.
5   *Corrupt leadership* The leader is willing to lie, cheat, or steal. To a degree that exceeds the norm, he or she puts self-interest ahead of public interest.
6   *Insular leadership* The leader minimizes or disregards the health and welfare of "the other" – that is, those outside his or her own group or organization.
7   *Evil leadership* The leader commits atrocities. He or she uses pain as an instrument of power. The harm done to men, women, and children is severe rather than slight. The harm can be physical, psychological, or both.[4]

The first three types of bad leadership tend to be bad in the sense that they are ineffective. The last four types tend to be bad by way of being unethical. Of course, in an untidy world, lines blur. Sometimes bad leaders are both ineffective and unethical.[5] And all too often, even though this situation may be dismissed as an aberration or outlier, it is possible for "bad leaders" to be apparently successful, effective, long-lived, and unethical.[6] As we will see, however, since bad leaders undermine the conditions for communal flourishing, they ultimately defeat the purpose of leadership.

Misleaders

Rather than using the phrase "bad leader," we prefer to use "misleader," a term we first encountered in the works of Peter Drucker.[7] Later we discovered it again, in the writings of the German theologian Dietrich Bonhoeffer. Bonhoeffer may not have coined the term, but his initial use of it is dramatically poignant and viscerally intuitive. He first used it in a February 1, 1933 radio speech entitled "The Younger Generation's Altered Concept of Leadership," in which he cautioned against the dangers of *der Führer* (the leader) – Adolf Hitler, the newly elected chancellor of Germany – becoming instead *der Verführer*.[8] In German, the term *Verführer* has several closely related meanings. The corresponding verb *verführen* can signify to "lead astray" or "mislead," but also to "tempt" or "seduce." We import all of these meanings into our use of the term *"Verführer*/misleader." Like a seducer, a "misleader" employs his or her apparent talents and charms to achieve power over others to destructive ends.

A word here needs to be said regarding our use of Adolf Hitler, the Nazi Party, and the Third Reich as examples of leadership, albeit of the kind we call "misleadership." Arguably the "dean of leadership studies" in America is James McGregor Burns. Burns avoids any reference to Nazism, because he feels that Hitler was a "naked powerwielder," demonically evil and immoral, and therefore should not be judged as a leader at all – not even one situated at the lowest end of the spectrum. Also, for years, there was an unofficial policy at National Public Radio not to make references or comparisons to Hitler or to the Nazi regime. The idea was that the real-world impact of Hitler's leadership was so large and devastating that to use it as a point of comparison would be excessive, inexact, and prejudicial. We are sensitive to the fact that careless comparisons and references to the Nazi regime should be avoided. However, given our thesis and Kellerman's, the destructive impact of the Nazis' use of power and the personal vision and message of Adolf Hitler are, unfortunately, a perfect example of the most malignant form of *misleadership* in our understanding of the concept. We think it would be an ethical and historical mistake not to address the power and violent consequences of Nazi ideology in this context.

For Bonhoeffer, the leadership principle was disastrously misguided and totally disconnected from the true objective of the office of leadership – the wellbeing of those whom the ones in this office should lead. Bonhoeffer argued that, whereas earlier forms of leadership were associated with a statesman, a father, or a benefactor, the new leadership of Germany, the *Verführer*, was self-derived, self-defined, self-justifying, and completely and terrifyingly authoritarian. Bonhoeffer went on to claim that this new *Führer Prinzip* (leadership principle) arose from the post-First World War generation in Germany, which was seeking meaning, guidance, direction, and purpose.[9] Both Bonhoeffer and Drucker suggest that the central idea of the *Führer Prinzip* is a bastardization of Friedrich Nietzsche's concept of the *Übermensch*, leader and superman. In Drucker's words:

> The "leader" is human only in the flesh. In the spirit he is beyond human fallibility, beyond human ethics, and beyond human society. He is "always right"; he can never err. His will determines what is good or evil. His position is outside and beyond society and does not rest upon any social sanction . . . The only basis of his claim, the only sanction for his position and power, is that he is above ordinary man . . . His authority is justified as long as he can inspire the masses with the belief which they crave in order to escape despair.[10]

Fear, confusion, and desperation led the German *Volk* (people) to embrace the autocratic mysticism and mythology of the Nazi Party. The *Verführer*'s exercise of power is not about true moral authority, human values, and faith in the rightness of rational action.[11] The *Verführer* rather claims: "I am the state! I am the *Volk*! I am the *Zeitgeist*! I am the supreme judge of all!" In so doing, says Bonhoeffer, "the leader makes an idol of himself and . . . mocks God."[12]

Bad Followers

Of course, it is important to understand that, in the leadership equation, misleaders are not the sole villains when things go wrong. At the level of both theory and practice, misleaders do not come to be entirely on their own. Nor do misleaders act alone. Misleaders, just like leaders, are dependent upon followers for exercising any power and authority.[13] Both leaders and misleaders achieve power either through the active cooperation or through the benign neglect of their followers. Historian Garry Wills reaffirms a point we previously made: that leaders need followers and, when followers are lacking, the best and the worst ideas have little or no effect. For Wills, followers set the terms of acceptance for leadership. Although "the leader is one who mobilizes others toward a goal shared by leaders and followers," leaders are powerless to act without followers. Leadership is always, and necessarily, a collective enterprise or activity.[14]

Kellerman argues that, at times, fatigue, frustration, coercion, or intimidation lead followers to cooperate with misguided or malevolent leaders. But, she says, it is quite another thing for followers to intentionally lend strong support to bad leaders. "Followers who knowingly, deliberately commit themselves to bad leaders are themselves bad."[15]

According to Kellerman, the most extensive study of bad followers that has been made to date is based on the example of Nazi Germany. This study divides bad followers during the Nazi regime into three groups: bystanders, evildoers, and acolytes. *Bystanders* went along with the regime but were not fervently committed to it. *Evildoers* supported the Nazi Party and its policy. They included many generals and military leaders who implemented Nazi policy. Finally, there were *acolytes*, the hardcore true believers, the zealots, the followers who were passionately committed to Hitler as a person and ideologically committed to his political agenda.[16]

In Hitler's Germany, bystanders behaved badly either because they had no issue with the Nazi agenda or because, if they did, they calculated that the cost of resisting was greater than the cost of doing nothing. Evildoers behaved badly because that's how they were told to behave. And acolytes behaved badly because behaving badly is what they wanted to do. Acolytes were so dedicated to the Führer that his wish was, literally, their command.[17]

Although the Nazi regime is an obvious target for condemnation and critique, Kellerman is convinced that this three-part typology of bad leadership can be applied to other, less violent political parties, and also to business organizations and groups. The financial swindles that occurred at World-Com, Enron, Tyco, Healthsouth, Lehman Brothers, AIG, and Countrywide Financial were perpetrated by top officers of these companies. But Kellerman suggests that the longevity, depth, and destructiveness of these corrupt activities were maintained and supported by a surrounding group of followers who knew what the score was, somehow participated actively in wrongdoing, stood to profit in some way from the fraudulent practices, and hence did nothing to stop it.[18]

A Few Examples

Some misleaders are simply pathetic egocentric scoundrels or selfishly vain adolescent narcissists, full of bluster and pomposity, who enjoy a bright moment and then are quickly and happily forgotten or dismissed. Consider the following figures and their likes: "pay-to-play" Rod Blagojevich – the impeached, indicted, and convicted governor of Illinois; the strutting peacock – Italian dictator Benito Mussolini; King Farouk, the corpulent playboy, pharaoh of Egypt; General Armstrong Custer, vainglorious Indian hater and fighter; Marie Antoinette, the foolish French queen who, when told that the poor had no bread to eat, is said to have replied: "Let them eat cake;" Joseph McCarthy, Wisconsin senator and self-styled inquisitioner of all things communist; and, finally, Donald J. Trump – a name, a brand, a television personality, and an outrageous pompadour.

Other misleaders are pathological liars, completely sociopathic in their interactions with others and utterly Machiavellian in their use of power. These are leaders whose actions have ruined the lives of individuals and nations, and who, in the business world, have destroyed large, once flourishing corporations. They are culprits whose villainy will not be forgotten soon. Such rulers include the following: Joseph Stalin of the Union of Soviet Socialist Republics, whose 23-year rule caused the death of at least 20 million of his own people; Jean-Bedel Bokassa, self-proclaimed head of the Central African Empire, who not only murdered his political enemies but apparently ate them as well; Pol Pot of the Khmer Rouge, who during his reign of terror created the never-to-be-forgotten "killing fields" of Cambodia; and Robert Mugabe of Zimbabwe, who began his political career as a revolutionary and resistance fighter, morphed into the role of democratic father of his country, and ended up a tyrant and a demagogue who destroyed the agricultural, financial, and social structure of one of the richest nations in Africa. Next come the less violent but equally vicious white-collar villains whose personal greed and desire for status, stuff, and success made them both utterly careless and indifferent to the financial wants, needs, and rights of others: Kenneth Lay and Jeff Skilling at Enron; hedge fund manager Bernard Madoff, who conducted the largest Ponzi scheme in history; and Angelo R. Mozilo at Countrywide Financial, whom Cable News Network (CNN) named as one of the "Ten Most Wanted: Culprits" of the 2008 financial collapse in the United States.

We agree with Kellerman's thesis that both historical and contemporary bad leaders/misleaders need to be studied and analyzed. In the words of English philosopher Francis Bacon, "knowledge is power." Without sufficient knowledge of the tendencies and techniques of such leaders as Kim Jong-Il (North Korea), Saddam Hussein (Iraq), Bernard Ebbers (World-Com), Muammar Gaddafi (Libya), and Dennis Kozlowski (Tyco), we will remain vulnerable to their perfidiousness and malevolent machinations.

In the 1930s, Winston Churchill was both out of power and out of favor in the corridors of Westminster Palace. No longer Lord of the Admiralty, now a mere "back-bencher" in Parliament, Churchill was looked upon as a failed, cranky old man who, in the midst of a worldwide depression, was excessively concerned about a rather insignificant politician in Germany by the name of Adolf Hitler. Even when Hitler came to power in 1933, Parliament paid Churchill little heed. He said of himself that he was "a voice in the wilderness."

But Churchill continued to warn his colleagues. He continued to hector for greater military preparedness and closer bonds with England's European allies. He denounced Neville Chamberlain's attempts at appeasement with Hitler as ignorant. He hammered away at the themes that Germany was preparing for war, that Hitler was evil, and that, if war should come, the stakes would be high. It would literally be "civilization versus barbarism."

On what did Churchill base his position and his warnings? Why did he assume the role of town crier? The simple fact was that Churchill did his homework. As a historian of political and military leadership, he had read *Mein Kampf* in its first English translation. As a journalist, he kept himself informed about day-to-day events in Germany and throughout the European continent. As a member of Parliament he had access to diplomatic dispatches and reports. Churchill's warnings about Hitler were based on research, reason, and analysis. He was a student of power and geopolitics and, for him, the mounting evidence regarding Hitler's real motives and aspirations was overwhelmingly clear. His "brief," his "case study," was, of course, accurate. And his warnings, in the long run, proved prescient and prophetic. As Joseph

Conrad has suggested, the "Heart of Darkness" cannot be defeated until it is known.

The contrast between these two titanic wielders of power – Churchill versus Hitler – also illustrates the key point on which we must insist: those who misuse power – misleaders – are not leaders at all. Centuries ago, Thomas Aquinas made a similar point with respect to unethical or wicked laws. Such laws (in our era they would include the apartheid laws of South Africa, or the Jim Crow laws of our once segregated South) are not laws but "perversions of law."[19] Aquinas defined "law" as "an ordinance of reason for the common good, made by him who has care of the community, and promulgated."[20] As a consequence, Aquinas maintained that unjust laws are not really laws at all; they are merely coerced impositions. The issue here is more than definitional. Aquinas believed that to use the word "law" to describe purely coerced impositions lends them a credibility and an authority they do not possess. Similarly, we argue that leaders who steer their organizations and followers in unethical directions are not leaders at all. Instead of the communal flourishing and creativity that genuine leaders foster, misleaders ultimately produce chaos.

Consider our two titans. Churchill left behind, and helped create, a new era of human freedom and global flourishing. His nation, despite its many ups and downs, remains an honored paradigm of Western values. In contrast, Hitler's Thousand Year Reich ended in rubble in little over a decade. The values of that empire have become a source of shame and a perpetual warning.

All real leadership is ethical. We align ourselves with this whole tradition of thought: all real leadership is ethical. In politics or business, unethical leadership may prosper for a time, but in the end it destroys the values that sustain the community. We must study misleadership to better understand and develop leadership, but we should not award the title "leader" to those who wield power only for themselves. These are not leaders: they undermine the conditions for the growth and perpetuation of both their communities and their values. Ethics is therefore essential not only to the practice of leadership, but to the very meaning of the term.

Notes to Chapter Two

1   Harry S. Truman, April 16, 1950, quoted in Ken Hechler, *Working with Truman: A Personal Memoir of the White House Years*. Columbia, MO: University of Missouri Press, 1996, p. 243.
2   Barbara Kellerman, *Bad Leadership: What It Is, How It Happens, Why It Matters*. Boston, MA: Harvard Business School Press, 2004, p. 11.
3   Ibid.

4   Ibid., pp. 40–46.

5   Ibid., p. 39.

6   Ibid., p. 219.

7   Peter F. Drucker, "Leadership: More Doing Than Dash." *The Wall Street Journal*, January 6, 1988.

8   Eric Metaxas, *Bonhoeffer: Pastor, Martyr, Prophet, Spy*. Nashville, TN: Thomas Nelson, 2010, pp. 138–139.

9   Ibid., pp. 141–144.

10   Peter F. Drucker, *The End of Economic Man: The Origins of Totalitarianism*. New York: Harper Colophon Books, 1969, pp. 229–231.

11   Ibid., p. xviii.

12   Denise Giardina, *Saints and Villains*. New York: Ballantine Books, 1999, 102.

13   Barbara Kellerman, *Bad Leadership*, pp. xiii, xiv.

14   Garry Wills, *Certain Trumpets: The Nature of Leadership*. New York: Simon & Schuster, 1994, pp. 13–16.

15   Kellerman, *Bad Leadership*, p. 25.

16   Ibid., p. 26.

17   Ibid., p. 27.

18   Ibid., pp. 24–25.

19   Thomas Aquinas, *Treatise on Law* (=*Summa theologiae*, Ia–IIae), translated by Fathers of the English Dominican Province. New York: Benziger Brothers, 1947, Question 95, Art. 2.

20   Ibid., Question 90.

CHARACTER AND LEADERSHIP

Let me state a personal bias that leadership is really a matter of character. The process of becoming a leader is no different than the process of becoming a fully integrated human being.

Warren Bennis[1]

Plato's *Republic* is arguably the first book ever written on the art of leadership. Even if you reject Plato's elaborate scheme for the organization of the state and the training of its leaders, it is difficult to overlook the intention and thesis of the text: What does justice mean, and how can it be realized in human society?[2]

Using Socrates as main interlocutor in the dialogue and presumably as his spokesman, Plato argues that the central problem of politics is to organize the state so as to place control in the hands of individuals who understand that you cannot make people happy by simply making them richer or more powerful than their neighbors. Socrates is convinced that, so long as knowledge is only valued as a means to power and wealth, the helm of the ship of state will be sought after by ambitious individuals who are only motivated by status and profit. Power, says Socrates, must only be given to those whose intelligence, character, and training compel them to do the right thing intentionally and for the right reason, no matter the cost to themselves. The goal of a state, he claims, is not to make any one class especially happy, but to secure the greatest possible happiness for the community as a whole.[3]

To achieve this end, says Socrates, we must identify and train a class of individuals who do not crave power, but who accept it and embrace it

10 Virtues of Outstanding Leaders: Leadership and Character, First Edition.
Al Gini and Ronald M. Green.
© 2013 John Wiley & Sons, Inc. Published 2013 by John Wiley & Sons, Inc.

as their duty and responsibility. He therefore proposes to create an elite cadre of rulers with the highest degree of intelligence, people trained in civic virtues and public policy, whose character and temperament have been rigorously tested and evaluated. These individuals – the guardian class – have real power, but they see their office as a social responsibility, a trust, a duty, and not as a symbol of their personal identity, prestige, or lofty status. Although Socrates' claims are utopian, his central argument is clear: character (intelligence, disposition, motivation, and training) is the *elemental* ingredient in leadership.

A detailed review of the philosophical literature on the role and function of character would take us through a number of books; even a cursory analysis of the topic is a daunting task. And yet, colloquially speaking, we all are more or less aware of what the term generally means. Social scientist James Q. Wilson argues that, when we describe people we admire or like, we rarely define them by any one trait. Rather we make judgments based on a set of traits: their character. By character, said Wilson, we mean two things: (1) a distinctive combination of personal qualities by which someone is known – that is, his/her personality; and (2) a distinctive combination of moral strengths, moral values, and integrity.[4]

The great philosopher and psychologist William James believed that the most interesting and important thing about a person, that which determines the person's perspective on the world, is his or her philosophy of life, values, ideals, and beliefs. These are the things a person chooses to hold as dear, important, and/or sacred; they are the road maps that help us decipher and explain what James calls the "booming, buzzing confusion" of reality. These are the things we are willing to act for and to act on. Our philosophy of life is defined by what we choose to value, and our character is defined by our actually living out that which we value. James believes that an honest person experiencing hard times will make every effort sooner or later to honor a debt, but that a dishonest person may never repay a debt even if he or she possesses more than sufficient resources to do so.

Ethicist Robert Solomon defines the virtues as lived behavior traits that contribute to and are essential for achieving happiness, getting along with others, and in general living well. Solomon, like Aristotle before him, sees the virtues as desirable traits of character that we choose, then make second nature through repetition and habit. Thus virtuous behavior is not an accident, or mere luck, or a one-time event. A virtuous act is doing the right thing for the right reason, and doing it habitually and purposefully. Ethics, says Solomon, is a question of one's whole character, not just a question of one particular virtue or another.[5]

Character and Integrity

Writing not long after Plato, Aristotle offers us, in the *Nicomachean Ethics*, a list of virtues that, he claims, are suitable for the "whole character" of the "great-souled person" – the *megalopsuchos*. Although this list has been criticized for being culturally specific and only reflecting Aristotle's idealized version of the "Greek gentleman," it has withstood the test of time and, at a minimum, it serves as a solid basis for a larger discussion of virtuous conduct. Humanities scholar Martha C. Nussbaum of the University of Chicago has created a useful chart, which lists the various spheres of human experience that trigger or necessitate a virtuous response.[6]

Sphere of experience	Virtue
1 Fear of important damages, especially death	Courage
2 Bodily appetites and their pleasures	Moderation
3 Distribution of limited resources	Justice
4 Management of one's personal property, where others are concerned	Generosity
5 Management of one's personal property, where hospitality is concerned	Expansive hospitality
6 Attitudes and actions with respect to one's own worth	Greatness of soul
7 Attitude to slights and damages	Mildness of temper
8 Association and living together and the fellowship of words and actions a Truthfulness in speech b Social association of a playful kind c Social association more generally	a Truthfulness b Easy grace (contrasted with coarseness, rudeness, insensitivity) c Nameless – a kind of friendliness (contrasted with irritability and grumpiness)
9 Attitude to the good and ill fortune of others	Proper judgment (contrasted with enviousness, spitefulness, and so on)
10 Intellectual life	The various intellectual virtues such as perceptiveness, knowledge, and so on
11 The planning of one's life and conduct	Practical wisdom

It can be argued that our moral character is the sum total of our values, virtues, and vices. The Romans had a perfect Latin word to describe and measure the quality of a person's character: *integritas*. Ethically speaking, integrity means *the state or quality of being entire or complete*. We encounter the Latin word today in our mathematical term "integer," which designates a whole number as opposed to a fraction. A person of integrity is "one thing," a unified self. Integrity means soundness of personality, being unimpaired, having all of one's component pieces fit together in a whole. Morally, it involves the attempt to adhere to a cluster of virtues and values that complement and reinforce one another. Integrity is about self-restraint, self-control, and self-mastery.

Integrity also means "living coherently," what the Greek Stoics called *to homologoumenōs zēn*, presenting to the world a sense of personal identity or honor. This is a matter of integrating the various parts of our personality into a harmonious, intact whole. A person of integrity is not "duplicitous," literally "two things." He or she does not do and say one thing when no one else is around and yet another when someone is present, or offer one face to the board of directors and another to customers. He does not speak with a forked tongue. Integrity is something that all morally serious people care about. To describe someone as exhibiting a lack of integrity is to offer a damning judgment:

> It carries the implication that this individual is not to be relied upon, that in some fundamental way they are not someone who [sic] we can, or should, view as being wholly unequivocally there. The foundations of self and character are not sound; the ordering of values is not coherent.[7]

In his 1996 bestseller *Integrity*, Stephen L. Carter suggests that integrity is a kind of *über*-virtue or a type of "philosophical cement" that contains and coordinates all of one's other virtues and values. By integrity, Carter understands having the courage of one's convictions. He suggests that, if ethics is living out what we value, then the integrity of a person's character, or lack thereof, is as good a yardstick as any to predict ethical conduct. Carter describes integrity as marked by three practices: (1) one takes pains to try to discern what is right from wrong; (2) one is willing to shape one's actions in accord with that discernment, even when it is difficult or painful to do so (as Walter Lippmann so eloquently phrased it: "He has honor if he holds himself to an ideal of conduct though it is inconvenient, unprofitable, or dangerous to do so"); and (3) one is willing to acknowledge publicly what one is doing. In short, a person of integrity is reflective, steadfast, trustworthy, and whole. "A person of integrity," says Carter, "is a whole person, a person somehow undivided."[8]

According to *Chicago Tribune* columnist Eric Zorn, a person of character is someone who has a conscience. Unfortunately, to most modern ears, says Zorn, the word "conscience" is too abstract, ephemeral, and old-fashioned to be used in most conventional conversations. For many people, the term evokes the image of a little person sitting on your shoulder, whispering in your ear, and offering advice and judgment on the moral goodness or blameworthiness of your actions. Nevertheless, Zorn argues, even though the word is rarely used, its meaning, function, and purpose are neither obsolete nor irrelevant.[9]

The philosopher Immanuel Kant defined conscience as "the moral faculty of judgment, passing judgment upon itself";[10] but our conscience is not just a nagging, faultfinding superego or policeman. "Conscience" implies care for, concern with, or (at the very least) recognition of others. The word comes from the Latin *conscire*, "to be conscious," "to know." Conscience is the faculty, the power, the instinct, and the ability to reflect on, be sensitive to, evaluate, and make judgments about our interactions with others. It is not an infallible instinct. It is not a polygraph or a lie detector that always distinguishes right from wrong. But, if we are lucky, if we are not totally lost in the maze of our own narcissism, conscience at the very least forces us to ponder our relationships with others and to make judgments about what we consider to be acceptable or unacceptable behavior in their regard.

If character is living out what we value, conscience is its inner counterpart, that part of us that makes judgments and evaluations about when, how, and with whom that value should or should not be applied. Conscience is frequently the first step in making a moral decision, the internal uneasiness that prompts us to ask ourselves some hard questions, which may well take the following shape:

- Is it legal?
- Is it right and fair for others as well as for myself?
- Can I truthfully defend my decision to others: family, friends, and colleagues?
- Would I feel comfortable seeing my action reported in the news media?
- Can I live with my conscience as well as with the consequences of my action?
- Am I treating others in the same way I would have them treat me or the people I know and love?

In the words of Carol Gilligan, conscience requires us to listen to "other voices." In 1982 Gilligan published her landmark book *In a Different Voice:*

Psychological Theory and Women's Development. In Gilligan's view, caring for others, being responsive to others, and helping others begin with talking and listening to them. According to Gilligan, "the moral person is one who [hears others, and] helps others; goodness is service, meeting one's obligations and responsibilities to others."[11] For Gilligan, the most basic moral imperative is the "injunction to care, [the] responsibility to discern and alleviate the 'real and recognizable trouble' of this world."[12] According to her, we are by nature interdependent, not independent, creatures. We have a responsibility to care for and to help others. In an ethical predicament neutrality is unacceptable. In this regard, Gilligan's thinking echoes Dante's in the *Divine Comedy*, when he suggested that the hottest places in hell are reserved for those who, in a period of moral crisis, maintain their neutrality.[13]

To lift a page from an older tradition, one might say that Gilligan saw each one of us as having the responsibility to be a *mensch*. The word *mensch* (rhymes with "bench") is Yiddish (an Ashkenazi Jewish language written in the Hebrew alphabet, with a primarily but not exclusively German vocabulary). A *mensch* is a person of character, an individual of recognized worth and behavior. James Atlas says that a *mensch* is a person of fundamental decency, a person of high values and standards. A *mensch* is both compassionate and proactive in relationships with others. A *mensch*, whether male or female, tries to do the right thing, for the right reason, purposefully. A *mensch* is not a saint or a hero, or someone always perfect in conduct, but she does always see her life in the context of others and, when necessary, in the service of others. Perhaps the concept of *mensch* is best understood by offering an example of its opposite. In the words of Mma Precious Ramotswe, the fictional Botswanian female detective of the *No. 1 Ladies' Detective Agency* fame: "He was a bad man, a selfish man who never once put himself out for another – not even his wife."

Being a person of character is an ongoing activity and not a one-time affair or an episodic experience. Ethical character is formed over time and withstands the test of time. Character, like a skill, athletic ability, or musical talent, must be practiced in order to be perfected and maintained. And yet some mistakes, some actions, some behavior, whether intended or not, can change our lives and our reputations forever. As Warren Buffet said, "[i]t takes 20 years to build a reputation of character and five minutes to ruin it."[14]

Character development is part of what Plato means by the "examined life." In *The Apology* he (or rather the character Socrates) argues that the first question and the first principle of philosophy is to be able to grasp and understand the admonition of the oracle of Apollo at Delphi: *Gnothi seauton*, "Know thyself." For Plato, the question of self ("Who am I?") precedes all other considerations, including that of self and others ("What ought I to do with others?"). In his view, only persons who know themselves both in their strengths and weaknesses can be balanced individuals and effective leaders. As he suggested in the *Republic*: Someone who would rule the world must first rule himself.[15]

Assuming the leadership of an organization – whether a club, a sports team, or a global corporation – is a daunting and dangerous thing to do; to attempt it without a solid understanding of who you are (your character) and without a clear sense of what you are willing and unwilling to do (your integrity and conscience) is a formula for public failure and personal tragedy. What one political observer said about others also applies to oneself:

> Find out what a person truly believes in and what they want to be. Don't just judge a candidate by what they say. Especially, by what they say in front of a camera or a microphone.[16]

The Dark Side of Character

When philosophers and psychologists talk about character and use this term, they sometimes use it as if it were a finished product and/or a predetermined state of being. Character is commonly thought of as a *bonum delectabile* ("a pleasurable good"), and a natural end-state of development. Many people, consciously or not, associate character with the classical Aristotelian model of character: a person who is a paragon of virtue, a person who is complete – a model of excellence and a bedrock of integrity. Too many of us assume, commonsensically, that a person of character is a person of enlightened egalitarian standards and of benevolent aspirations. But "character," like "ethics" and "leadership," is a normative term, a term that must be analyzed, evaluated, measured and weighted in order for us to determine its meaning and value. As we indicated in Chapter 1, "character" is an "essentially contested concept." The word is one we immediately recognize and regularly use, but its exact meaning and defining characteristics can vary widely. Ultimately its meaning is dependent upon custom, personal subjectivity, time/place, cultural circumstances, and aesthetic choice.

According to Robert Solomon, character is a vessel that needs to be filled up by life. Character results from what life gives us and exposes us to. It is the result of our experiences in the world and of the choices we make in the world. Hence, suggests Solomon, while the Aristotelian model of character may in fact be a paradigm to aspire to, it's only one possible outcome among many. There are no guarantees. But, whatever the final outcome, Solomon insists that character defines who we are. It organizes our life's geography, informs our understanding of human nature, and shapes our philosophy of life.

This all means that character formation is experiential, value-laden, idiosyncratic, and diverse. All character types are driven or motivated by philosophical perspectives that may or may not prove to be ethical in ways we recognize or like. In consequence, although we regularly praise the character of Lincoln, Churchill, and Gandhi, villains such as Hitler or Stalin or cynics like Machiavelli, like it or not, are persons of character as well, because their lives were formed through enduring choices and through values that shaped their personalities. In leadership the role of character is not in question. The real questions are: What kind of character does a leader possess? Is that character good or bad?

Niccolò Machiavelli (1469–1527), for example, saw the world very differently. All of life is about politics, and the world is divided between those who possess power and those who seek it. Power is the goal – the end of politics and life. Without it, said Machiavelli, no other goal, good or bad, will be accomplished and no form of stability (or sinecure) will be possible within a state. For Machiavelli, the virtuous politician, the politician of character, is one who covets, desires, and recognizes the value and purpose of power as an end in itself and pursues it monomaniacally, without concern for the well-being of others.

In 1513 Machiavelli wrote (but never published) *The Prince*. His intention was to give the book as a gift to his Prince (Giuliano de' Medici) in hopes of advancing his own political career. *The Prince* is not an abstract treatise. It is, rather, a concise manual for those who would acquire or increase their power and status as a leader. Perhaps a more contemporary title for *The Prince* would read: *How to Succeed in Leadership and Politics and Live Long Enough to Talk about It*. Historically, *The Prince* became a handbook for aspirants to political power and leadership. People such as Cardinal Richelieu, Frederick the Great, Otto Von Bismarck, or Georges Clemenceau publicly extolled its virtues. Many scholars have credited it with establishing modern political science (*realpolitik*). Benito Mussolini referred to it as "a necessary tool for statesmen."[17] Bertrand Russell called it a "handbook for gangsters."[18] Indeed, what other description would fit a book that teaches lessons such as these:

- Princes ought to eliminate entirely the families of rulers whose territories they wish to possess securely.
- Princes ought to murder their opponents rather than confiscate their property, since those who have been robbed, but are not dead, can plot revenge.

- Men forget the murder of their fathers sooner than the loss of their patrimony.
- If one has to choose between inflicting severe injustices and inflicting light injustices, one ought to inflict severe ones.[19]

For Machiavelli, ethics and leadership do not mix. He believed that judgments of good/bad, right/wrong, moral/immoral exist only in the personal sphere of life. Leadership is an entirely different matter. He maintained that it is naïve to think that a leader should follow the same moral code as the one that governs the conduct of private individuals. According to him, the moral purview and license of a leader is entirely different from that of an ordinary individual. He was convinced that the character and moral qualities of a prince "are virtues or vices only as they help or hinder his political functioning."[20]

For Machiavelli, there is no injustice or paradox in a leader's ruthless pursuit of power. He believed that all human beings are corrupt, greedy, and desirous of the possessions and positions of others. Therefore, in a world that knows no goodness and is a struggle of all against all for power and place, leaders must be stern, cruel, and fanatically committed:

> It is the nature of people to be fickle; to persuade them of something is easy; but to make them stand fast in that conviction is hard. Hence things must be arranged so that when they no longer believe they can be compelled to believe by force.[21]
>
> Any Prince who tries to be good all the time is bound to come to ruin among the greater number of those who aren't good![22]

We need not, of course, return to the Italian Renaissance to find examples of flawed character development and questionable leadership standards. We need only look at the fictional and real world of American big business at the start of the twenty-first century to come up with more than a few examples.

In 1987 director Oliver Stone created *Wall Street*, a film that critiques the mindset of many high-stake players in the financial world: players who embrace a value system that places profits and wealth, "doing the deal," and winning above all other considerations. In 2010 Stone released *Wall Street: Money Never Sleeps*, which further develops and updates his indictment of self-centered, predatory trading practices that can take the entire world to the brink of a complete economic meltdown. (The tension and drama of *Wall Street II* was, of course, enhanced by the real-life implosion of American International Group (AIG), Lehman Brothers, Bear Stearns, and the entire sub-prime mortgage industry in 2008.)

The main character and the villain in both of these movies is Gordon Gekko – a name, said movie critic Roger Ebert, "no doubt inspired by the lizard that feeds on insects and sheds his tail when trapped."[23] Gekko, played by a chiseled-faced and raspy-voiced Michael Douglas, is a hunter, a warrior, a survivor who is more interested in winning the game and going on to the next game than in spending the profits. In winning he is utterly unconcerned about the collateral damage that occurs.

Although in the second film the Gekko character evidences a brief moment of fatherly feeling when he attempts to reconcile himself with his daughter and grandson, he is still a player, and everything is still about winning the game. In *Wall Street I* he famously declares: "Greed is good!" In *Wall Street II* he claims to be proven right: "Greed is good. [And] now . . . it's legal . . . Everyone is drinking the same Kool Aid."

Gordon Gekko is an iconic movie personality that is both a model of bad character and a classic example of being a *misleader* in all aspects of his life. Gekko's worldview is narrowly and narcissistically focused. Like Machiavelli's Prince, Gekko seeks exclusively the satisfaction of his own desires and goals and is essentially unconcerned about the wellbeing of the community, the organization, or even the family he belongs to. For him,

> Greed is right, greed works. Greed clarifies, cuts through, and captures the essence of the evolutionary spirit. Greed in all its forms – greed for life, for money, for love, for knowledge – has marked the upward surge of humankind.

Nowhere in his repertoire of personal and professional skills and strategies does he ever compute the possibility that all players have social obligations because the action of each player affects everyone.

Fiction aside, it doesn't take much time to come up with a long list of companies and characters on which Gekko is modeled: AIG, Lehman Brothers, Bear Stearns, and so many others. Enron, which now only exists in the title of a Broadway musical, will long remain the poster child for corporate mismanagement, mischievousness, and *misleadership*.

How did Enron become the tainted icon of an era? How did it transform itself from one of America's paragons into one of its pariahs? How can it be that Enron could literally declare bankruptcy overnight? How can it be that the sixth largest energy corporation in the world wound up being vilified in the press as running a vast Ponzi scheme on its customers and stockholders?

Catastrophes like these are usually brought about by people's choices and actions; they are rarely ever a matter of happenstance or luck. Someone decides to do the wrong thing on purpose. In the case of Enron, CEO and chairman Kenneth Lay was the unquestioned driving force behind the birth and initial stellar growth of the company. He took it from a few oilrigs in Oklahoma to number seven on the Fortune 500 list. The company was further propelled into the stratosphere when Lay hired Jeffery Skilling and eventually promoted him to CEO. According to Harvard business scholars P. M. Healy and K. G. Paleph, Enron quickly reached unprecedented heights:

> From the start of the 1990s until year-end 1998, Enron's stock rose by 311 percent, only modestly higher than the rate of growth in the Standard & Poor's 500. But then the stock soared. It increased by 56 percent in 1999 and a further 87 percent in 2000, compared to a 20 percent increase and a 10 percent decline for the index during the same years. By December 31, 2000, Enron's stock was priced at $83.13, and its market capitalization exceeded $60 billion, 70 times earnings and six times book value, an indication of the stock market's high expectations about its future prospects. Enron was rated the most innovative large company in America in *Fortune* magazine's survey of Most Admired Companies.[24]

Yet within a year Enron's stock prices plummeted to nearly zero, and on December 2, 2001 Enron lawyers filed for bankruptcy.

As the title of the award winning documentary of the same name suggests, Lay and Skillings thought themselves to be, and acted as if they were, "The Smartest Guys in the Room."[25] For a long time, and for all of their supporters and many of their detractors, this seemed to be true. They created a corporate culture that relentlessly pursued creativity and continuous growth. They stressed risk taking, pushing the envelope, and testing the outer limits of every venture they entered into. Both in relation to the usual standards and practices of finance and accounting and in relation to the energy industry, they altered the rules, they changed the rules, they abandoned the rules whenever they thought it to be necessary or in their best interest.

In the end, by means of highly questionable "mark-to-market" accounting practices, "structural financing," "special purpose entities," "ricochet arbitrage," "pump and dump" stock pricing practices, and unfettered self-dealing, Lay, Skilling, and their henchman, CFO Andy Fastow, created a totally fantasy business entity that, while theoretically worth a fortune, was over $35 billion in debt, and on October 16, 2001 announced a third quarter operating loss of $618 billion. To borrow the words of Gertrude Stein – "there was no there, there."[26]

The first question that must be answered is, why? Why would someone making millions of dollars a year risk his safety for more? The explanation is altogether human, but not altogether rational. This is all about the thrill of the game. The excitement of the risk. The emotion and intellectual pleasure of the challenge. It's about the need to win, no matter the odds. It's about the palpable rush of breaking the rules knowingly. It's about the narcissistic illusion of invincibility. It's about feeling smugly superior to those ordinary mortals who don't take chances. And, every time you get away with it, it's about the arrogant certainty of your infallibility.

While the Enron saga sounds like a melodramatic rewrite of Tom Wolfe's *The Bonfire of the Vanities*, it is shamefully true. And it all comes down to the prime movers in the story: Lay and Skilling. At the center was their indifference to others and their wish to be "Masters of the Universe."[27]

While it can be argued, at least theoretically, that Lay and Skilling did not initially and intentionally set out to misappropriate and misdirect billions of dollars of investors' money, the same argument cannot be made for Bernard Madoff. Even though he said, somewhat disingenuously, that he "always meant to stop," the reality is that, from the outset, he ran a scam that ended up being a $65-billion Ponzi scheme. As he admitted to his sons, it was "one big lie."[28] Madoff's intention was always to "make off" with the money.

Madoff founded the Wall Street firm Bernard L. Madoff Investment Securities LLC in 1960, and his basic strategy was neither novel nor dependent on a complicated algorithm. Essentially it was a straightforward Ponzi or pyramid scheme. A financial investor (the schemer) promises lucrative returns on the original investment. The schemer then creates an illusion of legitimacy and solvency by paying earlier investors from investment capital raised from later ones. Paid off investors tend to invest more money or to encourage their friends to invest in what they believe to be a safe bet, too good to pass up. As long as the schemer can continue to bring in new investors to pay off the old ones, there may be no end to a Ponzi scheme. That is, as long as a critical number of investors do not want their money back. (In fact the original Ponzi scheme, initiated by Charles Ponzi, lasted for only about nine months, from 1919 to 1920, and involved about 40,000 people and $15–$20 million dollars.)[29]

Madoff's twist on the basic Ponzi scheme approach was subtle and clever. In a standard Ponzi scheme you need a continuous stream of investors. You need dupes, and more dupes. Any dupes will do. But, since schemers can't be choosers, they often wind up with some weak or unreliable dupes who need their profits back, and therefore the scheme is always vulnerable to sudden collapse. Madoff's gimmick was to never let an unknown or ordinary dupe invest in his scheme. He was cautious. He was selective. He didn't want people who needed short-term returns. He wanted investors with deep pockets, who clearly wanted/demanded a solid return, but who would never touch their initial investment. Using his vast network of wealthy friends, family and business acquaintances, Madoff created an impressive list of wealthy investors, who in turn spread the word to their wealthy friends and associates, creating an air of elitism by means of an "invitation only" policy. Madoff promised his approximately 13,500 individual investors annual returns of 10 percent to 12 percent every year, regardless of market conditions.

Madoff's scheme worked so long as markets kept rising and investors didn't need to call on their principle. But in 2008, as global financial conditions worsened, investors became increasingly nervous about market stability and a large number of them went to Madoff seeking to reclaim some or all of their initial investment. In December 2008 Madoff confided to his sons and his wife that he was "struggling to meet $7 billion in redemption." He told them that he was "finished," that he had "absolutely nothing left," and that his investment fund was a fake and nothing more than a "giant Ponzi scheme."[30] On December 11, 2008 Madoff was charged with eleven counts of securities fraud and surrendered to federal authorities. He is now serving a sentence of 150 years, the maximum allowed, in the Federal Correctional Institution near Butner, North Carolina.

Differences and nuances aside, we believe that it is obvious that the Gordon Gekko character in the two *Wall Street* dramas and the real-life Ken Lay, Jeff Skillings, and Bernie Madoff can all be described in the same way. Factual or fictional, they are players. They view business as a zero-sum, win-or-lose game. They wanted to be winners. They needed to be winners. They defined themselves by their wins, not by their losses. As far as they were concerned, losers deserved whatever happened to them, and non-players didn't even matter. As players, all four characters reveled more in the risk of the game than just in the possible financial rewards; and, worst of all, they were all utterly unconcerned about possible repercussions to others.

Gekko, Lay, Skillings, and Madoff may have all been charismatic, intelligent, shrewd financial wizards; but they were not men of principle. Historian J. Rufus Fears argues that there are four central ingredients to leadership: a bedrock of principles; a moral compass; a vision; and the ability to build a consensus in order to achieve that vision.[31] Our four tycoons of trickery possessed all of these ingredients, all of these talents and abilities, but in a perverted form. Their "principles" were purely pecuniary; their moral compass and vision was narcissistic; and the consensus they sought was chimerical. These are all men of character, but of *bad* character. In a negative way, they define the importance of character just as much as some of those leaders we admire most.

Character as Goodwill

The thesis of this book is straightforward. Leadership is not just a set of learned skills, a series of outcomes, a career, a profession, or a title. Leadership, at its core, is about character: specifically, a character attuned to its ethical responsibilities to others. The kind of character that, in regard to others, always tries to do the right thing, for the right reason, on purpose.

Kant argued that the good will or character, a person's good moral disposition, is the precondition for achieving the moral life. Everything else that happens in a person's life, whether good or bad, can be chalked up to accident or coincidence, said Kant; but good will is acquired intentionally, and it is the stimulus for ethical behavior:

> Nothing in the world – indeed even beyond the world – can possibly be conceived which could be called good without qualification except *a good will*. Intelligence, wit, judgment, and the other talents of the mind . . . or courage, resoluteness, and perseverance as qualities of temperament, are doubtless in many respects good and desirable. But they can become extremely bad and harmful if the will, which is to make use of these gifts of nature and which in its special constitution is called character, is not good.[32]

Like the moral life, leadership is about dealing with others. As Drucker observes, leadership is not good in itself, it is not an end in itself; rather it is a means to an end. The purpose and the justification of all forms of leadership, says Drucker, is that it makes life bearable, meaningful, and productive. Leadership, he insists, is for and about human beings. Leadership is about growing and developing the collective human experience.[33]

Paradoxically, perhaps, the critical and final "end" task or job of a leader is to make oneself irrelevant or unnecessary. That is, the "end" task of leadership is to make everyone a leader of his or her own job or unit. Leadership is not a sacred totem in itself. Leaders exist only for the sake of the society they serve. And what distinguishes the ethical leader from the *misleader* is that for ethical leadership it is more important to do the right thing than to do the thing right.

Notes to Chapter Three

1   Warren Bennis, quoted in David Ulrich, Jack Zenger, and Norm Smallwood, *Results-Based Leadership*. Boston, MA: Harvard Business School Press, 1999, p. 14.

2   Plato, *The Republic*, translated and with an Introduction by Francis MacDonald Cornford. New York: Oxford University Press, 1968, p. 1.

3   Ibid., p. xxix.

4   James Q. Wilson, *The Moral Sense*. New York: Free Press, 1993, pp. 240–241.

5   Robert Soloman, *A Handbook for Ethics*. Orlando, FL: Harcourt Brace, 1996, pp. 83–88.

6   Martha C. Nussbaum, "Non-Relative Virtues: An Aristotelian Approach." In M. C. Nussbaum and Amartya Sen (eds.), *The Quality of Life*. Oxford: Clarendon, 1993, pp. 246–247.

7   "Integrity." In *The Routledge Encyclopedia of Philosophy Online*. At http://www.rep.Routledge.com/Article/L134SECT1.

8   Stephen L. Carter, quoted in Gilbert Meilaender, "Integral or Divided?" *First Things*, 63, 1996: 49–71, at p. 32.

9   Eric Zorn, "'Conscience': Old-Fashioned but not Obsolete." *Chicago Tribune*, May 23, 2002.

10   Immanuel Kant, *Religion within the Limits of Reason Alone*, translated by Theodore M. Greene and Hoyt H. Hudson. New York: Harper & Row, 1960, p. 174.

11   Carol Gilligan, *In a Different Voice: Psychological Theory and Women's Development*. Cambridge, MA: Harvard University Press, 1982, p. 66 (parentheses added).

12   Ibid., p. 100.

13   The reference to Dante's *Divine Comedy* in this context was made by President John F. Kennedy, who gave this quotation in a speech in Tulsa, OK on September 16, 1959; see Fred R. Shapiro, *The Yale Book of Quotations*. New Haven, CT: Yale University Press, 2006, p. 420.

14   Roger Lowenstein, *The Making of an American Capitalist*. New York: Random House, 1995, p. 111.

15   Plato, *The Republic*, translated by C. D. C. Reeve. Indianapolis, IN: Hackett, 2004, p. 96 (from Book IV): "And if any of them seems to be immune to sorcery, preserves his composure throughout, is a good guardian of himself and of the musical training he has received, and proves himself to be rhythmical and harmonious in all these trials – he is the sort of person who would be most useful, both to himself and to the city. And anyone who is tested as a child, youth, and adult, and always emerges as being without impurities, should be established as a ruler of the city as well as a guardian. . ."

16   Steve Edwards, Chicago Public Radio – WBEZ-FM: "A Political Round Up." Aired on January, 12, 2008.

17   "I believe Machiavelli's *Prince* to be the statesman's supreme guide. His doctrine is alive today because in the course of four hundred years no deep changes have occurred in the minds of men or in the actions of nations." Benito Mussolini, quoted in Robert Bingham Downs, *Books that Changed the World*. New York: Penguin Group, 2004, p. 201.

18   See Jonathan Powell, *The New Machiavelli: How to Wield Power in the Modern World*. London: Random House, 2010, p. 4.

19   Leo Strauss, "Machiavelli the Immoralist." In Niccolò Machiavelli, *The Prince*, translated and edited by Robert M. Adams. New York: W. W. Norton, 1977, p. 180.

20   Niccolò Machiavelli, *The Prince*, translated and edited by Robert M. Adams. New York: W. W. Norton, 1977, p. 56, n. 8 (translator's footnote).

21   Ibid., p. 18.

22   Ibid., p. 44.

23   Roger Ebert, "Empire of the Sun." *Chicago Sun-Times*, December 11, 1987.

24   Paul M. Healy and Krishna G. Palepu, "The Fall of Enron." *Journal of Economic Perspectives*, 5(2), 2003: 3.

25   "The Smartest Guys in the Room," directed by Alex Gibney. Documentary. Magnolia Home Entertainment, 2005.

26   Gertrude Stein, *Everybody's Autobiography*. New York: Random House, 1937, p. 298. Full quotation at http://www.huffingtonpost.com/matt-werner/oakland-in-popular-memory_b_1560227.html (last accessed November 20, 2012).

27   Denis Collins, "Enron: The Good, The Bad, and the Really Ugly." In Al Gini and Alexei M. Marcoux (eds.), *Case Studies In Business Ethics*, 6th ed. Upper Saddle River, NJ: Pearson-Prentice Hall, 2009, pp. 104–115.

28   David Voreacos and David Glovin, "Madoff Confessed $50 Billion Fraud before FBI Arrest." *Bloomberg News*, December 13, 2008. At http://www.bloomberg.com/apps/news?pid=newsarchive&sid=atUk.QnXAvZY (last accessed November 20, 2012). See also: "SEC: Complaint SEC against Madoff and BMIS LLC" (PDF). US Securities and Exchange Commission, December 11, 2008. At http://www.sec.gov/litigation/complaints/2008/comp-madoff121108.pdf (last accessed December 29, 2008); and Binyamin Appelbaum, David S. Hilzenrath, and Amit R. Paley, "All Just One Big Lie." *The Washington Post* (Washington Post Company), December 13, 2008. At http://www.washingtonpost.com/wp-dyn/content/article/2008/12/12/AR2008121203970.html?hpid=topnews (last accessed December 13, 2008).

29   "National Affairs: Take My Money!" *Time*, January 31, 1949. At http://www.time.com/time/magazine/article/0,9171,794507,00.html (last accessed November 20, 2012).

30   Appelbaum, Hilzenrath, and Paley, "All Just One Big Lie."

31   J. Rufus Fears, *Churchill*. Chantilly, VA: The Teaching Company, 2001, p. 4.

32   Immanuel Kant, *Foundations of the Metaphysics of Morals*, translated by Lewis White Beck. Indianapolis, IN: Bobbs-Merrill, 1976, p. 9.

33   Peter F. Drucker, "Leadership: More Doing Than Dash." *The Wall Street Journal*, January 6, 1988.

LEADERSHIP AND BUSINESS EXCELLENCE

4

Nothing great ever happens until leadership shows up.

Mike Singletary[1]

President Calvin Coolidge was more than a little right when he said: "The business of America is business." Business of all kinds is the economic backbone of this society. "No group in America is more influential than business persons. Their influence, for good and evil, enters every life and every home."[2] Like it or not, business serves as the moral metronome for society. The meter and behavior established by business and business leaders help to set the tone, develop the vision, and shape the patterns of behavior for all of us.

When most of us think of business, we tend to think big. We think Fortune 500. We think mega-corporations – American Express, Coca-Cola, General Electric, the Home Depot, McDonald's, Microsoft, and Verizon. Many of us think, naïvely, that business is what large corporations do. We are partially correct; but, if we only stopped there, we would be overlooking a vibrant and pulsating community of commercial entrepreneurs operating right down the block and all around us – Bonnie's Bakery, Danny's Deli, Tony's Tailor Shop, Sally's Hair Stylings, Barbara's Bookstore, Claire's Copy Shop.

In America – and in the world – big businesses have clout because, whether they exist within a democratic government or not, big businesses make big money. Dollars have influence, dollars vote, and, in big business(es), big money gets to vote early and often. Nevertheless, in spite of the depth and power of an estimated 5,868,849 corporations with total revenues in excess of $28,762,923,553,000 (that's nearly 29 trillion dollars), small businesses play a

10 Virtues of Outstanding Leaders: Leadership and Character, First Edition.
Al Gini and Ronald M. Green.
© 2013 John Wiley & Sons, Inc. Published 2013 by John Wiley & Sons, Inc.

major role in our economy and in the way we live. Recent census data indicate that there are 29.6 million small and family businesses in America, and 99 percent of them employ fewer than 500 people each.[3]

Statistics aside, "business" as a concept, as a definition or description, is not an entity, a factory, a company, or a place. Nor is it a particular product, service, or thing. The essence of business is an action, an activity that occurs between two or more individuals. Business is something we do. Business is, most fundamentally, a transaction or a trade. We engage in trade by relinquishing some property rights (or services) and by acquiring other property rights (or services) through an exchange with another person. For example, you relinquish two dollars to acquire a pack of six Pilot pens at Staples. Staples relinquishes a six-pen pack to acquire two dollars. Or you agree to provide legal services for a fee to Staples. You perform and they pay you. In all these cases you have each relinquished and acquired, or exchanged, property rights or services. So, at its most fundamental level, business is the activity of executing exchange transactions. If Staples didn't engage in exchange transactions, it wouldn't be a business firm.

Ethics in Business

The issue of ethics in business arises at the very core, the nexus of what we mean by business – transactions, actions in regard to others. Both business and ethics begin with the admission that we are not alone in, or the center of, the universe. We are communally living creatures. We are in need of each other. We are dependent upon each other to survive and thrive. Our collective existence requires us to continually make choices, be they good or bad, about "what we ought to do" in regard to others.

For R. Edward Freeman of the Darden School of Business, two competing paradigms are firmly entrenched in our collective psyche and give rise to what he calls "The Problem of the Two Realms." One realm or paradigm is the realm of business. It is the realm of hard, measurable facts: market studies, focus groups, longitudinal studies, production costs, managed inventory, stock value, research and development, profit and loss statements, quantitative analysis. The other realm is the realm of philosophy or ethics. This is the soft realm, says Freeman, the realm of the seemingly ineffable: myth, meaning, metaphor, purpose, quality, significance, rights, and values. While the realm of business can be easily dissected, diagnosed, compared, and judged, the realm of philosophy is not open to precise interpretation, comparison, and evaluation. For Freeman, in a society that has absorbed and embraced the adage "the goods of life are equal to the good life," these two realms are accorded separate *but* unequal status. Only in moments of desperation, disaster, or desire does the realm of business solicit the commentary and insights of the realm of ethics. Otherwise, the realm of business operates under the dictum of legal moralism: *Everything is allowed which is not strictly forbidden.*[4]

For Freeman, the assertions that "business is business" and that ethics is what we try to do in our private lives simply do not withstand close scrutiny. Business is a human institution, a basic part of the communal fabric of life. Just as governments come to be out of the human need for order, security, and fulfillment, so too does business. The goal of all business, labor, and work is to make life more secure, more stable, and more equitable. Business exists to serve more than just itself. No business can view itself as an isolated entity, unaffected by the demands of individuals and society. As such, business is required to ask the question: "What ought to be done in regard to the others we work with and serve?" For Freeman, business ethics, rather than being an oxymoron, a contradiction in terms, is really a pleonasm, a redundancy in terms. As Henry Ford, Sr. once said: "For a long time people believed that the only purpose of industry is to make a profit. They are wrong. Its purpose is to serve the general welfare."[5]

What business ethics advocates is that people apply in the workplace those commonsensical rules and standards learned at home, from the lectern, and from the pulpit. The moral issues facing a person are age-old, and these are essentially the same issues facing a business – only writ in large script.[6] According to Freeman, ethics is

> how we treat each other, every day, person to person. If you want to know about a company's ethics, look at how it treats people – customers, suppliers, and employees. Business is about people. And business ethics is about how customers and employees are treated.[7]

What is being asked of the business community is neither extraordinary nor excessive: a decent product at a fair price; honesty in advertisements; fair treatment of employees, customers, suppliers, and competitors; a strong sense of responsibility to the communities it inhabits and serves; and a reasonable profit for the financial risk taking of its stockholders and owners. In the words of General Robert Wood Johnson, former president of Johnson & Johnson:

> The day has passed when business was a private matter – if it ever really was. In a business society, every act of business has social consequences and may arouse public interest. Every time business hires, builds, sells or buys, it is acting

for the . . . people as well as for itself, and it must be prepared to accept full responsibility for its acts.[8]

Workplace Ethics

As we mentioned earlier, when people talk about business in a general sense, they are usually referring to mammoth organizations. But, at a more personal level, when people talk about the world of business, commerce, and trade, their point of reference is more parochial. They think about *their* work, *their* jobs, *their* careers, how *they* earn a living, and how it all adds up and affects *their* lives.

No one is neutral about the topic of work. As adults, work preoccupies our lives. There is, in fact, nothing we do with our lives more than we work. We will not sleep, recreate, and spend time with our family and friends as much as we work. In the most general sense, work can be defined as any activity we need to do (show up at the office every day) or want to do (paint the garage, plant tulip bulbs) in order to achieve the basic requirements of life or maintain a certain lifestyle.

Work, however, is not just about earning a livelihood. It is not just about getting paid, about gainful employment. Work is also one of the most significant contributing factors to one's inner life and development. Beyond mere survival, we create ourselves in our work. Because work preoccupies our lives and is the central focus of our time and energies, it not only provides us with income, but it also literally names us, identifies us, to both others and ourselves. Even when we are dissatisfied with or dislike the work we do, our choice of occupation irrevocably "labels" us. *Where* we work, *how* we work, *what* we do at work, and the general climate and culture of the workplace mark us for life.[9]

Given the centrality of work in our lives, given the sheer number of hours we put in on the job, given the money we make and the stuff we are able to acquire, given the kinds of status and success we can achieve on the job, how can work not affect our values and sense of ethics? How is it possible to retain a purely private sense of objectivity, untouched by our work experience? How is it possible to not be swallowed by the needs and demands of the workplace? How is it possible not to be at least swayed, if not totally compromised, by the work environment that sustains us? The habits we acquire on the job, what we are exposed to, what is demanded of us, the pressure of peers – *can* change, influence, and/or erode our personal conduct and standards. At the very least, *when everybody else in the workplace is doing "it" (whatever "it" is), isn't it natural to at least ask yourself: "Why not me too?"*

Leaders as Role Models

As students of business ethics, we are convinced that, without the continuous commitment, enforcement, and modeling of leadership, standards of business ethics cannot and will not be achieved in any organization. The ethics of leadership – whether good or bad, positive or negative – affects the ethos of the workplace and thereby helps to form the ethical choices and decisions of the workers in the workplace. Leaders help to set the tone, develop the vision, and shape the behavior of all those involved in organizational life. As we have said, the critical point to understand here is that, like it or not, business and politics serve as the metronome for our society. Leaders set the patterns and establish the models for our behavior as individuals and as a group.

Both directly and indirectly, both consciously and unconsciously, leaders create and sustain the culture of an organization through their conduct and choices. Leadership sets the pace, communicates the standards, and establishes the mission and the vision, as well as the morale of day-to-day mundane reality. Ethical ideas, standards, and values may originate anywhere within the structure of an organization. But without the backing, encouragement, and *imprimatur* of leadership the best intentions and ideas wither on the vine. Without leadership, ethics doesn't happen. Although the phrases "business ethics" and "moral leadership" are technically distinguishable, in fact they designate inseparable components, neither of which can exist without the other in the life of an organization.

The fundamental principle that underlies our thesis regarding leadership and ethical conduct is age-old. In his *Nichomachean Ethics*, Aristotle suggested that morality cannot be learned simply by reading a treatise on virtue. The spirit of morality, said Aristotle, is awakened in the individual only through the witness and conduct of a moral person. The principle of "witnessing another," or what we now refer to as "patterning," "role modeling," or "mentoring," is predicated on a four-step process. The first three of these read as follows: (1) As communal creatures, we learn to conduct ourselves primarily through the actions of significant others. (2) When the behavior of others is repeated often enough and proves to be peer-group positive, we emulate these actions. (3) If and when our actions are in turn reinforced by others, they become acquired characteristics or behavioral habits.

According to B. F. Skinner, who takes only these three steps into account, the process is now complete. By affecting the actions of individuals through modeling and reinforcement, the leader in question (in Skinnerean terms, "the controller of the environmental stimuli") has succeeded in reproducing the type of behavior sought after or desired. For Skinner, the primary goal of the process need not take into consideration either the value or worth of the action or the interests or intent of the reinforced or operant-conditioned actor. From Skinner's psychological perspective, all that is important is the response evoked.[10] From a philosophical perspective, however, even role modeling that produces a positive or beneficial action does not fulfill the basic requirements of the ethical enterprise, either at the descriptive or at the normative level. Modeling, emulation, habit, results – whether positive or negative – are not enough. There is a fourth and final step in the process. This step must include reflection, evaluation, choice, and conscious intent on the part of the actor, because ethics is always "an inside-out proposition" involving free will.[11]

The American philosopher John Dewey argues that every serious ethical system rejects the notion that one's standard of conduct should simply and uncritically derive from acceptance of the rules of the culture one happens to live in. Even when custom, habit, convention, public opinion, or law are correct in their mandates, to embrace them without critical reflection does not constitute a complete and formal ethical act and might be better labeled "ethical happenstance" or "ethics by virtue of circumstantial accident." According to Dewey, ethics is essentially "reflective conduct"; he believes that the distinction between custom and reflective morality is clearly marked. The former bases the standard and the rules of conduct solely on habit; the latter appeals to reason and choice.

When we insist that workers or followers derive their models for ethical conduct from the witness of leaders, we are not denying that workers or followers share a responsibility for the overall conduct and culture of their organization. We do not want to reduce the responsibility of workers, but rather to explain the process involved: the witness of leaders both communicates the ethics of institutions and establishes the desired standards and expectations that leaders demand. Although it would be naïve to assert that employees unreflectively absorb the manners and mores of the workplace, it would be equally naïve to suggest that they are unaffected by the modeling and standards of their places of employment. As we said, work is how we spend our lives. The lessons we learn there play a part in the development of our moral perspective and of the manner in which we formulate and adjudicate ethical choices. As business ethicists, we believe that, without the active intervention of effective moral leadership, we are doomed to wage a rear-guard action forever. Students of organizational development are never really surprised when poorly managed, badly led businesses do unethical things.

A Culture of Narcissism

Not all forms of leadership should be emulated, because not all leaders are concerned about the people they lead. Bad leaders – whom we have called misleaders – are primarily focused on their own self-serving exercise of power and not on their constituents' concerns and needs. Misleaders mismanage and misdirect the people and companies they lead, and they do so in the pursuit of ephemeral status and success (money, power, prestige) that ultimately prove to be destructive to them, their organizations, their communities, and the business system as a whole.

Howard S. Schwartz, in his underappreciated management text *Narcissistic Process and Corporate Decay*, argues that too many businesses fail to be bastions of benign, other-directed ethical reasoning. The rule of these businesses, Schwartz believes, remains the "law of the jungle," "the survival of the fittest." The goal of survival engenders a combative "us against them mentality," which condones the moral imperative of getting ahead by any means necessary. Schwartz calls this phenomenon "organizational totalitarianism" – a self-contained, self-serving world view, which rationalizes anything done on behalf of its perpetrators and does not require justification on any grounds outside of their own interest. Within such a "totalitarian logic," neither leaders nor followers – neither rank nor file – operate as independent agents. To "maintain their place," to "get ahead," all must conform. The agenda of "organizational totalitarianism" is always the preservation of the status quo.[12]

In his landmark book *Moral Mazes*, Robert Jackall parallels much of Schwartz's analysis of organizational behavior, but he does so from a sociological rather than a psychological perspective. For Jackall, many American business organizations are examples of "patrimonial bureaucracies" wherein "fealty relations of personal loyalty" are the rule and the glue of organizational life. Jackall argues that corporations are often like fiefdoms of the Middle Ages, wherein the lord of the manor (the CEO, the president) offers protections, prestige, and status to his vassals (the managers) and serfs (the workers) in return for homage (commitment) and service (work). In such a system advancement and promotion are predicated on loyalty, trust, politics, and personality as much as – if not more than – on experience, education, ability, and actual accomplishments.

Jackall maintains that, as in the model of a feudal system, employees of a corporation are expected to become functionaries of the system and supporters of the status quo. Their loyalty is to the powers that be; their duty is to perpetuate performance and profit; and their values can be none other than those sanctioned by the organization. Jackall contends that the logic of organizations (places of business) and the collective personality of the workplace conspire to override the wants, desires, and aspirations of the individual worker. No matter what a person believes off the job, said Jackall, on the job all of us are required, to a greater or lesser extent, to suspend, bracket, or only selectively manifest our personal convictions:

> What is right in the corporation is not what is right in a man's home or his church. What is right in the corporation is what the guy above you wants from you.[13]

These are dark perspectives. Within the scope of Schwartz and Jackall's allied analyses, "normative" moral leadership is not possible. The model offered is both absolute and inflexible, and only "regular company guys" make it to the top. The maverick, the radical, the ethical reformer are not tolerated. The "institutional logic" of the system does not permit disruption, deviance, or default. We do not agree. Although these perspectives present one side of corporate life, they ignore the role – and even the possibility – of ethically informed leadership.

According to ethicist Georges Enderle, business leadership would be relatively simple *if* business only had to produce a product or service, without being concerned about employees; *if* management only had to deal with concepts, structures, and strategies, without worrying about human relations; *if* businesses just had to resolve their own problems, without being obligated to take the interests of individuals or society into consideration.[14] But, as we have insisted, this is not the case. Leadership is always about self and others. Like ethics, labor, and business, leadership is a symbiotic, communal relationship. It's about leaders, followers, constituencies, and all the stakeholders involved. And, like ethics, labor, and business, leadership is an intrinsic part of the human experience.

In the end, all leadership is about the establishment and maintenance of a successful productive community of individuals who recognize and respect their mutual need for each other. Critical (practical) thinking and moral (prudential) thinking are fundamental tasks of leadership. Ethical leadership, whether in business or elsewhere, is not an outlier or an oxymoron. It expresses the true nature of the leadership challenge. In the chapters ahead we go beyond asserting this point, to demonstrate its truth in the lives of a series of outstanding leaders.

Notes to Chapter Four

1   Mike Singletary, quoted in "Mike Singletary Happy to Get Chance with 49ers." *Chicago Tribune*, October 26, 2008. At http://articles.chicagotribune.com/

2008-10-26/sports/0810250536_1_coach-ditka-49ers-safety-ronnie-lott-bears/2 (last accessed November 20, 2012).

2   Raymond C. Baumhart, S.J., *An Honest Profit*. New York: Holt, Rinehart & Winston, 1968, p. xiii.

3   "Sales by Firm Structure." In *Other Useful Industry Statistics*, Bizstats.com, 2007. At NOhttp://www.bizstats.com/useful-industry-data.php (last accessed April 11, 2011).

4   R. Edward Freeman, "The Problem of the Two Realms." Lecture delivered at Loyola University Chicago, The Center for Ethics, Spring, 1992.

5   Henry Ford, Sr., quoted by Thomas Donaldson, *Corporations and Morality*. Englewood Cliffs, NJ: Prentice Hall, 1982, p. 57.

6   Ibid., p. 14.

7   Freeman, "The Problem of the Two Realms."

8   General Robert Wood Johnson, quoted by Frederick G. Harmon and Garry Jacobs, "Company Personality: The Heart of the Matter." *Management Review*, 74(10), 1985: 10, 38, 74.

9   Everett C. Hughes, "Work and the Self." In John H. Rohrer and Muzafa Sherif (eds.), *Social Psychology at the Crossroads*. New York: Harper, 1951, pp. 313–323.

10   B. F. Skinner, *Beyond Freedom and Dignity*. New York: Alfred A. Knopf, 1971, pp. 107–108, 150, 214–215.

11   Stephen R. Covey, *The Seven Habits of Highly Effective People*. New York: A Fireside Book, 1990, pp. 42–43.

12   Howard S. Schwartz, *Narcissistic Process and Corporate Decay*. New York: New York University Press, 1990.

13   Robert Jackall, *Moral Mazes*. New York: Oxford University Press, 1988, p. 6.

14   Georges Enderle, "Some Perspectives of Managerial Ethical Leadership." *Journal of Business Ethics*, 6, 1987: 657.

THE TEN VIRTUES

Many things are formidable, and yet nothing is quite so formidable as man.
Over the gray sea and the storming south wind,
Through the foam and welling of the waves, he makes his perilous way;
The Earth also, highest of the deities, who never shows fatigue, nor exhaustion, nor decay,
Ever he furrows and ploughs, year on year, with his ploughshare, muzzles and horses . . .
He, the cunning one,
And by his arts he achieves mastery of the savage game, of the creatures who wind their way upon the heights, tamed through his wondrous art,
And the defiant steed he bends to his will under the bit . . .
Supplied with cleverness of every imaginable type,
He ventures once towards evil, and then towards good.
If he honors the laws of the land and the right attested by the Gods,
Then may his city prosper. But homeless shall he be if he boorishly debases himself.

Sophocles, Antigone, "Ode to Man"[1]

The discipline of ethics begins with the Greeks. The great philosophers of ancient Greece – Socrates, Plato, and Aristotle – were among the first people to bring human reason and experience to bear on the question: "How should we live our lives?" While these intellectual giants disagreed on many details, they shared two fundamental convictions. One was that individual and social flourishing depend on the moral character of a community, its leaders, and its members. The second was that character flows from human moral excellences or virtues.

10 Virtues of Outstanding Leaders: Leadership and Character, First Edition.
Al Gini and Ronald M. Green.
© 2013 John Wiley & Sons, Inc. Published 2013 by John Wiley & Sons, Inc.

These core convictions ring forth in Sophocles' magnificent "Ode to Man." We humans are clever animals. We ply the raging sea in fragile vessels and subdue the resistant earth. With cunning we domesticate wild creatures. If we have the wisdom to honor the divinely inspired moral laws of right, we prosper. But, if we depart from these laws, our community collapses and we are cast out, homeless, from our city.

What was true thousands of years ago remains so today. The quality of life of a community, whether it is a political unit or a business corporation, depends on the character of all its members and on the virtue of its leaders. Our ten virtues of outstanding leaders belong to this intellectual tradition.

The term "virtue" may seem old-fashioned. As Gabriele Taylor notes, it "often implies not praise but rather the suspicion of a certain primness, or perhaps a more or less self-conscious do-gooding."[2] It is sometimes applied only to sexual conduct (as when a woman loses her "virtue"). But, to recover the meaning and value of the term, we must understand its origin. The Greek word that we translate as "virtue" is *aretē*. It literally means "excellence," and was routinely applied to everyday objects or activities. In the Greek view, all things have a characteristic "function" (*ergon*). When something performs its function well, it displays excellence. A knife that cuts well has *aretē*. A skilled athlete who masters his sport and functions at peak performance also exhibits *aretē*.

Against this background, it was natural for the Greeks to apply the term to human beings generally. A man or woman of *aretē* is someone of the highest effectiveness; a person of virtue uses all his or her faculties, strength, bravery, intellect, and cunning, to achieve real results. She performs her human *ergon* excellently.

When virtue is understood as excellence in function, its link to another key Greek idea becomes clear. This is the concept of *eudaimonia*. Usually translated "happiness" or "flourishing," *eudaimonia* is a word composed of *eu*, meaning "good," and a derivative of *daimōn*, which designated a supernatural spirit. Thus *eudaimonia* is better thought of as a state of being favored by the gods: "blessedness" might be a better translation. Since human virtue involves the excellent exercise of human functions, it is not surprising that it naturally leads to *eudaimonia*. An individual who functions excellently usually experiences wellbeing. A city or organization filled with well-functioning people is likely to be a happy one – a community favored by the gods.

Up until now we have said nothing about moral virtue. In their ancient and core employments, both *aretē* and *eudaimonia* referred to the whole array of human activities, from athletics or theatrical performances to military arts or politics. Any of these could be spheres for the exhibition of human excellence. A politician who shrewdly manipulates voters by deceiving them about his real intentions could exemplify political *aretē*. Moral goodness has nothing to do with it. Though it sounds odd from our standpoint, in the ancient Greek way of thinking, a courtesan who parlayed her charms into wealth or power would be a virtuous (or excellent) prostitute.

One of the achievements of the great classical philosophers, however, was to connect these basic ideas and convictions to morality and ethics. Socrates, Plato, and Aristotle all argued that the good life, the life characterized by *eudaimonia*, was inseparable from the exercise of the explicitly moral virtues, especially justice, temperance, courage, and practical wisdom. Justice is the ability to determine the appropriate balance between self-interest and the rights and needs of others; temperance is the ability to practice self-control, moderation, or abstinence in the face of temptations such as those of food, drink, drugs, sex, or luxury; courage is the ability to face and overcome fear; and practical wisdom is the ability to select proper goals and the ways to achieve them in particular situations. Each of these virtues has the effect of constraining the heedless pursuit of purely selfish goals. Each one subordinates one's own impulses to the governance of reason and to the common good. Only by practicing self-discipline, the philosophers argued, can individuals and their communities really flourish and enjoy the *eudaimonia* at which everyone aims.

At the level of the individual, these grand claims for the link between moral virtue and happiness never went unchallenged. The sophists, a group of paid itinerant teachers who were widely viewed as valuing power over virtue (because this is how they publicized themselves), argued that people who ignored the constraints of virtue in selfish pursuits could enjoy prosperous and satisfying lives and achieve *eudaimonia*. In Plato's *Republic*, the character Glaucon introduces the tale of the "ring of Gyges," which renders its wearer invisible and allows him to rob and grab sexual pleasures with impunity. The suggestion is that only fear of punishment and concern for one's reputation make virtue necessary. Anyone lucky enough to put these aside would pursue unfettered gratification and achieve *eudaimonia*. Socrates, Plato, and Aristotle denied this. They were confident that real flourishing could not be achieved without the self-restraint of moral virtue.

At the level of the individual we can question this confidence. Good people do not always end well. Indeed, even Socrates suffered death for his devotion to virtue. But, at the level of organizational and community life and where the success of the leaders that guide them is at stake, the connection is much more solid. As James Wallace observes, while it is not the case that "a good human being invariably flourishes," it is true that, "the more good people there are in a community, the better life generally in the community is apt to be."[3] Leaders who cannot control their own impulses, who mistreat subordinates, who exploit and degrade organizational excellence, or who ignore the larger social contexts on which their community depends inevitably undermine their community's flourishing. Such leaders are *misleaders*. The communities and organizations headed by misleaders may flourish for a brief time, but the misleader usually implodes, pulling the community down with him. From Sadaam Hussein, the cruel tyrant of Iraq, to the heedless auto industry executives who led GM into bankruptcy, or to Dominique Strauss-Kahn, the sexually predatory head of the International Monetary Fund, misleaders who lack a sense of justice, self-control, or sound moral judgment invariably bring ruin on themselves and on those who depend on them. Thus moral character and successful leadership are inextricably linked. Thousands of years of human experience have only reinforced the wisdom of the great Greek philosophers: for organizational life, virtue is essential to the achievement of *eudaimonia*.

The Greek philosophers wrote for those who would lead a city-state (*polis*). Their lists of virtues remain as relevant as ever. But the modern business corporation raises new issues and new challenges. Success and flourishing in a world of high technology and global decision-making calls for an updated list of virtues. We offer ten such items. Some of them are clearly moral virtues, like those of the ancient writers, and even draw on their wisdom. Others represent new traits that are essential to the function, *ergon*, and excellence, *aretē*, of a modern leader.

Like the classical virtues, these ten virtues are traits of character. They describe not just the actions a leader performs, but the basic dispositions and motives that underlie those actions. They describe a leader's way of reasoning, his or her most basic beliefs, and the emotions associated with those beliefs. Thus the first of our ten virtues, "deep honesty," involves not just the outward fact that a leader usually tells the truth. Rather it describes the leader's basic commitment to the truth, the fundamental belief that the others deserve the truth, and a sense of shame or anger when deceitfulness replaces truth-telling. As a virtue, deep honesty is a character trait that "goes all the way down" into the leader's personality.

As Neera Badhwar put it, Aristotle saw virtue "as a habitual emotional and rational disposition to feel, choose, and act in the right way for the right ends."[4] Like all Greek philosophers, he believed that virtues are literally habit-forming: their hold on our personality grows through repetition, is strengthened through use, and can fade through neglect. The same is true of our ten modern virtues. Although some leaders are gifted in their possession of these virtues, even they must exercise and reinforce them through practice. Virtues neglected or not activated in repeated and challenging situations of choice cease to exist.

Finally, these virtues are fragmentary. They can exist apart from one another, and not every leader possesses all of them. Most of the great leaders stand out for their extraordinary possession of only a subset of what is on this list. Another way of saying this is that not even excellent leaders are paradigms of virtue; and they should not be expected to be such, since this is to lose focus on the excellences they do possess. Winston Churchill, one of the greatest leaders of all time, smoked cigars and drank to excess. This prompted teetotaling Hitler to dismiss him as a drunkard. Churchill's love of adventure sometimes caused him to champion daring military expeditions that some regarded as foolhardy. As a result, throughout his career, political opponents described him as lacking judgment. But the critics were wrong. Churchill, like all really great leaders, possessed the key virtues needed for the leadership of his embattled country, and his minor vices did not impair his performance. In judging leaders, therefore, we don't just tote up their score in relation to our list. We ask which of these virtues are central to a leader's situation and challenges and how well the leader exercises them. In trying to form our own character as leaders we must do the same thing. Examining ourselves in relation to this list, we ask: "How can I minimize my weaknesses and strengthen the virtues I possess?"

What follows is an introduction to the ten virtues. Introduction is the right word, because the meaning of each of these virtues only becomes apparent as it is lived and exemplified in the special lives we frame in the chapters ahead.

Deep Honesty

Outstanding leaders abhor deception and misrepresentation. They recognize the value of honest communication as an essential expression of respect for others and for themselves. They do not regard honesty as just the best policy – a tool for achieving one's goals – but as a commitment prior to all policy-making, as a fundamental requirement of sound communal life.

Lying and deception are probably the most common vices of misleaders. As Sissela Bok observes, deceit is linked to violence. Most of the harms that violence inflicts on victims can also come to them through deceit. "Both can coerce people into acting against their will . . . But deceit controls more subtly, for it works on belief as well as action." When lying succeeds, Bok adds, it "can give power to the deceiver – power that all who suffer the consequences of lies would not wish to abdicate."[5]

Lying is instrumental in almost every form of wrongdoing. It is needed for the manipulation of public opinion in one's favor and for the perpetration of fraud, theft, and even murder. Once another serious wrong has been done, lying supports the cover-up that is used to erase one's tracks and to deflect opposition.

In contrast, truthfulness strengthens trust and loyalty among followers. "Trust," says Bok, "is a social good to be protected just as much as the air we breathe or the water we drink." She adds:

> The function of the principle of veracity as a foundation is evident when we think of trust. I can have different kinds of trust: that you will treat me fairly, that you will have my interests at heart, that you will do me no harm. But if I do not trust your word, can I have genuine trust in the first three?[6]

Outstanding leaders appreciate the value of truthfulness as the foundation of widespread mutual trust within their organization. They also recognize that, like cancer, deception is malignant. Once begun, lying spreads easily through imitation or retaliation, until misinformation and mistrust permeate the whole life of the company or community.

None of this means that outstanding leaders are totally transparent. Transparency is definitely a virtue in organization life, where it stands for honesty in financial or environmental disclosure, openness of budgetary reviews and audits, and a willingness to periodically open and report key meetings to stakeholders. Deeply honest leaders are committed to organizational transparency in this sense; but they are not personally transparent in the sense that they make themselves open books. Since leaders inevitably deal with sensitive and confidential information, they must often modulate their words to protect organizational values and people. Deep honesty means that they sometimes play their cards close to their chest. Their honesty is not superficial but goes deep, because they realize that they must protect the rights and claims of all stakeholders and that careless disclosure can sometimes put people and values at risk.

But leaders exhibiting deep honesty also know that this never warrants lying or misrepresentation. Faced with tough questions, answering which may, at a given moment, sabotage important work in progress or even cause serious harm, deeply honest leaders seek truthful alternatives that protect confidential information. At the extreme, they have the courage to say "no comment." This takes courage because, unlike a lie, the reply "no comment" arouses curiosity and renders one vulnerable. It may prompt questioners to try to ferret out the truth. It requires the confidence that organizational security is strong enough to withstand such efforts. Yet truthful refusals to disclose sensitive information are infinitely better than lies, misrepresentations, or cover-ups. Deeply honest leaders orient themselves in this world of tensely balanced considerations, always appreciating the value of fundamental honesty and showing this in the way they lead.

Moral Courage

One of the most ancient virtues ever mentioned, courage was always associated with the bravery of warriors. Our English term stems from the Latin word for heart (*cor*). Great political and military leaders had the strength of heart to face and overcome the terrifying fears of death and defeat in battle. This martial context has lessons for today. Courage still involves standing fast, though not always on a field of battle. It involves the ability to overcome things like death, which almost everyone fears. And it often involves exercising control not only over external threats, but also over the powerful internal feelings, the pounding heart, which prompt one to waver or flee.

But the courage of outstanding leaders goes well beyond the response to physical threats or death encountered on the battlefield. More relevant to leadership today is "moral courage." Here one confronts a multitude of things that terrify people: fear of criticism or embarrassment; fear of poverty or job loss; fear of losing friends or being ostracized – even fear of being seen to be in the wrong. Overcoming self-doubt can be an expression of courage. Courageous leaders hold fast to their key purposes when these fears assault them and when there is no certainty that the leader will prevail. The pastor and ethicist Earl Shelp offers a compelling definition of courage when he describes it as

> the disposition to voluntarily act, perhaps fearfully, in a dangerous circumstance, where the relevant risks are reasonably appraised, in an effort to obtain or preserve some perceived good for one self or others recognizing that the desired perceived good may not be realized.[7]

This definition evokes several important features of the virtue of courage. For one thing, the courageous person acts voluntarily. Someone threatened or compelled to undertake a dangerous act is not courageous, since that person's motivation is fear. Nor is the courageous person fearless. He or she experiences fear; but courage is precisely the ability to master fear, to act despite it, and to move ahead toward one's goals. Courage does not involve unreasonable fear either. Someone who consistently overestimates the dangers of action is not brave. Indeed, such conduct exemplifies the opposite of bravery: the vice of cowardice, which can involve excessive fearfulness as well as flight before the fearful situation. Courage thus involves the exercise of good judgment about risks and dangers, followed by the considered willingness to carry on in the face of these dangers. The courageous person lacks the certainty of success but dares to act on the basis of a reasoned assessment of the risks.

The need for a calculation of risks led Aristotle to argue that virtue represents a "mean" or mid-point between non-virtuous (or vicious) extremes. Thus courage lies mid-way between the extreme of cowardice and the extreme of foolhardiness, understood as too much confidence in one's ability to surmount dangers. The Aristotelian doctrine of the mean does not work well for some virtues. For example, what is the extreme of which justice or fairness is the mean? How can one be too fair or too just? But Aristotle's doctrine points up how important a measured judgment of the risks is in each courageous act.

Where leadership is concerned, one of the distinctive features of courage is that it facilitates the pursuit of all other virtues. Unlike honesty or compassion, where moral motives – telling the truth, helping other people – are the goal of conduct, courage, like the virtue of self-control, is not an aim in itself but supports *other* moral aims. For this reason, the philosopher Robert Merrihew Adams calls courage a "structural virtue." He states:

> However excellent they may be as strengths, structural virtues by themselves cannot make one a morally good person. That depends above all on "having one's heart in the right place," on what goods one is for, and thus on motivational virtues.[8]

One implication of this is that even vicious leaders or misleaders can possess and exhibit the virtue of courage. Osama Bin Laden or the terrorists who followed him may be examples.

Nevertheless, even though courage only supports other virtues, in its form as moral courage – the willingness to stand up for one's deepest values – it is absolutely essential to great leadership. A leader committed to the highest moral values – honesty, compassion, or fairness – is useless unless he or she also possesses courage. Real leadership always involves facing internal and external obstacles and the fears that they give rise to. An outstanding leader must be able to assess these fears properly, neither overestimating nor underestimating them, and, when the obstacles and fears seem daunting, must be able to carry on. While courage may be an ancient virtue that first showed its worth on the battlefield, it is needed for every one of the engagements that mark the course of outstanding leadership.

Moral Vision

Great leaders have moral vision. Not only do they exhibit moral courage, they are also able to *understand* the meaning of the values they fight for and the importance of ethics both in human life and in the life of organizations and communities. When a crisis looms, they perceive its moral dimensions and act to identify, preserve, and protect key ethical values. If values conflict, as they often do, great leaders understand which ones should be prioritized. At their best, such leaders are able to articulate this moral vision and to share it with their followers.

Moral vision presupposes good practical reasoning, the ability to select appropriate means in specific situations in order to achieve moral ends. This quality of practical reasoning and judgment – what the Greek philosophers called *phronēsis* – is a necessary part of moral vision. But it is not the whole thing. In addition to good judgment, moral vision involves genuine moral wisdom. It goes beyond the intelligent choice of means and involves a wise understanding of the ends of moral life, along with an assessment of how these ends can best be preserved in the immediate situation. In their handbook of character strengths and virtues, the psychologists Christopher Peterson and Martin Seligman indicate some of the qualities associated with wisdom of this sort. Wise individuals, they observe, are able to realize larger patterns of meaning or relationship. They have a wider perspective, and are "able to see to the heart of important problems."[9]

Another way of putting this is to say that outstanding leaders have a good moral compass. They know where they have come from, they know where they are going – and they know why. Frequently, they are able to communicate their vision through outstanding rhetoric. When stress and turmoil cause those around them to lose their moral bearings and to succumb to questionable values or policies, great leaders stay on course. In challenging circumstances, this trait of great leaders sometimes causes consternation among followers. When others are ready to capitulate or bend, such leaders can appear stubborn and inflexible. In their most challenging moments, leaders like Lincoln, Churchill, Rosa Parks, or Martin Luther King, Jr. sometimes looked behind and saw their most committed followers losing heart or fleeing. Criticism or abandonment at such times can weaken the resolve of even good leaders. But, when assaulted by criticisms they know to be unjustified, great leaders follow their moral compass until others return and renew pursuit of their common goal.

Compassion and Care

Whatever their intellectual strengths, great leaders also have an important emotional and affective side. They are able to connect with and resonate to the needs of their followers. They experience and display compassion. This word, combining the Latin preposition or prefix *cum* ("with") and the verb *patiscor, pati, passus sum* ("to suffer"), tells us that outstanding leaders are able to imagine, be moved by, and literally *feel with* the suffering or distress of others and are motivated to relieve it. Compassion has many synonyms. They include empathy and sympathy, kindness, altruism, and care.

Peterson and Seligman observe that the opposite of these traits is solipsism, a state of mind in which the self sees others only in terms of how they contribute to his or her agenda and are therefore considered useful. "Kindness and altruistic love," they observe, "require the assertion of a common humanity in which others are worthy of attention and affirmation for no utilitarian reasons but for their own sake." They add that the affective or emotional ground of this trait

> distinguishes it from a merely dutiful or principle based respect for other persons. Such affective states are expected to give rise to helping behaviors that are not based on an assurance of reciprocity, reputational gain, or any other benefits to self, although such benefits may emerge and need not be resisted.[10]

In modern treatments of ethics, this distinction between a principle-based moral reasoning and the emotional traits of kindness and compassion has led to an emphasis on "care" as opposed to "justice." In her 1982 book *In a Different Voice*, Harvard psychologist Carol Gilligan reported that, when young people are confronted with ethical dilemmas such as whether someone may or may not steal an overpriced drug to save his wife's life, men frequently responded in terms of basic "rights" and an organized hierarchy of principles ("A human life is worth more than money." "The judge would probably think it was the right thing to do."). In contrast, young women tended to ease the dilemma by emphasizing the emotional and relational aspects of the situation ("What would happen to the person's wife if he is caught stealing and sent to jail?" "Can't he persuade the druggist to work out a payment schedule?").[11]

Since this landmark study appeared, Gilligan and others have qualified the role that gender plays in this difference. Both men and women are now seen to exhibit traits of justice and care. What endures is the insight that care, as an emotional relation to others and as an empathetic, compassionate response in situations of choice, is an important component of the moral life. It cannot and should not replace principled concern with justice and rights. A leader who responded only emotionally to the needs of others could act unfairly and establish dangerous precedents for organizational life. But care – like emotional responsiveness, empathy, and the capability of being moved by the plight of others – is an undeniable complement to justice-based codes and rational moral reasoning.

One of the obvious issues in leadership studies is the relative absence of women as leaders. Even though women have been moving into the workplace and now constitute 50 percent of the US workforce, they are significantly underrepresented in leadership positions. Consider the following:

- Women hold 12 CEO positions in the Fortune 500 companies.
- Women hold 14 CEO positions in the Fortune 501-1000 companies.
- Women hold 15.7 percent of board seats in the Fortune 500 companies.
- Women hold 14.4 percent of executive officer positions in the Fortune 500 companies.
- Women represent 7.6 percent of top earners in the Fortune 500 companies.
- Women hold the governorship in seven states.
- Women hold approximately one sixth of the seats in the House of Representatives and one fifth in the Senate.[12]

Despite this slowly changing picture, women are moving into leadership at an accelerating rate. Three of our last secretaries of state have been women. According to *Inside Higher Education* in 2012 women constituted 23 percent of college and university presidents, and we are beginning to see executives like Marissa Mayer move into the leadership of even traditionally male technology firms like Yahoo. As Judith Rosener reports in a widely read *Harvard Business Review* article entitled "Ways Women Lead," a new generation of women entering higher management is adopting a leadership style Rosener describes as "interactive."[13] Instead of relying on authority and position, these women see themselves as leading by attempting "to enhance other people's sense of self-worth and to energize followers." This is an approach and an environment whose presence will certainly influence leadership studies and will bring virtues like care and compassion even more to the fore.

Compassion and care also express a positive moral dimension of another trait of leadership: charisma. Literally meaning "gift of grace," it specifies a magical quality of personal attraction that lets some individuals stand out and positions them for leadership roles. John F. Kennedy and Nelson Mandala exuded charisma, whereas presidential candidates George McGovern or Minnesota Governor Tim Pawlenty found their efforts plagued from the start by concerns that they lacked this crucial quality.

To some extent, charisma is in the eyes of the beholder. The German sociologist Max Weber, who introduced this concept in leadership discussions, focused on the unique two-way relationship between leader and follower, which reflects an intense reverence for and loyalty to the leader and a strong sense of empowerment and willingness to offer voluntary compliance coming from the follower. Leaders and followers need each other. Where this two-way relation exists, the leader's charisma is perceived as potent, but those outside the relationship may not see it at all. We still wonder why cult leaders like Jim Jones or David Koresh could lead their followers to death.

A leader able to exhibit caring and compassion in the eyes of his or her followers will be perceived as charismatic. Yet charisma can also have a "dark side." Frequently a leader will be perceived as caring in ways that foster an intense, even self-sacrificial response from followers. But such caring may be a pretense aimed at gathering power, with little thought given to the welfare or fate of the followers. Jones, Koresh, Hitler, Saddam Hussein all exhibited this dark or "destructive" side of charisma. Constructive charismatic leaders, in contrast, seek power in order to render service. Robert House and Jane Howell put this contrast in terms of their distinction between "personalized" and "socialized" charismatic leaders. Personalized leadership is based on "personal dominance and authoritarian behavior," "serves the self-interest of the leader and is self-aggrandizing," and is "exploitive of others." Personalized leaders "tend to be narcissistic, impetuous, and impulsively aggressive." Socialized charismatic leadership, in contrast, "is based on egalitarian behavior," "serves collective interests and is not driven by the self-interest of the leader," and "develops and empowers others."[14]

The fact that even destructive charismatic leaders usually develop an impressive show of compassion and that their followers often regard them as deeply caring tells us how important these traits are for sustaining charisma and leadership authority. By developing this veneer of compassion – sometimes supported by bewitching rhetorical displays – misleaders gain and wield power for aims that ultimately destroy both the leaders and their communities. Great leaders, in contrast, are just what they seem to be. They exercise and display real empathy. They care about the welfare of followers and others outside their community or organization. And, when others suffer, in both word and deed great leaders exhibit compassion that runs deep and is genuine.

Fairness

Fairness is one of the most studied and important virtues of outstanding leaders. Leadership fairness comprises what has been described as procedural fairness (or justice) as well as distributive fairness. The former is associated with leaders who set up and support equitable organizational policies and procedures. The latter involves a leader's bestowal of rewards and punishments in a fair and consistent way.[15] Many commentators have noted that the best leaders typically establish and respect fair organizational procedures, are able to restrain personal opinions and biases in making decisions, are willing to explain their decision-making processes to others, and entertain appeals when people feel they have been wronged.

Fairness, like honesty and compassion, is crucial to fostering trust in a leader. Indeed studies of leadership fairness indicate that its greatest importance is in reinforcing followers' trust. Trust is always important in situations where one chooses to make oneself vulnerable to the actions of another person and where you cannot monitor or control that person.[16] When I place my life and health in my doctor's hands, I have to trust her. I must trust my lawyer when I disclose sensitive confidential information that he needs in order to defend my interests. And I must trust my organization's or my community's leader when I put my career or life in his or her hands. In trusting a leader, I assume that he or she will not act impulsively and will respect the organization's rules on which I base my conduct. Because of this, I am confidently able to make my best efforts. As one study of leadership fairness observes, when leaders are perceived to be fair in executing policies, followers are assured that their efforts will be recognized and awarded, and they are "motivated to make extra efforts for the benefits of the collective above and beyond the call of duty."[17]

While a leader's fairness is always crucial to encouraging followers' best performance, it becomes critically important when followers misbehave and punishment is due. Because it sounds so negative, punishment is never a popular topic. But displaying the willingness to punish is both an unavoidable and an important part of a leader's tasks. If violations of key group norms are ignored and "bad apples" are allowed to flourish, everyone receives the message that norms don't count. Punishment, therefore, is the other side of the coin of establishing fair and productive organizational rules. Outstanding leaders punish fairly. As Gail Ball and her associates have pointed out, the best senior business managers

> follow the organization's rules, administer punishment in a private and timely manner, suppress biases toward the punished individual, provide an adequate explanation of the reasons for the punishment, avoid negative demeanor, and allow employees to express their viewpoint of the situation.[18]

In terms of severity of punishment, good leaders administer punishments in such a way that those who are punished "feel they have been treated equitably in comparison to others who have committed similar infractions."[19]

In some respects, giving compassionate attention to an individual follower while ignoring rules and procedures can erode organizational justice and fairness, just as treating everyone without bias and "strictly by the rules" can undermine the perception that a leader cares. Thus a leader can be fair without caring and caring without being fair. But these two virtues are synergistic. When brought together, they amplify a leader's authority and power. As difficult as it may be, great leaders exhibit compassion and kindness toward individual followers while always preserving the justified perception that they will not allow personal preference to compromise their commitment to fairness.

Intellectual Excellence

Outstanding leaders are open to the world. They are curious about their natural and social environment, about new insights being developed in politics, science, and culture that can affect their understanding of things. They value learning about others' ideas and opinions on matters of importance. The opposite trait, the vice that corrodes leadership, is intellectual self-sufficiency: a smug lack of interest in new information and the dismissal of others' opinions, especially when they challenge one's own views.

This virtue has two components that almost invariably go together. The first is curiosity, understood as an inquisitive habit of mind that leads to exploration, investigation, and a passion for learning. Some of the greatest US presidents exhibited this trait, and it contributed both to their ascent to leadership and to the excellence of their leadership. Thomas Jefferson's intellectual curiosity and breadth of interests find physical expression in his remarkable home, Monticello, which displays and reflects some of the finest achievements of eighteenth-century art, architecture, and technology. The voyage of Lewis and Clark, which opened up the American West to sustained exploration and settlement, grew directly out of Jefferson's intellectual curiosity. Over 150 years later, President John F. Kennedy welcomed a group of Nobel laureates to a White House dinner by saying: "I think this is the most extraordinary collection of talent, of human knowledge, that has ever been gathered together at the White House, with the possible exception of when Thomas Jefferson dined alone."[20] Kennedy drew the lesson of Jefferson's example when he said: "Leadership and learning are indispensable to each other."[21]

Abraham Lincoln's youthful love of learning freed him from his father's fate as a poor farmer and led him to a successful legal and political career. Although Lincoln had only one year of grade school education, his intellectual curiosity led him to read intensively – the Bible, Shakespeare, the law, and Euclid's geometry. This reading not only informed his decision-making, but also culminated in some of the most important and enduring political rhetoric in history. Even a speech as apparently simple as the Gettysburg Address resonates with Lincoln's intimate knowledge of history and the Bible.[22]

The second component of this virtue is open-mindedness. Peterson and Seligman define it as "the willingness to search actively for evidence against one's favored beliefs, plans, or goals, and to weigh such evidence fairly when it is available."[23] Outstanding leaders understand the possible limits of their own perspective and, without abandoning their core convictions, seek to test their own beliefs by engaging with others of differing views. This may take the form of picking up the telephone and seeking another opinion before acting. One outstanding university president exhibited this trait by adopting the practice, in important policy or personnel meetings, of going around the table and asking each participant to state what they believed were the arguments for and against the pending decision. As Deanna Kuhn puts it, intellectually engaged people "hold the implicit epistemological theory that treats argument as worthwhile."[24] It follows that open-minded leaders strive to avoid surrounding themselves by yes-men. They select strong associates who, within a framework of mutual respect, are willing to openly question and challenge the leader's positions.

The intellectual trait at the opposite pole from this might be called the vice of self-absorption. It has also sometimes been called "myside bias."[25] Poor leaders or misleaders cannot reach intellectually beyond their own thought horizon. They are threatened by unsettling information and new, differing, and challenging viewpoints. Psychological studies show that excessive self-focused attention interferes with curiosity and the exploration of the environment.[26] Faced with challenges to their worldview and with information or beliefs that don't please them, poor leaders shut down and reaffirm their own conclusions. In some cases they ignore, abuse, and sometimes even kill the bearers of bad news. Among the habits of spectacularly unsuccessful leaders, management theorist Sydney Finkelstein lists "thinking they have all the answers." Such leaders, he adds, close themselves off from learning new answers.[27]

Much leadership literature focuses on action-oriented traits such as decisiveness or courage and on emotionally appealing attributes like charisma. The virtue at hand tells us that really great leaders often are intellectuals, too: people who value the life of the mind and its creations. Intellectual achievements and developments are increasingly important in our information-oriented society, so today's great leaders must be able to understand and appreciate them. But, in addition, these traits of openness of mind are essential to the breadth of perspective and to the willingness to correct or modify one's views that sustain great leadership.

Creative Thinking

Are outstanding leaders artists? Although it may be surprising to say so, in two senses the answer may be yes. Great leaders share with creative artists – writers, painters, sculptors, designers, architects, filmmakers, and musicians – a tendency toward independence and creativity in thinking. In the case of a leader, this may not have an explicitly aesthetic side, but it may show itself instead in new ways of accomplishing organizational goals, and even of redefining those goals.

We designate this virtue "creative thinking." In research on creativity, a consensus has emerged that views it as not confined to the aesthetic domain but also applying to the production of novel, socially valued products or services.[28] Although business managers or organizational leaders are rarely described as creative human beings,[29] these studies consistently demonstrate the existence of a strong relationship between leader performance and creative capacities.[30]

Studies also show that original and creative thinkers tend to exhibit a similar roster of cognitive skills and personality traits. These include lack of conventionality, imagination, aesthetic taste, decision skill and flexibility, and drive for accomplishment and recognition.[31] Although artistically creative individuals tend to display the aesthetic dimensions of this profile, the profile itself applies as well to original and creative leaders in non-artistic spheres. This supports the claim that originality and aesthetic creativity are part of a broad spectrum of traits that are increasingly valuable in leadership roles.

It might be thought that an organizational leader cannot live the free, solitary, or bohemian lifestyle associated with great artists or musicians. It is true that organizational life imposes limits on creativity. Nevertheless, Michael Mumford and Mary Connelly, who have studied the link between leadership and creativity, insist: "The social nature of leadership and organizational life does not prohibit creativity." The social nature of organizational life may require the leader, unlike the solitary artist, to place "greater emphasis on social considerations in initial idea generation and require more time to be devoted to solution implementation and monitoring than is required in more independent creative endeavors."[32] In other words, creative organizational leaders must work with their followers to generate support and buy-in for their own innovative ideas and approaches. But within this constraint they can still be identified, because of the originality they bring to group projects.

The importance of independence, creativity, and originality of thinking has increased exponentially, given the nature of organizational life today. As

Mumford and Connelly point out, creative problem solving typically occurs in "ill-defined domains, where the nature and existence of a problem is poorly specified and, in fact, must often be generated by the individual."[33] This well describes the circumstances of many modern business, political, military, educational, or cultural organizations. In an era of accelerating change, the "old ways" of doing things seldom work well, and a premium is placed on leaders who can come up with original solutions or approaches, who can literally "think outside of the box." Mumford and Connelly add:

> When it is recognized that leaders are constantly grappling with changing environmental conditions as they seek to define and bring about goal attainment, it is difficult to see how noncreative individuals could perform effectively in organizational leadership positions.[34]

Aesthetic Sensitivity

Some great leaders also have distinctly creative aesthetic interests and abilities. They appreciate the creation of beauty and, in their role as a political, organizational, or business leader, they turn this appreciation to organizational advantage. It is not happenstance that the intellectual qualities of originally minded organizational leaders overlap with those of artistically inclined personalities, since both types share the qualities of imagination and novelty. In addition, the rapidly changing modern environment, marked as it is by an environment of highly competitive global production, rapid information exchange, and the emergence of new industries catering to cultural desires, rewards leaders who are sensitive to issues of design and to the aesthetic dimensions of products or organizational life. The days when Henry Ford could pioneer leadership in the automotive industry by offering the customer a car "painted any color that he wants so long as it is black" are long gone. Indeed Robert Lutz, a modern leader of that same industry, now argues: "I see us being in the art business. Art, entertainment and mobile sculpture, which, coincidentally, also happens to provide transportation."[35] Nor is it a matter of increasingly satisfying a sophisticated consumer. By paying attention to the aesthetic dimensions of their enterprise, outstanding leaders pioneer new products and services and actively shape the tastes of millions. Lady Gaga and Steve Jobs are worlds apart, but, as leaders of their respective domains, they have shared this understanding of the importance of aesthetic creativity.

In his best-selling business book *A Whole New Mind*, Daniel Pink argues that we need to think about doing business in new ways. Pink says that we no longer live in the Industrial Age, which strived to produce what people needed. We now live in a Conceptual Age, and the task of business is to produce not simply functional products, but rather products that embody utility, significance, and design. To do this, Pink maintains, we have to move beyond linear, logical thinking and become more creative. In our new age, he says, aesthetics matters, and we need to design products that can give us pleasure, beauty, and utility. For Pink, our new Aesthetic Age has changed all the rules. "The MFA is the new MBA."[36]

Good Timing

Timing may not be everything, but it is crucially important to leadership excellence. The old Kenny Rogers song "The Gambler" says that you need to "know when to hold 'em, know when to fold 'em." This is a reminder not only of prudent risk taking, but also of how important it is to know when to act.

Good timing is another structural virtue: not morally desirable in itself, but necessary for the pursuit of any worthy goal. Great leaders possess this virtue and exercise it in their most important strategic decisions. Timing is crucial even in smaller managerial actions. For example, management scholars Gail Ball, Linda Treviño, and Henry Sims have pointed out how important good timing is in a manager's decisions about punishment. Punishment delayed "may be perceived as a violation of organizational due process"; but punishment should not be too swift either. "When punishment occurs so immediately that the employee feels that the leader has not given the event careful consideration, the leader may be perceived as 'lashing out.'"[37] The authors add that arguments about the timeliness of punishment suggest a curvilinear relationship, perceptions of injustice being expected when punishment is either too immediate or unreasonably delayed.

Like deep honesty, good timing defies superficial outer appraisal. A leader who awaits the precise moment to act may appear indecisive to those who urge a quicker response. Such a leader must also have the courage to weather criticisms. Think here of Lincoln's timing of the Emancipation Proclamation. Its delay drew the wrath of some of his firmest abolitionist supporters. In retrospect, however, they – and we – appreciate the sensitivity of the president's understanding of where the country was, emotionally and politically. He knew that the nation was not ready for this dramatic step until the moment when the experience and the needs of war made it inevitable. Good timing was crucial, and Lincoln brilliantly exhibited this virtue, as he did so many others.

Deep Selflessness

The willingness to sacrifice oneself is central to outstanding leadership. It may seem odd to say this in an era when the dominant examples of leadership appear to involve utter selfishness. In the business world we see fantastic and ever-increasing CEO salaries and perks compared to those of ordinary workers. In politics we witness elected leaders promising devoted service but selling their votes to the most well-heeled lobbyists. But we shouldn't be confused. These are examples of *misleadership*. Great leaders are prepared to sacrifice themselves to organizational or communal goals. When they do so, they take their group, community, or movement to new levels of achievement. We think here of such outstanding political leaders as Mahatma Gandhi or Nelson Mandela. In the business world, Lee Iacocca comes to mind. When Chrysler faced bankruptcy in the 1970s, Iacocca reduced his annual salary to one dollar in order to turn the company around.[38]

Empirical research has consistently shown a positive link between leaders who try to serve their group rather than themselves and the effectiveness of those leaders in marshaling group energies and commitment.[39] Theorists have proposed specific psychological mechanisms for this. A key idea is that superior leadership is particularly demanded in moments of great organizational uncertainty, when standard ways of handling challenges are inadequate and only new thinking can chart the way. At such moments followers are often required to exercise extraordinary degrees of commitment, involvement, and loyalty. This is when a leader's willingness to model the self-sacrifice to which everyone is called is crucial. As management scholars Yeon Choi and Renate R. Mai-Dalton observe:

> A leader's self-sacrifice in such a situation could send a clear message as to what kind of conduct is needed to overcome the crisis and how earnestly the leader is committed to the cause of the organization. It conveys to followers the leader's strong conviction that "we can do it," and is an earnest invitation to participate.[40]

Just as deep honesty does not mean total transparency, deep selflessness does not require total self-abnegation. A deeply selfless leader may exhibit forms of self-regard, or even self-indulgence. This can include a needed retreat from others in order to gather strength, or private behaviors that may assault conventional sensibilities. For example, Gandhi exercised his philosophy of spiritual purity (*brahmacharya*) by ceasing to have sexual relations with his wife and by sleeping (non-sexually) with younger women.[41] Martin Luther King, Jr. engaged in extra-marital affairs that drew the attention of his critics and enemies. King explained these affairs as "a form of anxiety reduction."[42] But none of these self-indulgences eclipsed either Gandhi's or King's utter devotion to their people and their causes, a devotion that eventually cost each one of them his life. Deep selflessness is not a veneer developed to impress followers. Nor is it the indication of a life of perfect self-renunciation and unmitigated altruism devoid of self-concern. But it shows an unwavering, fundamental commitment to one's cause, and the willingness, if necessary, to subordinate one's own concerns to the welfare of one's community.

In his extraordinarily successful management book *Good to Great*, Jim Collins argues that the single most critical component of modern business success is what he calls "level 5 leadership." Collins argues that level 5 leadership runs counter to the popular assumption that successful companies are always run by larger-than-life personalities, who make the headlines and become celebrities. Collins observes that level 5 leaders tend to shun public adulation. They act "with quiet, calm determination," relying "principally on inspired standards not inspiring charisma." Above all, the level 5 leader "channels ambition into the company, not the self."[43] In our terms, level 5 leaders exhibit the virtue of deep selflessness.

In the forthcoming chapters we will look at the complex ways in which great leaders in different sectors of life – politics, the military, business, or the cultural sphere – have exercised these virtues. Our aim is to illustrate the meaning of these virtues in practice and their vital importance. These virtues can be lived and, when they are, outstanding leadership and *eudaimonia* – flourishing – are the result. As Sophocles wrote over 2,000 years ago, when leaders and followers conduct their lives in accordance with these virtues, "their cities prosper."

Can virtue be taught? All the Greek philosophers believed so. We share this confidence. Each of the leaders we examine had an intuitive and natural sense of how to exercise the virtues that made him/her great; but all of us can learn from their experience. By witnessing the *lived* display of deep honesty, moral courage, moral vision, compassion and care, fairness, intellectual excellence, creative thinking, aesthetic sensitivity, good timing, and deep selflessness we can begin to develop these virtues in our own lives in order to become very good, if not great, leaders.

Notes to Chapter Five

1   Translation by Scott Horton, after Hans Jonas; available at http://short-schrift. blogspot.com/2007/05/ode-to-man.html.
2   Gabriele Taylor, *Deadly Vices*. Oxford: Clarendon Press, 2006, p. 8.

3 James D. Wallace, *Virtues and Vices*. Ithaca, NY: Cornell University Press, 1978, p. 161.

4 Neera K. Badhwar, "The Limited Unity of Virtue." *Nous*, 30, 1996: 306–329, at p. 306.

5 Sissela Bok, *Lying: Moral Choice in Public and Private Life*. New York: Pantheon, 1978, pp. 18 and 22.

6 Ibid., p. 31n.

7 E. E. Shelp, "Courage: A Neglected Virtue in the Patient–Physician Relationship." *Social Science and Medicine*, 18, 1984: 351–360, at p. 354.

8 Robert Merrihew Adams, *A Theory of Virtue: Excellence in Being for the Good*. Oxford: Clarendon Press, 2006, p. 34.

9 Christopher Peterson and Martin E. P. Seligman, *Character Strengths and Virtues: A Handbook and Classification*. New York: Oxford University Press, 2004, p. 182.

10 Ibid., p. 326.

11 Carol Gilligan, *In a Different Voice: Psychological Theory and Women's Development*. Cambridge, MA: Harvard University Press, 1982.

12 *Women CEOs of the Fortune 1000*. Catalyst, November 2010. At http://www.catalyst.org/publication/322/women-ceos-of-the-fortune-1000 (last accessed January 20, 2011); *Women on Boards*. Catalyst, December 2010. At http://www.catalyst.org/publication/433/women-on-boards (last accessed January 21, 2011); *2010 Catalyst Census: Fortune 500 Women Executive Officers and Top Earners*. Catalyst, December 2010. At http://www.catalyst.org/publication/459/2010-catalyst-census-fortune-500-women-executive-officers-and-top-earners (last accessed January 20, 2011); *Women In Congress*, January 20, 2011. At http://womenincongress.house.gov/member-profiles/ (last accessed November 5, 2012); Karen Tumulty, "Female Candidates Made Big Gains in the 2012 Election." *Washington Post*, November 7, 2012. At http://www.washingtonpost.com/politics/decision2012/female-candidates-made-gains-in-the-2012-election/2012/11/07/9b2e6f02-291c-11e2-b4e0-346287b7e56c_story.html (last accessed November 9, 2012).

13 Judith Rosener, "Ways Women Lead." *Harvard Business Review*, 68(6), 1990: 119–125.

14 R. J. House and J. M. Howell, "Personality and Charismatic Leadership." *Leadership Quarterly*, 3, 1992: 81–108, at p. 84.

15 C. Shawn Burke, Dana E. Sims, Elizabeth H. Lazzara, and Eduardo Salas, "Trust in Leadership: A Multi-Level Review and Integration." *Leadership Quarterly*, 18, 2007: 606–632, at p. 618.

16 D. M. Rousseau, S. B. Sitkin, R. S. Burt, and C. Camerer, "Not so Different after all: A Cross-Discipline View of Trust." *Academy of Management Review*, 23, 1998: 393–404.

17 Jeewon Cho and Fred Dansereau, "Are Transformational Leaders Fair? A Multi-Level Study of Transformational Leadership, Justice Perceptions, and Organizational Citizenship Behaviors." *Leadership Quarterly*, 21, 2010: 409–421, at p. 412.

18   Gail A. Ball, Linda Klebe Treviño, and Henry P. Sims, Jr., "Understanding Subordinate Reactions to Punishment Incidents: Perspectives from Justice and Social Affect." *Leadership Quarterly*, 3/4, 1992: 307–333, at p. 326.

19   Ibid., p. 315.

20   President John F. Kennedy, Remarks at a Dinner Honoring Nobel Prize Winners of the Western Hemisphere, April 29, 1962. *Public Papers of the Presidents of the United States: John F. Kennedy*. Washington, DC: US Government Printing Office, 1962–1964, p. 347.

21   John F. Kennedy, Remarks Prepared for Delivery at the Trade Mart in Dallas, November 22, 1963. At http://www.jfklibrary.org/Research/Ready-Reference/ JFK-Speeches/Remarks-Prepared-for-Delivery-at-the-Trade-Mart-in-Dallas- November-22-1963.aspx (last accessed 9 November, 2012).

22   Elton Trueblood, *Abraham Lincoln, Theologian of American Anguish*. New York: Harper & Row, 1973, Ch. 3.

23   Peterson and Seligman, *Character Strengths and Virtues*, p. 144.

24   Deanna Kuhn, *The Skills of Argument*. Cambridge: Cambridge University Press, 1991, p. 201.

25   Ibid., p. 144. See also A. G. Greenwald, "The Totalitarian Ego: Fabrication and Revision of Personal History." *American Psychologist*, 35, 1980: 603–618.

26   J. R. Rodrigue, K. R. Olson, and R. P. Markley, "Induced Mood and Curiosity." *Cognitive Therapy and Research*, 11, 1987, 101–106. See also R. W. Plant and R. M. Ryan, "Intrinsic Motivation and the Effects of Self-Consciousness, Self-Awareness, and Ego-Involvement: An Investigation of Internally Controlling Styles." *Journal of Personality*, 53, 1985: 435–449.

27   Sydney Finkelstein, "The Seven Habits of Spectacularly Unsuccessful Executives." *Ivey Business Journal*, 68(1), 2004: 1–6.

28   T. M. Amabile, "A Model of Creativity and Innovation in Organizations." *Research in Organizational Behavior*, 10, 1988: 123–167; L. Briskman, "Creative Product and Creative Process in Science and Art." *Inquiry*, 23, 1980: 83–106; T. V. Busse and R. S. Mansfield, "Theories of the Creative Process: A Review and a Perspective." *Journal of Creative Behavior*, 14, 1980: 91–103; H. Gardner, "Creativity: An Interdisciplinary Perspective." *Creativity Research Journal*, 1, 1988: 27–51.

29   E. P. Torrance, "Predictive Validity of the Torrance Tests of Creative Thinking." *Journal of Creative Behavior*, 6, 1972: 236–252.

30   B. M. Bass, *Bass & Stogdill's Handbook of Leadership: Theory, Research, and Managerial Application*, 3rd ed. New York: Free Press, 1990, p. 104.

31   Robert J. Sternberg, "Implicit Theories of Intelligence, Creativity, and Wisdom." *Journal of Personality and Social Psychology*, 49, 1985: 607–627, at p. 622; R. G. Lord and R. J. Foti, "Schema Theories, Information Processing, and Organizational Behavior." In H. P. Sims & D. A. Gioia (eds.), *The Thinking Organization*. San Francisco, CA: Jossey-Bass, 1986, pp. 161–185.

32   Michael D. Mumford and Mary S. Connelly, "Leaders as Creators: Leader Performance and Problem Solving in Ill-Defined Domains." *Leadership Quarterly*, 2/4 (1991): 289–315, at p. 297.

33   Ibid., p. 296.

34   Ibid., p. 297.

35   Quoted in Daniel Pink, *A Whole New Mind*. New York: Riverhead Books, 2006, p. 53.

36   Ibid., p. 54.

37   Ball, Klebe Treviño, and Sims, "Understanding Subordinate Reactions to Punishment Incidents."

38   Lee Iacocca and William Novak, *Iacocca: An Autobiography*. New York: Bantam Books, 1984.

39   Yeon Choi and Renate R. Mai-Dalton, "The Model of Followers Responses to Self-Sacrificial Leadership: An Empirical Test." *Leadership Quarterly*, 10, 1999: 397–421; David De Cremer and Daan van Knippenberg, "How Do Leaders Promote Cooperation: The Effects of Charisma and Procedural Fairness." *Journal of Applied Psychology*, 87, 2002: 858–866; Stefani L. Yorges, Howard M. Weiss, and Oriel J. Strickland, "The Effect of Leader Outcomes on Influence, Attributions, and Perceptions of Charisma." *Journal of Applied Psychology*, 84, 1999: 428–436.

40   Yeon Choi and Renate R. Mai-Dalton, "On the Leadership Function of Self-Sacrifice." *Leadership Quarterly*, 9/4, 1998: 475–501.

41   Eric Erikson, *Gandhi's Truth: On the Origins of Militant Non-Violence*. New York: Norton, 1970, pp. 192, 404.

42   David Garrow, *Bearing the Cross: Martin Luther King, Jr. and the Southern Christian Leadership Conference*. New York: William Morrow, 1986, pp. 375–376.

43   Jim Collins, "Level 5 Leadership: The Triumph of Humility and Fierce Resolve." *Harvard Business Review*, 83(7/8), 2005: 136–146.

PART II

LEADERSHIP IN ACTION

JAMES BURKE AND THE TYLENOL POISONING EPISODES

DEEP HONESTY

Somehow or other this organization functions the way I think a business institution ought to function. And I think it does because of its value system.[1]

James E. Burke

I would think within a year it [is] going to be very tough to find any product with the name Tylenol on it, unfortunately"[2] . . . I don't think McNeil can sell another product under that name. There may be an advertising person who thinks he can solve this, and if they find him I want to hire him, because I want him to turn our water cooler into a wine cooler.[3]

Jerry Della Femina, marketing expert

On Wednesday morning, September 29, 1982, 12-year-old Mary Kellerman of Elk Grove Village, Illinois, awoke early with a sore throat and a runny nose. Her parents gave her a Tylenol capsule. At 7 a.m. they found her dying on the bathroom floor. Mary was the first of seven people to die in the Chicago area after ingesting cyanide-laced capsules of Extra-Strength Tylenol. As news reports filtered in, police cruised the streets of suburban Chicago warning people to throw away their Tylenol capsules. Thus began an unprecedented episode of pharmaceutical terrorism, and a landmark case in business ethics.[4]

Tylenol's maker, McNeil Consumer Products, a subsidiary of the large pharmaceutical firm Johnson & Johnson, had been on a heady financial ascent with its over-the-counter pain reliever. After years of selling Tylenol to physicians and hospitals as a prescription medication, McNeil had secured Food and Drug Administration (FDA) approval to market it as an over-the-counter product. "Hospitals trust Tylenol" became a major selling point for the brand. By 1982

10 Virtues of Outstanding Leaders: Leadership and Character, First Edition.
Al Gini and Ronald M. Green.
© 2013 John Wiley & Sons, Inc. Published 2013 by John Wiley & Sons, Inc.

sales had reached over $500 million, making Tylenol the market leader with over 35 percent of sales for over-the-counter pain relievers. News of the Chicago poisonings not only rocked the staid New Jersey-based company, but also threatened the unique American system of direct shelf access to over-the-counter medications.

Burke's Rise to Leadership

At the center of this vortex was James E. Burke, J&J's 57-year-old CEO. Raised in Slinglands, New York – a small town outside Albany, New York – Burke came from a middle-class family.[5] Years after the Tylenol episodes, Burke reflected on the role his background played in preparing him for that event:

> I guess partly because of the way I was brought up – I had a set of values that I knew I was going to have difficulty compromising ever. I never had any doubts to speak of about right and wrong because my father had no doubts . . . My mother was extraordinarily bright, and loved intellectual ferment. She taught us all to challenge everything. Our dinner table – or every meal – was a constant arguing over anything and everything.[6]

After attending the rigorous Vincentian Catholic High School in Albany, Burke went on to Holy Cross. A brief stint in the navy was followed by the Harvard Business School. He joined J&J in 1953 as brand manager for Band-Aids and quickly rose through the ranks. By 1976 he was named CEO. Under his leadership J&J experienced strong growth. Burke played a major role in the success of the Tylenol brand, overseeing its move from a prescription analgesic to an over-the-counter pain medication. At one point Tylenol's future was seriously jeopardized, when competitor Bristol-Myers reduced the price on its acetaminophen product Datril and began an aggressive advertising campaign highlighting Datril's lower cost. At Burke's urging, McNeil responded by slashing Tylenol's price. Burke now argued that the Datril ads were misleading. After failing to get Bristol-Myers to withdraw them, he went to the leading television networks and persuaded them either to not run the ads or to require changes in them. This episode hinted at Burke's toughness and at his willingness to use the issue of truthfulness and honesty to competitive advantage.[7]

Despite the growth of J&J under his leadership, Burke was troubled by what he saw happening around him at the company. During the 1940s the company's legendary chairman, General Robert Wood Johnson II, had penned a "Credo" embodying what he believed were the company's core values. The Credo, which often hung on walls around the company's Brunswick headquarters, proclaimed that J&J's "first responsibility" was to "the doctors, nurses, and patients, to mothers and fathers and all others who use our products and services."[8] Responsibilities to employees, management, communities, and stockholders followed – in that order.

The new CEO had come to believe that the Credo had lost its influence in the organization. Speaking to senior managers, Burke said:

> The Credo sits in somewhere between a hundred and fifty and two hundred of our locations, hangs on the walls at least, and if the Credo doesn't mean anything we really ought to come to that conclusion and rip it off the walls and get on with the job. I think if it's there as an act of pretension its not only valueless but has a negative effect.[9]

To reinvigorate the Credo, J&J mounted a series of "Credo challenge" meetings, where company executives were invited to debate the Credo and its continuing relevance. What emerged from those meetings was the conviction that the values of the Credo had been instrumental in J&J's success for nearly a hundred years, and that the company and all its employees had to actively recommit to them.

Response to Crisis

These initiatives served J&J well during the poisoning episodes, when major decisions had to be made quickly, while lives were at stake and hundreds of millions of dollars were on the line. When those decisions were being made, the Credo served as a kind of sea anchor, maintaining the company's direction despite the turbulent forces that pulled it one way or the other.

Under Burke's direction, J&J took two vital actions in the earliest stages of the Tylenol crisis. The first was to give all available information to the press. "We all agreed . . . because the public was at stake, we were going to have to be deeply involved with the media and tell them everything and anything."[10] Daily press conferences with extensive opportunities for question and answer (Q&A) persuaded reporters that nothing was being held back. This openness to the press, a key expression of the honesty to which Burke was committed, played a major role in preserving public trust in the company. If doctors, nurses, patients, and those who used the products were the first priority, they deserved to hear directly from the company's leadership: not just in staged or in published announcements, but also in face-to-face meetings with journalists able to detect evasions and to ask hard questions. As the crisis progressed, this openness to the media built trust. In Burke's words: "The media became in many respects our handmaiden . . . for the most part because they understood right from the beginning that they had an issue of public safety." One television commentator told Burke: "We consider you as much the victims as anybody."[11]

The company's other significant action was national withdrawal from the market of all Extra-Strength Tylenol capsules. Burke and his crisis team knew that pulling capsules would be costly. Estimates rose to $100 million. More worrisome was the loss of shelf space. With Tylenol gone from this fiercely competitive marketplace, the makers of similar pain relievers would claim the vacant space – and Tylenol's market share with it.

Complicating the decision was pressure from the Federal Bureau of Investigation and from the Food and Drug Administration not to recall the capsules. Senior administrators at both organizations believed that a recall would encourage new terrorist episodes. With Halloween looming, they feared that many more "crazies" would be heartened by a J&J retreat.

But there was the Credo. It told Burke and his team that their "first responsibility" was not to the FBI, not to the FDA, not even to shareholders or employees, but to the people who used their products. To go against that value now, when people's lives were on the line, was unthinkable. Among other things, it would have made the Credo challenge process a joke. Within a matter of days, in the most costly product recall on record, J&J pulled all Tylenol capsules off the shelves.

At the start of the crisis Burke had assembled a task force of top J&J staff. The task force was to meet at 8 a.m. and 6 p.m.; in fact, as Burke said, they "ate, slept, drank, yelled and screamed at each other" for the six-week duration of the crisis.

> We had a value system, we had a lot of very smart people here and a lot of smart people outside of here that we tried to suck into the vortex of the process, and then we let the debate rage. A lot of what happens in this kind of a thing, I think, is to get solutions through controversy. Let everybody say what they goddamn well believe. Fight like hell. Call everybody names. Get rid of the tension that everybody's got. We were all scared to death.[12]

Hard decisions continued to impinge. At the start of the crisis, Burke and his J&J task force colleagues were encouraged by evidence suggesting that the poisoned capsules had been tampered with *after* leaving the factory. This evidence included the fact that the poisoned capsules, which had been found only in the Chicago area, came from widely separate factories that produced for the national market. Task force members had also been led to believe that no cyanide was present in the McNeil plants, a fact that Burke and others had conveyed to the press and media in the almost daily press conferences during the crisis.

Then, like a bombshell, Burke learned that this vital piece of information was wrong. Cyanide was in fact present in the manufacturing plants, in small amounts, as part of the product testing process. Although it was made clear to Burke that this was not the cyanide used in the poisonings, the information threatened to unravel Burke's and J&J's public posture and to make their efforts look like a cover-up.

Once again, with the Credo and Burke's whole upbringing exerting their force, he took the hard decision. At a press conference, he communicated the news about the in-plant cyanide, but assured the public that company scientists were confident that this substance was not involved in the poisonings. After a brief flurry of headlines, the issue vanished from public attention. Thanks in no small part to Jim Burke's forthrightness, the press and public remained convinced that J&J was not a perpetrator of the disaster, but one of its victims.

James Burke's performance at this crucial juncture vividly illustrates what we mean by the virtue of "deep honesty." This is not the same thing as absolute transparency. Deep honesty does not require ongoing disclosure of every item of one's affairs to all the questioners. Nor does it mean volunteering information that is not needed or whose disclosure is not appropriate. Deep honesty requires the exercise of moral judgment and a determination of what one's key stakeholders need to know and have a right to know. A business manager or leader exercising deep honesty realizes that many of the people and processes leading up to a policy require confidentiality. Such a leader respects these needs and measures his or her communications accordingly. But necessary confidentiality and discretion are never an excuse for dishonesty, misrepresentation, or lying. Finally, deep honesty does not mean failing to be tough when others shade the truth. Burke's aggressive attack on Bristol-Myers for what he regarded as deceptive advertising shows that one's own commitment to honesty can be a powerful motivating factor, and even a source of competitive advantage.

Lying can also take subtle forms. As J&J struggled to save the brand, many leading marketing experts predicted that it was doomed.[13] The name Tylenol, these experts said, had become synonymous with death. A leading marketing expert, Jerry Della Femina, boldly predicted: "You'll not see the name Tylenol in any form within a year."[14] Della Femina and others, of course, were not recommending that J&J get out of the lucrative acetaminophen market. Their advice was that, to overcome customers' fears, J&J repackage the same product under another name. But neither Burke nor J&J chose this course.

They recognized that merely renaming the brand was a form of misrepresentation, suggesting that somehow the new product was different from the one that had been associated with the Tylenol deaths. They also recognized that the Tylenol name was a huge asset, into which years of effort had been invested. The challenge was to assure the public that in the future they could safely rely on Tylenol.

Extensive polling told the company that there were many consumers who depended on the strength of the capsule form of the product and on its ease of use. The immediate need was to make the capsules more secure. To achieve this, J&J took the lead in spearheading a joint industry/government effort to develop new "tamper-evident" packaging. While no one could absolutely prevent tampering in the open environment of US drug and food stores, three levels of sealing were put in place, to alert customers to any penetration of the product. Working night and day, J&J employees were able to develop the new packaging, secure government and industry-wide approval of it, prepare advertising informing consumers of the new packaging, and – well ahead of the competitors – restock shelves with the newly packaged Tylenol. Within a year, sales of Tylenol would meet and exceed their pre-poisoning levels. By putting its efforts into addressing the basic problem rather than choosing to mislead or manipulate customers, J&J saved the brand.

A Further Challenge

Despite this success, J&J, Tylenol, and Jim Burke were not out of the woods. Although the tamper-evident packaging put an end to the Chicago-area episodes, three years later another Tylenol-related poisoning shocked the nation. On February 8, 1986, a 23-year-old woman from Westchester County, New York, Diane Elsroth, died after taking two Extra-Strength Tylenol capsules purchased at a local A&P store. A skilled perpetrator was apparently able to penetrate the product's packaging, insert cyanide into several capsules, and reseal the package. Several days later, technicians at a US FDA laboratory discovered the same type of cyanide in another bottle of Tylenol capsules, recalled from a Woolworth's store two blocks away from the one where the Tylenol responsible for Elsroth's death had been sold.

James Burke once again found himself in the spotlight. In the wake of Elsroth's death, J&J moved quickly to recall all capsules and, at a cost of $150 million, had rushed to introduce Tylenol caplets, a compressed and coated capsule-shaped tablet that had been under development for several years. But this did not spare Burke or the company criticism. They were now blamed for ever having reintroduced capsules.

The complaint came to a head on a national evening news program, where an angry correspondent confronted Burke: "The mother of Diane Elsroth, the girl who was killed, says that she feels that Johnson & Johnson was three years too late. What is your response to that?"[15]

Putting oneself in Burke's shoes and freeze-framing this question in order to reflect, one can see what a challenge it poses. Anything Burke says could imperil his company. An admission of culpability would subject J&J to law suits, with Burke's own public remarks offered as evidence. No wonder that, in such situations, CEOs typically stonewall. They usually offer extended arguments to the effect that the company took every reasonable step to avoid the tragedy, or they just offer some form of "no comment." Johnson & Johnson had in fact made substantial efforts to render over-the-counter Tylenol safe while meeting strong customer demand for a product that represented a third of its Tylenol business. Who could predict that a clever killer would evade all of these efforts? Could the company be held responsible for such fiendishness?

But this was not the kind of answer Burke chose. Instead, replying to the reporter's question, he said simply:

> My response is that if I were the mother of Diane Eslroth, I'd say the same thing, and I'd feel the same thing. And with the benefit of hindsight which is 20–20, I wish we had never gone back on the market with capsules.[16]

In this reply Burke avoided both rationalization and self-justification. Identifying with the pain and suffering that J&J's decisions had caused, he admitted that the company made a mistake. Although there is no public record of the legal or financial implications of this honest answer, the brand survived and continued to dominate the pain relief markets.

Burke's leadership during these trying episodes was not perfect. He and J&J probably could have moved faster to remedy problems associated with the capsules. Nevertheless, throughout these events he took responsibility for all his decisions, remained open to his critics, and managed to ensure the survival and flourishing of the Tylenol brand. His conduct throughout this episode of ethical and business crisis remains a vivid illustration of the meaning of deep honesty.

Notes to Chapter Six

1   "James E. Burke: A Career in American Business." Harvard Business School Case Video Supplement by Richard S. Tedlow, 54 minutes. Publication date: Feb 15,

1990. Production number: 890550-VID-ENG at time 2 minutes and 29 seconds. All references to this video are to minutes and seconds from the start of the video.

2   Ibid., at 28 minutes and 26 seconds.

3   Richard S. Tedlow and Wendy K. Smith, "James Burke: A Career in American Business (B)." Harvard Business School Case Number 9-390-030. Publication date: 1989, revised October 20, 2005, p. 3.

4   For a focused ethical analysis of this case, see Ronald M. Green, *The Ethical Manager*. New York: Macmillan, 1994, pp. 208–226.

5   An account of Burke's life and career is offered in the Harvard Business School case "James Burke: A Career in American Business (A) and (B)." Case numbers 9-389-177 and 9-390-030.

6   "James Burke: A Career in American Business." HBS Video Supplement at 3 minutes 9 seconds.

7   Harvard Business School case "James Burke: A Career in American Business (A)," pp. 15–16.

8   The latest version of the Credo is found online at: http://www.jnj.com/wps/wcm/connect/c7933f004f5563df9e22be1bb31559c7/jnj_ourcredo_english_us_8.5x11_cmyk.pdf?MOD=AJPERES

9   "James Burke: A Career in American Business." HBS Video Supplement at 23 seconds.

10   "James Burke: A Career in American Business." HBS Video Supplement at 20 minutes 35 seconds.

11   "James Burke: A Career in American Business" HBS Video at 33 minutes 42 seconds.

12   "James Burke: A Career in American Business." HBS Video Supplement at 26 minutes 43 seconds.

13   *Business Week*, October 10, 1982, p. 43.

14   One year later, Della Femina admitted he had made a mistake in offering this advice. "I was absolutely wrong," Femina said. "Good products win out." To remind Della Femina of his errant prediction, Compton Advertising, the agency that handled Tylenol, sent him a water cooler filled with wine. N. R. Kleinfield, "Tylenol's Rapid Comeback." *The New York Times*, September 17, 1983 (available online at: http://www.nytimes.com/1983/09/17/business/tylenol-s-rapid-comeback.html).

15   "James Burke: A Career in American Business." HBS Video Supplement at 38 minutes 33 seconds.

16   "James Burke: A Career in American Business." HBS Video Supplement at 38 minutes 41 seconds.

ABRAHAM LINCOLN/ROSA PARKS

MORAL COURAGE

> It is curious – curious that physical courage should be so common in the world, and moral courage so rare.
>
> Mark Twain[1]

The concept of courage is usually associated with physical acts of derring-do that involve danger, risk, and behavior that overcomes seemingly insurmountable obstacles and odds. The word "courage" conjures up images of individuals performing difficult actions while risking physical injury or death. A courageous act is one in which the actor disregards concern for personal safety or wellbeing and exerts himself or herself in the service of others. The courageous act is thus seen as a heroic act. In popular culture, we use the word "hero" to honor soldiers, firefighters, rescue workers, and others who act with little regard for themselves. From this perspective, courage is a supra-virtue, an extraordinary achievement, and not part of the common repertoire of traits and behaviors associated with the more mundane and pedestrian aspects of our lives. It is something special, rare, and publicly significant.

From a philosophical and ethical point of view, moral courage is not an "extra" or a "supererogatory" virtue, but rather a critical human quality that serves as a necessary precondition for all other forms of human conduct. Moral courage is about our willingness to act on an idea, a belief, or a value. Moral courage is the readiness to endure danger for the sake of principle.[2] Moral courage rejects voyeurism and seeks engagement. As Nelson Mandela has suggested, moral courage is not the absence of fear, but the strength to triumph over one's fear and to act.[3] Moral courage is the ability to put ethics into practice.

10 Virtues of Outstanding Leaders: Leadership and Character, First Edition.
Al Gini and Ronald M. Green.
© 2013 John Wiley & Sons, Inc. Published 2013 by John Wiley & Sons, Inc.

Moral courage is the first of human qualities, because it is the one that generates and guarantees all others. Moral courage means the willingness to take on ethical issues and questions, to extend ourselves, to put ourselves in harm's way in the name of our moral ideals. Without moral courage to propel us forward, we become captives to our own selfish needs and desires. Moral courage allows us to see beyond our self-contained universe of personal concerns. It allows us to become, if only momentarily, more selfless than selfish. Moral courage allows us to develop our moral vision of the world and to act on that vision. We believe that Abraham Lincoln and Rosa Parks, two people who lived decades apart and who stood on opposite sides of America's racial divide, nevertheless both exemplify courage, and remain classic examples of physical and moral courage. Each had a vision of the world and each possessed the bravery and tenacity to act, even though their actions put their personal safety at risk.

Courage: Physical and Moral

In the hard scrabble world of Lincoln's youth, manhood entailed more than just reaching a certain age. It meant strength, endurance, and physical contests of all kinds. At six foot, four inches tall with a well-muscled physique, thanks to years of heavy farm work, Lincoln could hold his own against boys and men alike. In 1832, as a militia volunteer in the Black Hawk Wars, Lincoln was elected captain not only because of his affability and popularity, but also because he was the company's champion wrestler.[4] But, besides physical prowess and athletic ability, Lincoln also possessed a generous modicum of physical courage, which he demonstrated on numerous occasions during the course of his presidency.

The first example of this courage begins with Lincoln's attempt to enter Washington for his first Inauguration. On February 11, 1861 Lincoln left Springfield for a 12-day tour through Indiana, Ohio, Pennsylvania, New York, and Maryland, to make himself and his message better known to the general American public. The night before he was to pass through Baltimore and arrive in Washington, Allan Pinkerton, a private detective and later Lincoln's bodyguard, discovered an assassination plot and insisted that Lincoln change his announced plans and proceed incognito to Washington. Reluctantly Lincoln agreed, and traveling by night safely he arrived in Washington. According to historian Doris Kearns Goodwin, Lincoln was embarrassed by Pinkerton's scheme and wanted to reject it. He feared that people would think him a coward. He also feared damage to his moral position and that his conduct would engender ridicule and a loss of confidence in his new administration.

And yet he swallowed his pride, because he knew that, although "creeping into Washington" was undignified, his mission and his message were more important than his personal vanity.[5]

Upon arriving in Washington, Lincoln was faced with yet another dangerous situation. Although Washington was the capital of the Union, it was bordered on the south by the Confederate state of Virginia and on the north by the state of Maryland, which continuously vacillated in its primary allegiance. Also, the population of Washington was made up of a mixed constituency of both Union and Confederate sympathizers. To make matters worse, on Inauguration Day there were only a handful of regular troops in Washington. Winfield Scott, the 74-year-old commanding general, was forced to organize a few emergency regiments of older retired regulars who called themselves the Silver Gang, in order to protect the president.[6] In spite of his vulnerability, Lincoln refused to leave Washington and carried on the business of government, until a sufficient number of Union troops descended on Washington and took up defensive positions.

During the course of the war, at least two large Confederate army groups advanced directly on Washington. On more than one occasion Lincoln mounted the parapets to view the battle. Once, after Lincoln came under serious fire, the Union General in charge, Horatio G. Wright, "ordered" him to step away and seek better cover. When Lincoln did not leave, Wright threatened to have him forcibly removed.

> The absurdity of the idea of sending off the President under guard seemed to amuse Lincoln . . . he agreed to compromise by sitting behind the parapet instead of standing upon it.[7]

Lincoln came under fire inside the city's walls no less than when he was on top of them. During the heat of summer, the Lincoln family regularly retreated to a residence known as the Soldier's Home, which was situated in the shaded hills, three miles north of the White House. The location was a welcome relief both from the weather and from the frenetic activity of the city. Lincoln rode his horse Old Abe back and forth to his White House office, sometimes accompanied by guards and sometimes not. Late one night when Lincoln was riding home alone, a rifle shot rang out and Old Abe took off at breakneck speed. Arriving at the White House without his hat, Lincoln laughed off the incident and said: "I tell you there is no time on record equal to that made by the two 'Old Abes' on that occasion."[8]

Just as physical courage is the ability to transcend fear and to act, moral courage is the ability to act or endure risk for the sake of a principle. It is the ability to put beliefs into practice. Although the one does not always lead to the other, it can be argued that Lincoln's physical bravery was the foundation for the acts of moral courage that he exhibited during his presidency. An early example of this is his First Inaugural Address in 1861.

At the time of the Inaugural Address seven states had already seceded, Fort Sumter was under siege, and US ports and federal barracks had been seized. War was in the air. However, Lincoln used his speech not to lecture the South, not to warn it, not to condemn it for slavery, but to calmly and rationally plead for peace. He pledged that the North was not a threat to the South's way of life, happiness, or property. As president he had no constitutional right to interfere in the affairs of the original 13 states, and he promised not to interfere in the South. We have issues, said Lincoln, but they must be addressed rationally, patiently, and legally. "We are not enemies, but friends . . . Though passion may have strained, it must not break our bonds of affection."[9]

His foes thought the speech disingenuous and without real alternatives. Friends felt that the speech was too weak, too academic, and too amorphous. Abolitionists like Frederick Douglas found the speech apologetic, without nerve, and "vastly below what we had fondly hoped it might be . . ."[10] But, from Lincoln's moral point of view, it was his only chance to ask, to plead, to beg for peace.

> My countrymen, one and all, think calmly and well, upon this whole subject. Nothing valuable can be lost by taking time . . . In your hands, my dissatisfied fellow countrymen, and not in mine, is the momentous issue of Civil War. The government will not assail you.[11]

This moderate stand amid fearfully competing passions exemplified Lincoln's moral courage.

Team of Rivals

Another example of Lincoln's moral courage is his willingness to suspend his own feelings and to ignore differing and divergent political points of view and party lines concerning the men he chose to serve in his Cabinet – his now famous *Team of Rivals*.[12] When Lincoln was elected, never had conditions for a president-elect been so severe; and yet, according to his critics, never had anyone seemed – to go by their credentials – so poorly educated and ill prepared for the job. Lincoln's fifteen predecessors had included generals, vice presidents, secretaries of state, and seasoned veterans of Congress. Harriet Beecher Stowe said that we were a nation in crisis and the state was being led by a "plain working man," with no culture, instruction, or education.[13]

No matter how poorly educated and technically unprepared for the job, Lincoln completely understood his predicament and bravely sought out the "best and brightest" to help him in his task. He appointed Republicans, former Whigs, and even Democrats to his Cabinet. Some of them were detractors and opponents, both to himself and to one another. More often than not, Cabinet meetings were vociferous and contentious. Lincoln's three most controversial selections for the Cabinet were his three Republican opponents for the presidency: William H. Seward of New York (secretary of state); Salmon P. Chase of Ohio (secretary of the treasury); and Edward Bates of Missouri (attorney general). Lincoln also appointed Edwin M. Stanton as secretary of war. The prominent Ohio lawyer had served as a Cabinet member for Democratic President James Buchanan. Lincoln appointed him in spite of the fact that, in 1855 when Stanton was lead attorney at the famous McCormick Reaper patent trial, he fired Lincoln as co-counsel and publicly referred to him as a "long armed ape."[14]

All of these people were well connected and better known, better educated, and more experienced in public life than Lincoln. When he was challenged about his controversial appointments, especially in regard to his Republican opponents, Lincoln's response was simple, straightforward, and, from his point of view, commonsensical.

> We needed the strongest men of the party in the Cabinet. We needed to hold our own people together. I had looked the party over and concluded that these were the very strongest men. Then I had no right to deprive the country of their services.[15]

Finally, no checklist of Lincoln's courage and integrity would be complete without reference to his Second Inaugural Address. The war was almost over and victory was in sight. But, for Lincoln, it was not a time to celebrate. It was not a time to gloat, to point blame, to be righteously indignant. Lincoln rather had the courage to offer an olive branch. "Perhaps," he said, "God gave this war to both sides as a punishment for two hundred and fifty years of unrequited (slave) toil." Whatever the Lord's purpose, said Lincoln, we must now

> With malice toward none; with charity for all ... bind up the nation's wounds ... care for he who shall have borne the battle, and for his widow, and his orphan – to do all which may achieve and cherish a just and a lasting peace, among ourselves, and with all nations."[16]

An Important Bus Ride

At well over six feet in height, Lincoln was a big man who cast a giant shadow. Rosa Parks, on the other hand, at just over five feet, was a petite woman who nonetheless cast a shadow large enough to inspire a moral movement that would help transform American history. In an era when black men were in real danger of being beaten or killed for any infringement, Rosa Parks demonstrated remarkable physical and moral courage when she calmly and politely refused to give up her seat on a public bus to a white man.

Although Lincoln's Emancipation Proclamation and the Thirteenth Amendment had ended slavery, the bitter aftermath of the Civil War led to resurgent racism, Jim Crow laws, and the suppression of the rights of millions of African Americans. Black and white people were segregated in virtually every aspect of daily Southern life. Restaurants, neighborhoods, schools, stores, parks, playgrounds, restrooms, water fountains, and all forms of public transportation were separated along racial lines, black people always getting the lesser share.

Although bus and train companies did not provide separate vehicles for different races, they did enforce seating policies that allocated separate sections for blacks and whites. In Montgomery, Alabama, the first four rows of bus seats were reserved for white people. Even though 75 percent of the ridership in Montgomery was made up of black people, the "colored section" was located in the back of the bus. "White" and "colored" sections were not fixed in size, but they were determined by the placement of a portable sign. Black people could sit in the middle rows until the white section was full. Then they were forced to make a choice. They could move to the seats in the rear, stand, or, if there was no room, leave the bus.

On Thursday, December 1, 1955, after a long day at the Montgomery Fair department store, a tired 42-year-old Rosa Parks boarded her regular bus with nothing else on her mind except "the day is done, I want to go home."[17] Parks paid her fare and sat in an empty seat in the first row of the "colored section," which was behind the seats reserved for white people. As the bus followed its regular route, the white-only seats filled up and two or three white men were left standing. Following "standard practice" the bus driver moved the "colored section" sign behind, where Parks and three other black people were already sitting, and demanded that they give up their seats so that the white passengers could sit. At first, said Parks, "didn't anybody move. We just sat right there where we were, the four of us: Then he spoke a second time: 'Y'all better make it light on yourselves and let me have those seats.'"[18]

After a moment, said Parks, the man in the window seat next to her stood up, and the two other black women in the row also stood up. And, "suddenly," she said, "I decided not to get up." "I didn't give up my seat because I was tired . . . No, the only tired I was was tired of giving in." Besides, "I could not see how standing up was going to make it light for me."[19] In a 1992 interview with NPR, Parks recalled:

> I did not want to be mistreated, I did not want to be deprived of a seat that I had paid for. It was just time . . . there was opportunity for me to take a stand to express the way I felt about being treated in that manner. I had not planned to get arrested. I had plenty to do without having to end up in jail. But when I had to face that decision, I didn't hesitate to do so because I felt that we had endured that too long. The more we gave in, the more we complied with that kind of treatment, the more oppressive it became.[20]

Five days after Parks was arrested, she was tried and convicted for disorderly conduct and fined ten dollars and four dollars for court costs. Emboldened by her courage and integrity, a city-wide bus boycott was organized under the leadership of the then 26-year-old Martin Luther King, Jr. King urged all members of the African American community who patronized the Montgomery bus system to walk, arrange carpools, or find other means of transportation. King also filed suit in federal court on behalf of those discriminated against by the bus service. On June 2, 1956 the federal court ruled for the boycotters and declared segregated bus service unconstitutional. Although the ruling was appealed to the United States Supreme Court, on November 13, 1956 the lower court's findings were upheld. The boycott ended on December 20, 1956 – 386 days after Rosa Parks' arrest.

Rosa Parks' courageous decision to act by not acting, by not getting up, and her subsequent arrest and conviction on charges of disorderly conduct proved to be the "tipping point" for race relations and for the beginning of the Civil Rights Movement in America. According to activist and author Eldridge Cleaver, because of Rosa Parks, "somewhere in the universe, a gear in the machinery shifted."[21] Historian Douglas Brinkley points out that, within a year of the Montgomery boycott, 42 other local movements were organized in the South. The phrase "back of the bus" became a synonym for, and a rallying cry against, racial discrimination.[22]

Shared Convictions

Just as Abraham Lincoln deserves to be remembered for preserving the Union and for helping to eradicate the "sin of slavery," so too Rosa Parks deserves to be remembered as the "mother of the Civil Rights Movement." Each of these individuals had different talents and temperaments and they faced different kinds of challenges, in different circumstances, and in different times. What they shared was a similar series of ideals and beliefs. Both were committed to the notion of the "inalienable rights of man" and to the notion that "all men are created equal." And both believed it was wrong to earn one's bread "from the sweat of other men's faces." But, more than a common list of beliefs, they shared the conviction that the greatest ideas and the best of intentions are not enough. To be real, to be complete, these must be put into action and lived out with others. To be real, they require an act of moral courage: to endure risk for the sake of principle.

Notes to Chapter Seven

1   *Mark Twain in Eruption: Hitherto Unpublished Pages about Men and Events*, edited by Bernard De Voto. New York: Harper, 1940, p. 47.
2   Rushworth Kidder, *Moral Courage*. New York: Harper Collins, 2005, p. 7.
3   Richard Stengel, "Mandela: His 8 Lessons of Leadership." *Time*, July 9, 2008, pp. 20, 27.
4   Douglas L. Wilson, *Honor's Voice: The Transformation of Abraham Lincoln*. New York: Alfred A. Knopf, 1998, p. 295.
5   Doris Kearns Goodwin, *Team of Rivals*. New York: Simon and Schuster Paperbacks, 2006, pp. 305–312.
6   Ronald C. White, Jr., *Abraham Lincoln*. New York: Random House, 2009, p. 412.
7   David Herbert Donald, *Lincoln*. New York: Simon and Schuster, 1995, p. 519.
8   White, *Abraham Lincoln*, p. 647.
9   Lincoln's "First Inaugural Address." In Ronald C. White, Jr., *The Eloquent President*. New York: Random House, 2005, p. 346.
10   William Lee Miller, *President Lincoln*. New York: Alfred A. Knopf, 2008, p. 427.
11   Lincoln's "First Inaugural Address," p. 346.
12   Goodwin, *Team of Rivals*.
13   Joshua Wolf Shenk, *Lincoln's Melancholy*. New York: Mariner Books, 2006, p. 172.
14   Goodwin, *Team of Rivals*, p. 174.
15   Ibid., p. 319.
16   Lincoln's "Second Inaugural Address." In White, *The Eloquent President*, pp. 398, 399.
17   "Rosa Parks Quotes." BrainyQuote. Book Rags Media Network, June 29, 2011. At http://www.brainyquote.com/quotes/authors/r/rosa_parks.html (last accessed November 8, 2012).
18   Rosa Parks with Jim Haskins, *Rosa Parks: My Story*. New York: Dial Books, 1992, p. 115.
19   Ibid., pp. 115–116.

20　"Parks Recalls Bus Boycott: Excerpts from an Interview with Lynn Neary." *National Public Radio*, 1992, linked at Civil Rights Icon Rosa Parks Dies, NPR, October 25, 2005. At http://www.npr.org/templates/story/story.php?storyId=4973548 (last accessed June 29, 2011).

21　Douglas Brinkley, *Rosa Parks*. New York: A Lipper/Viking Book, 2000, p. 2.

22　Ibid., p. 2.

WINSTON CHURCHILL MORAL JUDGMENT AND MORAL VISION

May 1940: "The spring like a corpse was sweet with the smell of doom."

Graham Greene[1]

When lists of great leaders are compiled, the name of Winston Churchill always ranks near the very top. Churchill's deeds in saving his nation and the world from Nazi domination have become legendary. But it was not always so. Looking back through the lens of history, we see clearly what Churchill accomplished. But, as the year 1940 dawned, there were many in Britain and around the world who believed that what Churchill lacked above all was the capacity for sound leadership. Many in his own Tory party were prepared to oppose any ascent by him to the post of prime minister.

They had good reasons. Although Churchill had accomplished much during his four-decade-long political career, there were also notable blemishes on his record.[2] In 1911, while he was serving as home secretary, his presence at the scene of an anarchist-led standoff earned him a reputation as a publicity hound, and his forceful suppression of a miners' strike during the same period ignited the burning hatred of the labor unions. During the First World War, he was blamed (perhaps unjustly) for the military debacle at Gallipoli. As recently as 1937, Churchill's passionate defense of King Edward VIII in the face of widespread calls for the King's abdication as a result of his involvement with Wallis Simpson, an American divorcée, made Churchill an object of ridicule in both liberal and conservative circles.

Former Prime Minister Stanley Baldwin probably summed up much of the political opinion when he privately said of Churchill at the time of the abdication crisis:

10 Virtues of Outstanding Leaders: Leadership and Character, First Edition.
Al Gini and Ronald M. Green.
© 2013 John Wiley & Sons, Inc. Published 2013 by John Wiley & Sons, Inc.

When Winston was born lots of fairies swooped down on his cradle with gifts – imagination, eloquence, industry, ability – and then came a fairy who said "No one person has a right to so many gifts," picked him up and gave him such a shake and twist that with all these gifts he was denied judgment and wisdom. And that is why while we delight to listen to him in this House we do not take his advice.[3]

But Baldwin was badly mistaken. Yes, Churchill had many gifts and outstanding skills of leadership. But the most important of these was the very one Baldwin faulted: his moral judgment and moral vision. This is the ability to clearly understand the moral stakes of a decision and correctly prioritize those stakes when determining a course of action. In addition, it involves the ability to assess the moral character of key actors in a situation in order to accurately measure their advice or predict their likely actions. In these respects, Churchill was exemplary. His moral vision, insight and judgment were penetrating and guided him through difficult decisions when the fate of his country and that of the world were at stake. Nowhere is this truer than during five days in May 1940, from Friday, May 24 to Tuesday, May 28, when German tanks overran France and reached the English Channel, when French surrender loomed, and when it seemed as though Britain herself would soon fall before the Nazi onslaught.

Churchill versus Halifax

Historians Andrew Roberts and John Lukacs have extensively examined these five days in May.[4] Both writers focus on the encounter in the British Cabinet between Foreign Secretary Lord (Edward) Halifax and Churchill, newly named on May 10 as prime minister. Roberts, Lukacs, and other students of the period broadly agree on what happened during those five days, but they differ significantly in their interpretation of the causes and meaning of each man's decisions. Roberts argues that, while Halifax and Churchill disagreed on some details about the choices facing Britain, Halifax's position was broadly congruent with Churchill's. He perceives the differences between the two men as being of modest importance. Lukacs, in contrast, sees a sharp divide and argues that Churchill's conduct at this point was perhaps the most decisive event of the Second World War.

Halifax and Churchill came to May 1940 and to the questions of the war before them with different records and experience. Since the early 1930s Churchill had been a solitary voice in the wilderness, warning his countryman of the danger posed by the rise of Hitler's Germany. These warnings were largely ignored. The nation was exhausted by the bloodshed of the First World War and the economic hardship of the Great Depression. British governments drastically reduced military budgets. Military preparedness waned, and pacifist sentiments were widespread. Young people shared these views. In 1933 the mood of the country's emerging leadership was highlighted by a debate sponsored by the Oxford Union in which the undergraduates voted 275 to 153 for the motion "That this House refuses in any circumstances to fight for King and Country."

Among upper-class Britons, indifference to the threat represented by Nazi Germany was also fed by a fear of communism. To these people, Hitler was a possible bulwark against the Soviet Union. His angry speeches and threats of violence were dismissed as posturing, and his virulent anti-Semitism went largely ignored. Indeed, although British anti-Semitism was far more tepid than its German counterpart, it was prevalent among aristocrats and the well-to-do, who disliked the growth of economic power in the hands of what they regarded as Jewish upstarts.

Halifax shared these opinions. Throughout the 1930s, he was one of the leading proponents of "appeasement" of the dictators – Hitler and Mussolini. Although appeasement has become a term of opprobrium, during the thirties it had positive moral overtones. Many people thought that the provisions of the Versailles treaty had been unduly severe for Germany. They regarded Hitler's anger and his territorial claims as partly justified. By yielding to the dictator's demands, they believed that they could mollify him and once and for all remove the causes of tension that threatened European peace.

Acting on these beliefs, in October 1937 Halifax accepted an invitation to attend the International Hunting Exhibition in Berlin. The invitation was occasioned, in part, by Halifax's reputation as an avid foxhunter, a passion that, combined with his devotion to High Church Anglicanism, had earned him the nickname "the Holy Fox." Neville Chamberlain, the equally appeasement-minded prime minister, encouraged this visit by his future foreign secretary, seeing it as an opportunity for relaxed and informal face-to-face meetings with the Nazi leadership. Writing to his sisters, Chamberlain said that the visit could be the start of "the far-reaching plans I have in mind for the appeasement of Europe and Asia and for the ultimate check to the mad armaments race."[5] Halifax agreed. Shortly before the visit, in a letter to former Prime Minister Stanley Baldwin, he observed: "Nationalism and Racialism is a powerful force but I can't feel that it is either unnatural or immoral"; and on the eve of his departure he added: "I cannot myself doubt that these fellows are genuine haters of Communism, etc.! And I daresay if we were in their position we might feel the same!"[6]

Most historians agree that Halifax's visit was disastrous. In the course of a wide-ranging conversation at Berchtesgaden, Hitler's mountain retreat in southern Germany, Halifax volunteered the comment that the British government was open to "any alterations" regarding Danzig, Austria, and Czechoslovakia that might come about "through the course of peaceful evolution."[7] In these words Hitler probably saw an opening to the unopposed path he would follow in order to consolidate his power in Europe.

Behind these actions lay Halifax's deep misjudgment of the moral character of the Nazi leaders. From 1925 to 1931 Halifax had served illustriously as viceroy to India. During this period he met with the great leader of the Indian independence movement, Mahatma Gandhi, whom Halifax regarded as a tough and formidable bargainer. Writing to a friend after the Berchtesgaden meeting, Halifax stated: "if Hitler had worn a dhoti he [Halifax] could have mistaken his mystical approach to life for that of Mr. Gandhi." This was a dreadfully flawed comparison. Gandhi, for all his passionate commitment to his cause, was a man of peace, dedicated to non-violence and human dignity. Hitler, in contrast, was a hate-filled bully. In the five years preceding Halifax's visit Hitler had suspended civil liberties and press freedoms, banned all other political parties, murdered his ally Ernst Rohm and other leaders of the Storm Trooper movement in the 1934 "Night of the Long Knives," and sent thousands of other opponents to torture and death in concentration camps.

Halifax's misjudgment of character is nowhere better illustrated than in his response to the meetings with other Nazi leaders. Of Göring, who would soon unleash a pitiless bombardment of British cities, he wrote:

> I was immensely entertained at meeting the man himself. One remembered at the time that he had been concerned with the "cleanup" in Berlin on June 30th, 1934 [the Night of the Long Knives] and one wondered how many people he had been, for good cause or bad, responsible for having killed. But his personality, with that reserve, was frankly attractive, like a great schoolboy . . . a composite personality – film star, great landowner interested in his estate.[8]

Writing in his diary, Halifax added this about Josef Goebbels, Hitler's propaganda minister: "I had expected to dislike him intensely – but didn't. I suppose it must be some moral defect in me." Halifax was right. There was a moral defect in him, although it was one shared with many of his contemporaries: an inability to properly distinguish between a superficial display of good fellowship, and the deeper motives driving a personality. Such distinctions rest, in part, on an informed knowledge of a person's deeds and statements. That Halifax could confuse Goebbels' charm with his well-established record of manipulation and lies reveals a catastrophic lack of moral judgment.

Churchill's encounters – or, more precisely, non-encounter – with the Nazi leadership illustrate a directly opposite quality of moral judgment. The opportunity for such a meeting arose in 1932, before Hitler came to power, when Churchill was traveling in Germany as part of his research for a book on his ancestor, the Duke of Marlborough. While staying at a hotel in Munich, Churchill was approached by Putzi Hanfstaengl, a charming, Harvard-educated millionaire who was acting as Hitler's press secretary. Hanfstaengl asked Churchill whether he might like to meet with the Führer. At that time Churchill was a freelance journalist forced to earn his living through his writings, so the chance for an interview with Germany's rising political star was understandably attractive. But, instead of jumping at the offer, Churchill asked:

> Why is your chief so violent about the Jews? I can quite understand being angry with Jews who have done wrong or who are against the country, and I understand resisting them if they try to monopolize power in any walk of life; but what is the sense of being against a man simply because of his birth?[9]

The meeting never took place. Many years later, on September 11, 1940, as British cities were being devastated by a rain of German bombs during the Battle of Britain, Churchill addressed the British nation, describing Hitler as "[t]his wicked man, the repository and embodiment of many forms of soul-destroying hatreds." In these words we see that Churchill's estimate of Hitler's character, formed almost a decade earlier and before the tyrant's worst outrages had begun, only deepened with time and experience. Churchill brought this acuity of moral judgment to the fateful Cabinet meetings of May 24–28.

The War Cabinet Meets

As Friday, May 24 dawned, Britain's War Cabinet faced an impending calamity. Ten days before, German armored columns had broken out of the Ardennes forest and started an almost unopposed drive across the center of France. French counter-attacks from the south had been turned back with ease, the Belgian army was cut off and surrounded, and German forces were pressing closely against the British Expeditionary Force, which had retreated to a few Channel enclaves. The "Miracle of Dunkirk," by means of which those troops were evacuated without their weapons by a flotilla of large and small craft, lay almost a week away and was unimagined. France's surrender was imminent, and the British land army, with its back to the sea, seemed lost. Unbeknownst to the Cabinet that day, Hitler, fearful that his lines were overextended,[10] gave a halt order to his troops, providing British forces with a few days of precious time. Much of that day's Cabinet meeting was spent discussing the situation in Calais, and whether British forces should be withdrawn or ordered to resist encirclement.

The War Cabinet met nine times over the next five days. It was a tensely structured group of men. Headed by Churchill, who had assumed the post of prime minister on May 10 after a Tory uprising had forced Neville Chamberlain to resign, it included Chamberlain and Halifax and two representatives of the opposition Labour Party. Because the Labour members were new to power and had never exercised ministerial leadership, this meant that the Cabinet's deliberations would be shaped by Churchill and by the two men whose policies he had vehemently opposed for almost a decade. Churchill knew that he was on probation. In the last-minute jostling for the premiership, Halifax had been the leading alternative. He had stepped aside, ostensibly because he believed his membership in the House of Lords rather than in the House of Commons rendered him unsuited to be a wartime leader.[11] Although Churchill had been swept into power by a Tory revolt sparked by the events in France, he knew that many Conservative Party members were having second thoughts. Any missteps on his part could once again push him out of office and bring the appeasers back in.

It was not until the next day, Saturday, May 25, that the tensions in the War Cabinet began to make their appearance. At the morning session Halifax reported that, "at the invitation of a third party," a meeting had taken place between an adviser to the foreign office and a member of the staff of the Italian Embassy.[12] In the course of that meeting the Italian had suggested that his government would not rebuff a British approach "with a view to exploiting the possibilities of a friendly settlement." Here was the slender possibility of a negotiated peace, with Italy perhaps serving as a mediator between Britain and Germany. Halifax urged a further meeting, adding that "very likely nothing might come of all this." But Churchill was wary. Although he did not object to Halifax's arranging another meeting, he cautioned, "it must not, of course, be accompanied by any publicity, since that would amount to a confession of weakness."[13]

Later that Saturday afternoon Halifax met personally with Giuseppe Bastianini, the Italian ambassador to London, and he subsequently reported the conversation to the War Cabinet. Halifax said that he opened the conversation with Bastianini by stating "we had intended to make an approach, in appropriate form, to certain political questions . . ." Bastianini replied with a question: could he "inform his Government that His Majesty's Government considered it opportune now to examine the question at issue between our two countries within the larger framework of a European settlement?" By 1940, following nearly a decade of appeasement, the phrase "a European settlement" had become a code word for a negotiated peace between the dictators and their opponents. Halifax continued the conversation, saying that "it was difficult to visualize such wide discussions while the war was still proceeding." The ambassador replied, "once such a discussion were begun, war would be pointless."[14]

Two years later, in an account of this meeting with an official war historian, Halifax tried to obscure what had transpired. He asserted:

> There was certainly never the idea in the mind of His Majesty's Government then or at any time of asking Mussolini to mediate terms of peace between them and Germany

adding that the subject of the Bastianini conversation "had been solely neutrality from Italy and never mediation with Germany." But this clearly contradicted the wording of the conversations and was certainly not the way the meeting was understood in the War Cabinet over the next few days. As Andrew Roberts puts it: "'The Holy Fox' could hear the hounds baying for his reputation, but he could lay only the faintest of false trails."[15]

Thus the leading issue before the War Cabinet when it met on the morning of Sunday, May 26 was whether Britain should seek to use the offices of Mussolini to send a signal to Hitler that it was willing to discuss a negotiated peace to end the war, then and there, on the far shores of the English Channel. Halifax began the discussion by reporting:

> Signor Bastianini had clearly made soundings as to the prospect of our agreeing to a conference. The Ambassador had said that Signor Mussolini's principal wish was to secure peace in Europe.[16]

At this point Churchill intervened, observing that peace and security would not be achieved under a German domination of Europe and adding: "That we could never accept. We must ensure our complete liberty and independence." He was opposed to any negotiations that might lead to a derogation of Britain's rights and power.[17]

To back up his position, Churchill distributed a paper he had asked the chiefs of staff to prepare in response to the question of whether Britain could hold out against Germany single-handedly if France capitulated. Their answer, a paper "British Strategy in a Certain Eventuality," did not envision any way in which Germany could be defeated in the present circumstances, but it argued that Britain might resist invasion if two conditions were met: if it could count on increasing material support from the US; and if the Royal Air Force, together with the navy, could remain in control over Britain and thus "prevent Germany from carrying out a serious sea-borne invasion of this country."[18]

The War Cabinet broke for lunch, during which Churchill dined with French Prime Minister Paul Reynaud, who had flown over for the meeting. Reynaud conveyed to Churchill the near hopelessness of the French situation. Churchill told him that Britain would go on alone. "We would rather go down fighting than be enslaved to Germany." The Cabinet reconvened at 2 p.m. There was a short further discussion of whether Britain should make any approach to Italy. Halifax favored this. Churchill "doubted whether anything would come of an approach to Italy, but said that the matter was one which the War Cabinet would have to consider."[19]

Halifax now wanted a commitment. He asked: "If he [Churchill] was satisfied that matters vital to the independence of this country were unaffected," would he be "prepared to discuss such terms?" Churchill realized that, given his still fragile position as prime minister, both Halifax and Chamberlain, long-time advocates of dealing with the dictators, had to be treated carefully. If they chose to go public about disagreements with Churchill, or, worse, if they walked out of the Cabinet, Churchill's government could collapse, an unthinkable prospect at this critical moment in the war. Thus Churchill replied cautiously, saying that he

> would be thankful to get out of our present difficulties on such terms, provided we retained the essentials and the elements of our vital strength, even at the cost of some territory;

but he added that he did not believe in the prospect of such a deal.[20] In a final meeting that day, Halifax continued to champion an effort to reach out to Mussolini in pursuit of a general settlement, and Churchill continued to insist that this approach would produce little of value.

Only on the next day, Monday, May 27, which Lukacs calls "the most crucial of the nine War Cabinet sessions," did the dispute between Halifax and Churchill came to a head, as each laid out and defended the key assumptions that underlay their different positions. The session began with a discussion of a draft memorandum Halifax had prepared. Entitled "Suggested Approach to Signor Mussolini," the memorandum expressed his view that modest territorial concessions to Mussolini, combined with his own discomfort with a Europe totally dominated by Germany, might induce the Italian dictator to serve as a mediator with Hitler, to help end the conflict before it reached the British homeland. The War Cabinet knew that a similar position was being advocated at that very moment by the French premier, Reynaud.

Churchill now made a decisive intervention. He began by saying that he was increasingly oppressed with the futility of the suggested approach to Signor Mussolini, which the latter would certainly regard with contempt. He added that such an approach would do France's Reynaud far less good than if he made a firm stand. In Lucacs' indirect report or paraphrase, Churchill continued:

Anyway, let us not be dragged down with France. If the French were not pre-pared to go on with the struggle, let them give up, though he [Churchill] doubted whether they would do so. If this country was beaten, France became a vassal state; but if we won, we might save them. The best help we could give to M. Reynaud was to let him feel that, whatever happened to France, we were going to fight it out to the end . . . At the moment our prestige in Europe was very low. The only way we could get it back was by showing the world that Germany had not beaten us. If, after two or three months, we could show that we were still unbeaten, our prestige would return. Even if we were beaten, we should be no worse off than we should be if we were now to abandon the struggle. Let us therefore avoid being dragged down the slippery slope with France. The whole of this manoeuvre was intended to get us so deeply involved in negotiations that we should be unable to turn back. We had gone a long way already in our approach to Italy, but let us not allow M. Reynaud to get us involved in a confused situation. The approach proposed was not only futile, but involved us in a deadly danger.[21]

Lukacs adds here that "It is perhaps not unreasonable to assume that by naming Reynaud in the penultimate sentence Churchill also meant Halifax."[22]

Recognizing this, Halifax now spoke. Aware of how large the rift between him and Churchill had become, he said that "he was conscious of certain rather profound differences of point of view that he would like to make clear." He went on:

On the present occasion, however, the Prime Minister seemed to suggest that under no conditions would we contemplate any course except fighting to a finish. The issue was probably academic, since we were unlikely to receive any offer which would not come up against the fundamental conditions which were essential to us. If, however, it was possible to obtain a settlement which did not impair those conditions, he, for his part, doubted if he would be able to accept the view now put forward by the Prime Minister. The Prime Minister had said that two or three months would show whether we were able to stand up against the air risk. This meant that the future of the country turned on whether the enemy's bombs happened to hit our aircraft factories. He was prepared to take that risk if our independence was at stake; but if it was not at stake he [Halifax] would think it right to accept an offer which would save the county from avoidable disaster.[23]

Halifax then ended his discourse by putting a blunt question to Churchill and to the War Cabinet. The question revealed that all the talk of Mussolini was really a smokescreen for an approach to Hitler. Halifax asked:

> Suppose Herr Hitler, being anxious to end the war through knowledge of his own internal weaknesses, offered terms to France and England, would the Prime Minister be prepared to discuss them?[24]

Over the passage of years, and through this fog of words, it is hard to discern the contours of the sharp dispute that rose then to the surface. It was a dispute involving entirely different appreciations of the nature of Britain's situation, opposing estimates of the character of her foes, and, ultimately, different moral priorities.

Halifax's views were consistent with everything that had guided him through the past decade. Like many people, he had lost faith in both Hitler and Mussolini, but he continued to believe that the dictators were open to reasoned arguments. Hitler, satisfied with his conquest of France, might be open to a "general settlement" that would ensure his hegemony of Europe without any need for him to engage in a difficult cross-Channel invasion of Britain. Mussolini might be goaded by the promise of modest territorial gains (Malta, Gibraltar) to coax his stronger ally into concessions. Furthermore, continued resistance had its costs. It could lead to the bombardment of Britain, countless deaths, and the destruction of the airplane factories that were Britain's one hope for continued resistance; and it might still end in an invasion causing massive destruction. Was it not wiser to sue for peace now, and hope to survive to fight another day? In this logic of "yield now to avoid catastrophe and almost certain death," Halifax continued to follow the script that had guided him and Chamberlain through the Rhineland, Austrian, and Czechoslovak episodes.

Churchill's Judgment

But on a closer examination, which Churchill engaged in with laser-like moral precision, we can see that almost everything in Halifax's account was wrong. A key problem was his misreading of Hitler. "Satisfaction" was not a word in Hitler's vocabulary. A decade of experience had shown that every concession only whetted his appetite for more. It was highly unlikely that he would rest content with an independent Britain at his back, especially as he plotted his further and long-heralded moves to conquer Russia to the east. Nothing short of a totally subdued Britain would suit him. For Churchill, this meant massive British disarmament, perhaps a handing over of most of the British fleet, and the replacement of the existing government with a more compliant one. This could mean the premiership of Oswald Mosley, the notorious British fascist, or of the elderly former Prime Minister Lloyd George, an outspoken admirer of Nazi Germany.[25]

Added to this was Halifax's total misreading of Hitler's character. Given the dictator's proven record of disdain for solemn agreements, what reason was there to believe that he would honor the terms of any accord? After grabbing the Sudetenland in the Munich agreement of September 1938, and despite written assurances, Hitler had used the weakening of Czechoslovakia's border defenses to openly invade the country the following March. What would prevent him from using any respite he gave Britain and any weakening of her defenses as an opportunity to undertake a new and more decisive aggression? Roberts observes that the view

> that there was a rational solution to all problems and all that was needed was to find a modus vivendi comfortable to all parties was deeply ingrained in his [Halifax's] character and personality.[26]

But it can be a fatal mistake to impute either rational prudence or honor to a vicious tyrant.

It might be argued, as Halifax implicitly did, that this analysis misses a key point in reasoning about the choices facing the country. For, even if all these estimates of Hitler's character, intentions, and likely actions are right, what is lost by trying to negotiate and secure peace? The alternative, after all, was a war that Britain, given the circumstances, was most likely to lose. In that case the end result would be the same, and perhaps even worse than a violated truce. In either case, the country would be bludgeoned into submission; but thousands whose lives might be spared by peacemaking would survive. By entering negotiations, there was at least a chance of reducing the bloodshed.

But this analysis is wrong in terms of its estimate both of the costs of negotiating and of the costs of different kinds of defeat. As Churchill's War Cabinet remarks show, there was a huge price to be paid for entering into negotiations. News of such efforts would immediately weaken British resolve and undermine further resistance. More importantly, once negotiations were entered into, there would be no way back. This was the "slippery slope" to which Churchill alluded. True to form, Hitler would cleverly offer blandishments that would make further resistance appear unreasonable. In short order, the British would be pulled down into the dark tunnel that had consumed other free peoples before them.

But would not some lives be spared? Perhaps; but, in moral terms, there are fates much worse than death. Up to this point we have focused on Churchill's moral judgment and vision. But it is important to note that he also possessed moral courage. He had shown this when, as a young correspondent during the Boer War, he had escaped from a prison camp and evaded an Afrikaner manhunt. He showed it again during the First World War when, following his humiliation in the Gallipoli affair, he went off to France to join and lead soldiers in the trenches. Referring to an instance when, as a government minister, Churchill insisted on fulfilling a speaking engagement in Belfast's Unionist Hall despite threats to his life, the biographer Paul Johnson observes:

> This was one of many instances at the time which testify to his lack of physical fear. In this sense there has never been a more courageous politician. He courted danger, given the chance.[27]

Churchill's physical courage should not be confused with bravado or foolhardiness. It was rooted in the conviction that there are certain things worth risking one's life for, especially if they involve one's freedom and dignity. Churchill knew that a life in slavery or subservience was not worth living, and at this crucial moment he clearly perceived that this was what was at stake. Hitler was not, as the appeasers believed, merely another authoritarian ruler who would eventually mellow and become more moderate – who might even be welcomed as an alternative to the much worse alternative of Bolshevism. A decade of experience in Germany and more recent reports of Hitler's genocidal conduct in conquered Poland had convinced Churchill – and anyone else not blinded by illusions and false values – that Hitler was a demonic power without precedent. Just a few days later, on May 31, during a meeting in Paris with Paul Reynaud, Churchill remarked:

> If Germany defeated either ally or both, she would give no mercy; we should be reduced to the status of vassals *forever*. It would be better far that the civilisation of Western Europe with all of its achievements should come to a tragic but splendid end than that the two great democracies should linger on, stripped of all that made life worth living.[28]

Nineteen days later, when France had fallen, he reiterated this theme in his famous "Finest Hour" address. If Hitler wins and we fall, he said, then the whole world, including the United States, including all that we have known and care for, will sink into the abyss of a New Dark Age, made more sinister, and perhaps more protracted, by the lights of perverted science.[29]

Here Churchill was prophetic. Years before they were disclosed or even took place, he saw the horrors of Auschwitz. But Churchill was not a clairvoyant. He did not possess some magical ability to see into the future. His ability to predict the future grew out of his clear insight into the present: into what Hitler represented. It also reflected his non-negotiable commitment to a set of human values. It is often said that one of the great tragedies of Nazi oppression was that it was so complete that it denied millions of its victims – Poles, Frenchmen, Russian prisoners of war, Jews, and many others – the chance to resist and die fighting. Churchill saw this risk and wisely feared it more than death.

Churchill was still not ready to openly reject Halifax's proposals, realizing that doing so might split the War Cabinet. In the course of that day, Halifax, his anger rising, had obliquely suggested that he might be forced to resign, telling his undersecretary, Alexander Cadogan, "I can't work with Winston any longer." At Halifax's urging, Churchill and Halifax then took a walk in the garden. No record of that conversation remains, but Cadogan writes in his *Diaries* that Halifax visited him afterward and reported that "he had spoken to W., who of course *had* been v.[ery] affectionate!"[30] Churchill, still not in a position to put down the revolt that was brewing in his midst, was in a conciliatory mood.

Tuesday, May 28, saw the culmination of the clash between the prime minister and foreign secretary. Following a morning meeting devoted largely to discussion of the Belgian surrender, the War Cabinet met again, at four in the afternoon, in a private room in the House of Commons. Halifax reintroduced the possibility of an Italian mediation with Hitler and stressed the French support for that idea. Churchill resisted getting into that position, which he again described as a slippery slope. He read a statement reiterating his opposition and concluded the discussion by saying that "the chances of decent terms being offered to us at the present were a thousand to one against."

It was now 5 p.m. Asking the War Cabinet to adjourn for two hours, Churchill went to a previously scheduled meeting (also in the House of Commons) of the twenty-nine or thirty members of the Outer Cabinet, which included all the government's ministers. In the course of this hour-long meeting, Churchill admitted to thinking about whether it "was his duty to consider negotiations" with Hitler. But, he concluded, "[i]t was idle to think that, if we tried to make peace now, we should get better terms from Germany than if we went on and fought it out." The Germans would demand our fleet, he said, and we would become a slave state "under Mosley or some such person."[31] One member present recorded in his diary Churchill's main point: "There was nothing to be done at any rate until we have turned the tide, except fight all out."[32]

The ministers appeared to be emphatic in their support of Churchill's positions, some patting him on the back at the close of the meeting. Returning to the War Cabinet at 7 p.m., Churchill reported on this encouraging response. This marked the end of Halifax's efforts. Churchill had prevailed. Whether he had used the Outer Cabinet to stage a coup, as some have suggested, or whether it was merely his tenacity and conviction that wore Halifax down, no one can say. What is clear is that the crisis was over. There would be no negotiations. Britain would fight on alone. News of the astonishing salvation of nearly the whole British Expeditionary Force at Dunkirk over the next few days would make survival more likely. But Dunkirk never figured in Churchill's reasoning. From the start, his position was based on a shrewd and morally sensitive assessment of his country's options.

The Hinge of Fate

John Lukacs argues persuasively that these five days in London in May 1940 were most decisive ones shaping the outcome of the Second World War. These five days, he says, were *the hinge of fate*. If Hitler had subsequently won the air war over Britain, he would still have faced a formidable challenge in conquering the country, especially if the United States entered the war. If Hitler had not been turned back at the gates of Moscow and rebuffed at Stalingrad, he would have dominated Europe, but not the world. Had D-Day failed, the determination of the Anglo-American alliance to defeat the Third Reich would not have weakened. In other words, none of these events was decisive, none was "the hinge of fate."

But if Britain had entered negotiations with Hitler in May 1940, the slippery slope that Churchill feared might have become a reality. Deprived of her essential defenses, Britain, like Norway and France, would have slipped under the control of a fascist puppet regime. With no one threatening him from behind and with the US lacking a toehold in Europe, Hitler's conquest of Russia would have been easier. Soon the United States would have stood alone against the world-bestriding power of both Germany and Japan. The long dark age of brutality and genocide that Churchill foresaw might have come to pass, "made more sinister, and perhaps more protracted, by the lights of perverted science."

We owe it to Churchill that this did not happen. During those five days in May he showed many virtues, among them graciousness to old political opponents (Chamberlain and Halifax), shrewdness in political calculation, intellectual acumen, and physical courage. But what made this brilliant combination of character assets work, and what guided them all in the right direction, was the virtue of good moral judgment. Churchill remains the icon of outstanding leadership. But we must not forget what it takes to become an icon.

Notes to Chapter Eight

1   Graham Greene, *End of the Affair*. London: Heinemann, 1951, p. 59.
2   For an excellent brief account of Churchill's accomplishments and failures in the years preceding the Second World War, see Paul Johnson, *Churchill*. New York: Viking, 2009.
3   Ibid., p. 97.
4   John Lukacs, *Five Days in London*: May 1940. New Haven, CT: Yale University Press, 1999 and Andrew Roberts, *The Holy Fox: A Biography of Lord Halifax*. London: Weidenfeld & Nicolson, 1991.
5   Roberts, *The Holy Fox*, p. 63.
6   Ibid., p. 68.
7   Ibid., p. 71.
8   Ibid., p. 73.
9   Winston S. Churchill, *The Gathering Storm*. Boston, MA: Houghton Mifflin, 1948, pp. 83–4. In *His Father's Son: The Life of Randolph Churchill*. London: Weidenfeld & Nicolson, 1996, Churchill's grandson, Winston S. Churchill, quotes Hanfstaengl to the effect that Churchill added the following lines at the end of his reply: "Tell your boss from me that anti-Semitism may be a good starter, but it is a bad stayer," p. 93. Hanfstaengl records substantially the same remark in his *Hitler: The Missing Years*. London: Eyre & Spottiswoode 1957, p. 185.
10   Various reasons have been given for this halt order, but it was not immediately reported to the War Cabinet and apparently it did not enter into their deliberations. See Lukacs, *Five Days in London*, pp. 40–42, and Alistair Horne, *To Lose a Battle: France* 1940. New York: Penguin, 2007, pp. 610ff.
11   Roberts and others contend that this was only a superficial reason for Halifax's concession to Churchill and that his real motives included the belief that he could better restrain Churchill in a ministerial role and the belief that, if Churchill failed, he would be next in line for the post. See Roberts, *The Holy Fox*, pp. 198–199.
12   The advisor was Robert Vansittart, who until 1938 had served as permanent under-secretary of state and was known to oppose appeasement, a fact that Halifax probably believed strengthened his own proposal for a meeting with the Italians.

13   Lukacs, *Five Days in London*, p. 92.

14   Ibid., p. 93.

15   Roberts, *The Holy Fox*, pp. 227, 228.

16   Lukacs, *Five Days in London*, pp. 108, 109.

17   Ibid., p. 109.

18   Ibid., p. 107.

19   Ibid., p. 112.

20   Ibid., p. 113.

21   Ibid., pp. 148–149.

22   Ibid., p. 149.

23   Ibid., p. 150.

24   Ibid., p. 151.

25   Indeed, as Britain's prospects worsened over the next few days, Churchill himself proposed bringing Lloyd George into the Cabinet, perhaps in the belief that, if Britain was vanquished, it would be better to have the "old man" in charge rather than the traitor Mosley. See Lukacs, *Five Days in London*, pp. 177–178.

26   Roberts, *The Holy Fox*, p. 115.

27   Johnson, *Churchill*, p. 35.

28   Lukacs, *Five Days in London*, p. 217.

29   Ibid.

30   *Diaries of Sir Alexander Cadogan*. London: Cassell, 1971, p. 153.

31   Lukacs, *Five Days in London*, p. 183.

32   Leo Amery, *The Empire at Bay*. London: Hutchinson, 1988, p. 619.

OPRAH WINFREY

COMPASSION AND CARE

> Illuminating life as a web rather than a succession of relationships, women portray autonomy rather than attachment as the illusory and dangerous quest. In this way, women's development points toward a different history of human attachment, stressing continuity and change in configuration, rather than replacement and separation, elucidating a different response to loss, and changing the metaphor of growth.
>
> Carol Gilligan[1]

Talk shows, in one form or another, have been a part of programming almost from the beginning of television. Early on there were the intellectual insights of Edward R. Murrow. Then there was the cool and calming commentary of Dave Garroway on the early morning *Today Show*. During the day, Arthur Godfrey in his radio/television simulcasts chatted with guests, played his ukulele, and talked to his audience about anything that struck his fancy. At night, Steve Allen kicked off a television dynasty known as the *Tonight Show*. He was succeeded by Jack Parr, Johnny Carson, Jay Leno, and for a while by Conan O'Brien – and then by Jay Leno again. In the mornings, Phil Donahue captured huge national ratings by involving his studio and TV audience in lively discussions on the hottest topics of the day. Then in January of 1984 WLS-TV in Chicago hired a young unknown news anchor and talk show host from Baltimore to host a low-rated half-hour morning talk show called *AM Chicago*. Her name was Oprah Winfrey. The show was on the air in the same time slot as Donahue's. By the middle of March, Winfrey went from last place in the ratings to overtaking Donahue as the highest rated show in Chicago.

10 Virtues of Outstanding Leaders: Leadership and Character, First Edition.
Al Gini and Ronald M. Green.
© 2013 John Wiley & Sons, Inc. Published 2013 by John Wiley & Sons, Inc.

Four months later the station doubled the length of the show. By September of 1985 the show changed its name to *The Oprah Winfrey Show*. In the fall of 1986 it was broadcast nationally, and it quickly became the number one talk show in national syndication. In 1987 the show received three Daytime Emmy Awards, and in 1988 Winfrey was named the International Radio and Television Society's "Broadcaster of The Year." A star was born, and both the broadcast industry and the nature of talk shows were forever changed.[2]

Since rising to national prominence in 1986, Winfrey has become omnipresent in every facet of the media. Until her retirement from the show in May 2011, she regularly appeared on TV five days a week, claiming as many as 44 million viewers in the United States. Her show was broadcast in 147 countries, from Saudi Arabia to South Africa. She also had a daily presence on satellite radio. She has starred in a number of films, and was nominated for an Oscar for her performance in *The Color Purple*. She has done numerous made-for-television films, and her production company (HARPO, Oprah spelled backwards) is also deeply involved in television film production. She has a monthly magazine with a 2.4 million circulation. She has made investments in the cable channel Oxygen. Her website, Oprah.com, attracts approximately 6.7 million visitors a month. And a Google search of her name generates in excess of 8 million results.[3] In 2010 the *New York Times* estimated her net worth at more than $2 billion.[4] That same year *Fortune* estimated her net worth to be in excess of $3 billion.[5] Whatever the exact amount, as a stand-up comic put it: "She's so rich now that the Chinese government borrows money from her!"

In the summer of 2010 Oprah announced that the 2010/2011 season would be the last season of her daily talk show. Her new project, she said, is the launch of her new 24/7 cable network – *The Oprah Winfrey Network* or OWN in January 2011. Her ambition is to create 1,200 hours of original and acquired programming. Her goal is to change what's on TV and what people get out of watching TV. Neither her most ardent supporters nor her detractors are sure that she can succeed in this new high-risk media venture, and the effort has continued to struggle. But both camps agree that, if it can be done, Oprah can do it.[6]

Star Status and More

Winfrey's status in modern society transcends the titles of celebrity, star, media mogul, or corporate entrepreneur. She is all these things and more. An advocate for important public causes, she was the prime mover for the passage of the 1991 "National Child Protection Act," which created a database and helps to monitor the activity of all convicted child abusers. As unofficial biographer

Kitty Kelley points out, "Oprah Winfrey's career and life have left an indelible mark on society . . . She has made the American dream come true – for herself and for many others."[7]

She is also a philanthropist. Deeply involved in educational reform both in America and Africa, she singlehandedly established an all-girl's school in South Africa, the Oprah Winfrey Leadership Academy for Girls, to give academically gifted young women from impoverished backgrounds the chance to excel. One of the Academy's stated goals is to create leaders who will give back to the community, as Winfrey herself has tried to do. In the course of its brief history, the Academy has come under criticism for offering excessively lavish accommodations, for providing education for too few youngsters, and for having administrative problems, including an instance of sexual abuse by staff. Despite this, Oprah has not wavered in her commitment to her project. In response to the concerns that too much is being spent on a handful of students, she replied:

> I'm looking for the opportunity to change the paradigm, to change the way not only these girls think . . . but to also change the way a culture feels about what women can do.[8]

From a leadership point of view, Winfrey's cultural and financial success is directly connected to her level of popularity with her fans and followers. From a business perspective, leaders are often measured and judged by how intensely they affect co-workers, employees, and stakeholders. This standard business paradigm simply doesn't work in Oprah's case. Although she is CEO of HARPO, Inc. – a multi-media production company that directly employs about 800 people – and although her actions and decisions affect the lives of thousands of other workers in the media world, her real base, her real followers, her true stakeholders and constituents, and the ultimate source of all her power and success are her fans.

Over a period of 25 years the *Oprah Winfrey Show* was the most awarded, most successful, "most talked about," most influential single talk show in the history of television. Over the years she has garnered accolades from every segment of society. To name but a few: in 1997 *Newsweek* accorded her the title "Most Important Person in Books and Media" and *TV Guide* that of "TV Performer of the Year"; in 1998 the National Academy of Television Arts and Science bestowed on her the Lifetime Achievement Award; in 1999 the National Book Foundation gave her its Gold Medal; in 2002 she won the Bob Hope Humanitarian Award; in 2004 the United Nations rewarded her with the Global Action Award; in 2005 the National Association for the Advancement of Colored People (NAACP) presented her with its Image Hall of Fame Award;

in 2006 the New York Library gave her the Lion Award; in 2007 the Elie Wiesel Foundation gave her the Humanitarian Award; in 2010, for the seventh consecutive year, *Time* magazine placed her among its Top 100 Most Influential People in the World; and in December 2010 she was honored by the Kennedy Center for the Performing Arts.

Her Fan Base

All this recognition can be traced directly back to her fan base – the people who turn on the TV in order to watch Oprah specifically. These are the people who listen to her carefully, who believe in her, and, most importantly, who trust her. These fans are her followers. And without followership leadership, in any field or endeavor, cannot exist.

Pulitzer Prize-winning historian Garry Wills argues that we have long had a list of a leader's requisites – determination, focus, a clear goal, a sense of priorities, and so on. But we tend to overlook or forget leadership's first and all-encompassing need: "The leader most needs followers. When those are lacking, the best ideas, the strongest will, the most wonderful smile have no effect."[9] Followers set the terms in which leadership is accepted. Leadership is a "mutually determinative" activity on the part of leader and followers. Sometimes it's cooperative, sometimes it's a struggle, and often it's a feud; but it's always collective. Although "the leader is the one who mobilizes others toward a goal shared by leaders and followers," leaders are powerless without followers. In effect, Wills argues, successful leaders need to understand their followers far more than followers need to understand leaders.[10] Oprah Winfrey has understood this lesson well.

Initially *The Oprah Winfrey Show* followed the model established by other daytime talk shows, employing sensational stories and outrageous special guests to attract viewers. In the early 1990s a handful of talk shows abandoned the "fresh talk format" (spontaneous discussion of a topic with an interesting guest), and embraced a more extreme "flesh talk" or "smut talk format" (salacious subjects, titillating commentary, and the antics of outrageous guests). Oprah chose to distance herself from this innovation. After a number of years on the air it became clear to her that her most engaging interviews were with people who had an emotional experience to share and a real "human" story to tell. She realized that famous people with inspirational stories make for great television, to be sure; but so do non-famous people with inspirational stories. Winfrey was convinced that we all want to be heard – rich or poor, commoner or celebrity – and that the greatest pain in life is to be unheard, invisible, and without hope.[11]

Mirroring many of the ideas found in Carol Gilligan's feminist classic *In A Different Voice*, Winfrey came to believe that in talking to each other, in listening to each other, we are in effect saying "I'm like you, I've suffered like you, I understand you. If nothing else, perhaps something good can come out of all of this."

Although Winfrey never completely abandoned the entertainment aspect of her show and easily maintained lively banter with gossip columnists, rock stars, porn actors, or politicians in the news, she and her staff consciously changed the vision and mission of the show. The new focus was on "personal growth themes" and on the examination of issues and topics that could be of service to her audience. Winfrey described this shift in vision and mission as the desire to be a catalyst for transformation in people's lives. She wanted to help people "Live Their Best Lives."[12] She wanted people to make better choices as a result of using the experience and stories of others. "Our intention," she said, "is to create moments in which people can connect to the truest sense of themselves and build from there."[13] For Winfrey, the purpose of the show was to alter the ways people see themselves and the world. The goal was to uplift, enlighten, encourage – and, of course, to entertain.

Before each show Winfrey said to herself: "My prayer, my meditation, my thought for myself is, how can I best be used?"[14] After all,

> The only reason to do anything at this point is to be of some service to other people. I'm already in millions of homes each day. I certainly have enough attention, enough money, enough fame. The only reason [to keep doing this] is that you can use your life experience to enlighten someone else's . . .[15]

Over the years Winfrey has tried to make her show a "community of listeners," a "community of learners." She does this through her ability to relate to her guests, through her willingness to be emotionally open and vulnerable on camera, and by showing real passion and interest in her subject matter. During this period the choice of topics has been diverse and eclectic, and the topics themselves have usually been of interest to Oprah. Here are just a few of the topics and issues Winfrey has covered in the past 25 years and approximately 4,500 shows:

Meditation Techniques	The Death Penalty
The Need for Exercise	America's Poor
Diet and Lifestyle	Faces of Autism
Teenage Alcoholism	Lives of Young Prostitutes
Clinical Depression	Living on a Minimum Wage
Date Rape	Social Class

Spousal Abuse	The Message of the Media
Alternative Medicine	Heroes in the Headlines
Dads and Daughters	Ethnic Stereotypes
When I Knew I Was Gay	UFOs
Personal Finances	Going Green 101
Workaholism	The American Dream
Obsessive Love	New York City after 9/11
Divorce	Satanic Worship
Healing Childhood Wounds	The AIG (American International Group) Crisis
Children and Guns	Kidnapping
Clergy Abuse	The Need for Teachers
Multiple Personality Types	Teen Drivers
Belief and Spirituality	Knowing Your Limits

The Book Club

There is no better single example of Oprah's desire to uplift and enlighten her fans and followers than her decision in 1996 to start Oprah's Book Club. Both as a young child and as a teenager under her father's strict tutelage, she fell in love with the magic of books. Books were the way out. Books freed her from the limits and poverty of her day-to-day world. Books exposed her to options, alternative world views, and gave her hope. She started the Book Club to do the same thing for her television audience. Her aim was to promote literacy, to excite her viewers about reading, and to encourage the concept of lifelong learning. Each month Winfrey chose a book and discussed it with her audience and, when possible, with the book's author as well.[16]

The first book she chose was by the little known first-time author Jacquelyn Mitchard: *The Deep End of the Ocean*. Nine days after it was selected, it reached the top of *The Wall Street Journal*'s bestseller list; and two weeks later it made *The New York Times*' list. Thanks to the publicity, the publisher was forced to print an extra 540,000 copies immediately. The book eventually sold over 4 million copies. Of the Book Club's first 46 picks, every single one appeared on bestsellers lists, and each of them sold in excess of 1.5 million copies.

In 2003 Winfrey restructured the format of the Club and began to select also more classic works of literature, like Tolstoy's *Anna Karenina* or Gabriel Garcia Marquez's *One Hundred Years of Solitude*, as well as biographies and memoirs, like *The Measure of a Man: A Spiritual Autobiography*, by Sidney Poitier, and *Night*, by Elie Wiesel. Winfrey's first classic selection was John Steinbeck's *East of Eden*. It immediately jumped its Amazon.com ranking from 2,356,000 to 113, and in one week's time it topped *The New York Times* bestselling paperback fiction list. Surveying these numbers and her staggering Book Club Show ratings, Winfrey was convinced that the most significant accomplishment of the Club was

> getting people to think differently about themselves and their lives. It has done what I knew books could do, which is [to] open people up to the possibilities of their lives and extend the vision of these possibilities.[17]

She felt that the Book Club encapsulated her mission and purpose: "Be your best self."

The true test of the import and impact of the Club could perhaps best be seen when something went terribly wrong. In 2005 James Frey published a memoir, *A Million Little Pieces*, that recounted his lifelong addiction to alcohol and drugs, all of which led to a life of petty crimes, violent behavior, shattered relationships, and a long list of failed attempts at rehab. Or so he said. At first Winfrey was horrified and drawn to Frey's story. After all, as she pointed out: "Is there one family in this country untouched by alcoholism and addiction? I doubt it."[18] As far as Winfrey was concerned, Frey's story was riveting and his style was immensely readable. It was, for her, "a perfect teaching moment."

Within a month of Frey's book being selected and of his appearance on the show, nearly half a million copies of the book were sold. In a matter of weeks, *A Million Little Pieces* had the "triple crown" of book sales by being rated number one in *USA Today*, *The New York Times*, and *Publisher's Weekly*.[19] And then things started to come undone.

Little by little websites, critics, and commentators began to investigate and question the general authenticity of many of the book's claims. Frey defended himself on *The Larry King Live* show and admitted that "there were embellishments in the book" and that "in certain cases things were toned up." But, he maintained, "in the memoir genre, the writer generally takes liberties."[20] Oprah called into *The Larry King Show* and defended Frey:

> We support the book because we recognize that there have been thousands of and hundreds of thousands of people whose lives have been changed by this book . . . I feel . . . that although some of the facts have been questioned . . . that the underlying message of redemption in James Frey's memoir still resounds with me . . .[21]

But Winfrey's endorsement didn't stop the national attacks on Frey's basic details, and in fact his entire story was shown to be fictional much more than autobiographical. As the body of evidence mounted against Frey, Winfrey changed her mind. She remained convinced that Frey's "underlying message" warranted attention; but as a novel, a piece of creative, evocative fiction – not as a memoir. On January 26, 2006 Winfrey invited Frey back to her show and told him that she had revised her opinion of his book. "I feel duped," she said. "But more importantly, I feel you have betrayed millions of readers."[22] She went on to address the comments she had made on *The Larry King Show*.

> I made a mistake . . . I left the impression that the truth does not matter. And I am deeply sorry about that, because that is not what I believe . . . The truth matters.

As a leader, as a respected media presence, Oprah wisely recognized that her extraordinary career had invested her with authority over a broad range of issues and had a real impact on the lives of those who trusted her.[23] She knew that her word was both her bond and her brand, and she needed to save both in order to be who she is and to do what she does. "After all," said Oprah, "this is not about money. I would like to feel I could have an impact on people's lives in a broader venue."[24]

Leadership Is a Relationship

Opraholics and Oprahphiles worship her and study her. She is the subject of over three dozen PhD dissertations. The Harvard Business School published a case study on her corporate success. The University of Illinois offers an undergraduate course entitled "History #298 'Oprah Winfrey, the Tycoon: Contextualizing the Economics of Race, Gender, Class in Black Business in a Post-Civil Rights America'" And *The Wall Street Journal* defined "Oprahfication" as meaning "public confession as a form of therapy."[25]

But, when we ask what caused the extraordinary success and impact of this single individual, we cannot escape the conclusion that Oprah, above all, is perceived by her admirers as a caring individual and as someone whose concern and compassion for others animate every personal, professional, and career decision she makes. In her selection of topics for her show, in her private philanthropic endeavors, in her support for public causes, and in her constant ambition to reach out and elevate her followers, whether through literary initiatives or personal example, she is perceived as someone who cares about *you*, whether you are a celebrity or an ordinary person.

Are Oprah's compassion and care genuine? If Oprah has her fans, she has her detractors as well. Some skeptics argue that her push to build a media empire is fueled by a desire for money and an insatiable need to expand her power, fame, and media domination. Many critics are troubled, for example, by her need to be on the cover of every single issue of *O, The Oprah Magazine*. Others belittle and play down her themes of self-actualization and celebrity. Rather, they say, her shows are about self-actualization *through* celebrity. Her critics accuse her of placing herself on a pedestal and proclaiming to her fan base: "be like me" and then you'll be "your best possible self."[26] And now, they say, with the new *Oprah Winfrey Network*, sycophants and fans can be exposed to all that is Oprah and *Oprah-approved* 24/7! They wonder if fame and fortune have lulled her into believing that she possesses something akin to papal infallibility.[27]

No one can easily read a person's inner heart. Like all human beings, Oprah Winfrey is a complex mix of ego and altruism. Like all great leaders, she is far from perfect. As one media commentator observes:

> She's been doing it so long. She's under constant scrutiny. Sure, she makes mistakes. Sure, she gets too cute at times. Sure, some of her people [guests and experts] are just too kitschy. Frankly, no one who lives in a fish bowl the way she does could fake it that long! Besides, even when you can't buy into her latest idea, book, or celebrity *du jour*, she's always trying to raise the bar. She's always trying to reach out and have an effect on a public that she knows is watching every move she makes. No matter how schmaltzy she can seem, no matter how gushingly sentimental or self serving, the bottom line is she cares. And it shows![28]

Most of the leaders we have examined up to now commanded armies or multi-national corporations. If you leave out her business holdings, which are not inconsiderable, Oprah is a not a leader of this sort. Her followers are an inchoate mass of people who will – and have – followed her directions, example, and advice. She is less an organizational leader than a cultural one, a pacesetter who vastly influences many people through her initiatives and example. None of this makes her less of a leader than the general of an army would be – and indeed in the modern world it is just such cultural leaders who often have the greatest effect on history and culture.

In the end, leadership is not always about issuing orders in a clearly delineated organizational structure. At its most basic level, leadership is a relationship between individuals who share the same or similar aspirations and goals. From a leader's point of view, leadership is about commitment to a constituency of others and those others' commitment to the leader. The bond, the cement that holds that relationship together is an admixture of vulnerability, honesty, and trust. By living her life in front of a camera, Winfrey learned to listen both to others and to herself. In doing so she came to see life as complicated, contextual, and connected. Like Carol Gilligan, she began to understand that "[w]e know ourselves as separate only insofar as we live in connection with others."[29] Winfrey has spent a career advocating for, and living, an ethic of care and responsibility. Millions of people each week watch, listen, believe in, and trust her.

> For me, it's about getting . . . into the hearts of people's lives. I want to expand Americans' views of other people in the world . . . Playing small doesn't serve me. The truth is I want millions of [viewers]. I'm not one of those people who say, "Oh, if I change just one person's life . . ." Nope, [I'm] not satisfied with just a few. I want millions of people.[30]

Through Oprah, these millions learn that Oprah cares, and her demonstration of this fact leads them to care about both others and themselves. In her leadership, Oprah has undeniably made care and compassion an industry; but these values are no less genuine or important for that reason.

Notes to Chapter Nine

1 Carol Gilligan, *In a Different Voice: Psychological Theory and Women's Development*. Cambridge, MA: Harvard University Press, 1982, p. 48.
2 Bernard M. Timberg, *Television Talk: A History of TV TalkShows*. Austin: University of Texas Press, 2002, pp. 134–146.
3 Kitty Kelley, *Oprah: A Biography*. New York: Crown Publishers, 2010, p. xiv.
4 Paul Sullivan, "Oprah Winfrey Opts for Her Own Private Financial Advisor." *New York Times*, June 18, 2010.
5 Patricia Sellers, "Oprah's Next Act." *Fortune*, October 18, 2010, pp. 116–126.
6 Meg James, "Winfrey Network Ready to Roll." *Chicago Tribune*, Business, Section 2, December 26, 2010, p. 2.
7 Kelley, *Oprah*, p. 409.
8 "Oprah Wants to Change View of Women in Africa: Talk Show Host Opens School for Girls in Effort to Change the Culture." Today/Celebrities, January 1, 2007. At http://today.msnbc.msn.com/id/16455632 (last accessed November 26, 2012).
9 Garry Wills, *Certain Trumpets*. New York: Simon & Schuster, 1994, p. 13.
10 Ibid., p. 17.
11 Nancy Koehn, Erica Helms, Katherine Miller, and Rachel K. Wilcox, *Oprah Winfrey*. Harvard Business School Case, 809-068. Boston: Harvard Business School, 2009, p. 6.
12 Ibid., p. 15.
13 Ibid.
14 Ibid., p. 13.
15 Ibid., p. 15.
16 Ibid., p. 16.

17   Mike McDaniel, "Oprah's Strong Suit." *Houston Chronicle*, April 27, 1997.
18   Koehn, Helms, Miller, and Wilcox, *Oprah Winfrey*, p. 1.
19   Ibid., p. 286.
20   Interview with James Frey, CNN: *Larry King Live.* Aired January 11, 2006. At www.cnn.com.
21   Kelley, *Oprah*, p. 288.
22   Koehn, Helms, Miller, and Wilcox, *Oprah Winfrey*, p. 3.
23   Ibid., p. 4.
24   Ibid., p. 1.
25   Kelley, *Oprah*, p. 409.
26   James Poniewozik, "On Her Own." *Time*, January 10, 2011, p. 46.
27   Kelley, *Oprah*, p. 288.
28   Steve Edwards, Program Director, Chicago Public Radio, WBEZ-FM, 848 E. Grand, Chicago, Illinois 60611, December 15, 2010. This was a private interview I had with Mr. Edwards on the general topic of the media and leadership. I specifically asked him about Oprah, credibility, and continuing popularity as "media leader."
29   Gilligan, *In A Different Voice*, p. 63.
30   Sellers, "Oprah's Next Act," p. 126.

DWIGHT D. EISENHOWER, THE SICILIAN SLAPPING INCIDENTS

FAIRNESS

> I can't decide logically if I am a man of destiny or a lucky fool, but I think I am
> destined . . . I feel that my claim to greatness hangs on the ability to lead and
> inspire . . . I am a genius – I think I am.
>
> George S. Patton, November 3, 1942[1]

Like Lincoln, Churchill, Roosevelt, and de Gaulle – the four other great
wartime leaders we are examining in this book – Dwight David ("Ike") Eisenhower displayed multiple leadership virtues. Throughout his long military
and political career, Ike repeatedly evidenced moral judgment, moral courage,
intellectual excellence, compassion, deep honesty, and deep selflessness. He
added to these a host of other excellences, including an iron determination in
executing plans, an easygoing approachability, and a self-deprecating sense of
humor, which told others that he didn't take himself too seriously.

But, if one has to choose the single virtue that Ike exhibited most, from the
beginning to the end of his long military and political career, that would be
fairness. From his earliest years, when he was the bearer of his class color at
West Point, until the closing days of his presidency, when he issued a prophetic
warning about the growing power of the "military industrial complex" in
which he had spent his whole life, Ike was always an admired leader who rose
above favoritism and partisanship to act on behalf of the common good. His
assessments of the situation were always fact-informed, unbiased, and even-
handed. He was committed to treating subordinates justly and to basing his
judgments on their merit and performance, not his own or others' emotions
or prejudices.

10 Virtues of Outstanding Leaders: Leadership and Character, First Edition.
Al Gini and Ronald M. Green.
© 2013 John Wiley & Sons, Inc. Published 2013 by John Wiley & Sons, Inc.

Great leaders are not afraid to discipline. This is often required in order to uphold organizational standards and get rid of misbehaving or non-performing individuals. Ike understood this; but, while he was willing to discipline or fire subordinates, he always exercised fairness in this key leadership function. His recent biographer Jean Edward Smith observes that Ike did not belong to the "counsel and correct" school of military leadership. He believed that "officers that fail must be ruthlessly weeded out." An officer who underperformed in the course of the European campaigns "was summarily relieved and sent back to the United States."[2] Nevertheless, Ike's judgments were invariably regarded as just and fair, even by those who suffered under them.

The Slapping Incidents

Ike's fairness is nowhere better illustrated than in a set of decisions he made in August 1943 in the wake of the Allies' invasion of Sicily. Operation Husky, as the invasion was called, had been a striking success. With Eisenhower as supreme commander, a force of 160,000 American, British, and Canadian troops stormed ashore on a wide beachhead on Sicily's south coast, on the night of July 9/10. Led by General Bernard Montgomery, British and Canadian forces fought their way up the eastern side of the island, around the looming obstacle of Mount Aetna, toward Messina on the island's northeast corner. General George S. Patton led American forces through the island's center, to the city of Palermo on the northern coast, where his forces wheeled right and pushed through strong German resistance along the coastal road to Messina. On August 17, the troops of the Seventh Army, driven by Patton's relentless demands and exhortations, beat the British by hours in the race to Messina. Brute force had prevailed. The German army was driven off the island and the Allies had their first foothold in Europe.

On August 3, as Patton's men were driving forward against strong German opposition, Patton himself visited a frontline field hospital. The general was noted for such visits; he saw soldiers' bandaged wounds as a "recognizable badge of courage," epitomizing the military values he cherished.[3] As he made the rounds of the wounded, pinning the Purple Heart on some gravely wounded men, Patton came to a patient, 27-year-old Private Charles H. Kuhl, who was slouched on a stool midway through a tent ward. In the previous ten days Kuhl had been sent back from the front lines twice, with a diagnosis of moderate to severe "psychoneurotic anxiety" – or what had come to be known as battle fatigue. In the end Kuhl was found to be suffering from malaria and chronic dysentery, and he was running a fever of over 102 degrees.

Patton knew nothing of this. What happened next is chronicled in many places, including the film "Patton," but Rick Atkinson offers a lucid account in his history of the Sicilian campaign:

> Patton asked Kuhl where he was hurt. The soldier shrugged. He was "nervous" rather than wounded, Kuhl said. "I guess I can't take it," he added. To the astonishment of doctors and patients alike, Patton slapped the man across his face with his folded gloves. "You coward, you get out of this tent!" he shouted. "You can't stay here with these brave, wounded Americans." Grabbing Kuhl by the collar, he dragged him to the tent entrance and shoved him out with a finishing kick from his cavalry boot. "Don't admit this sonuvabitch," he bellowed. "I don't want yellow-bellied bastards like him hiding their lousy cowardice around here, stinking up this place of honor." Alternately barking at the doctors and the quailing Kuhl, Patton said, "You send him back to his unit at once. You hear me, you gutless bastard? You're going back to the front."[4]

A week later, on August 10, Patton repeated this behavior at a different field hospital, when he encountered another soldier suffering from battle fatigue. Patton yelled at the soldier, Private Paul G. Bennett, "[y]ou ought to be lined up against a wall and shot," and added: "In fact, I ought to shoot you myself right now." Patton then pulled out his pistol and waved it in the terrified soldier's face. He also slapped Bennett across the face with his gloves. Before leaving the hospital he repeated this gesture, hitting Bennett so hard that the soldier's helmet liner was knocked to the floor.[5]

News of the episodes spread like lightning among neighboring units, and word of Patton's antics quickly reached Eisenhower. A surgeon at one of the field hospitals, who, like the other medical professionals, was angered that a senior officer had arbitrarily overruled medical judgment, prepared an official report. This was followed within a few hours by a visit to Eisenhower by a group of newspaper correspondents who personally confirmed the details. Eisenhower immediately realized the gravity of these incidents. Although officers were permitted to discipline physically, and even to shoot, disobedient or malingering soldiers in combat situations, the US military code of justice required a formal judicial procedure for infractions committed behind the front lines. In addition to antagonizing the medical staff, Patton had committed a court-martial offense. The question before Eisenhower was what to do; and he knew he had little time to act. The reporters' presence told Ike that, if he did not move quickly to address the problem, he would soon have a public relations disaster on his hands that could threaten his future ability to command.

The Challenges Ike Faced

Several considerations sharpened Ike's problem. One was his close, emotionally charged relationship to Patton. The two had been friends since 1919, when they both served as young tank officers at Camp Meade, Maryland. Eisenhower graduated from West Point in 1915 and spent the First World War at various US military postings. Patton was five years older and six years Eisenhower's senior in the Regular Army (he had graduated from West Point in 1909). He had fought in France, returning as a decorated hero. There were also differences in background. While Ike descended from humble German immigrant roots (at the time Ike was born, his impoverished father was working as a menial laborer in a Texas railroad yard), Patton traced his lineage to English nobility – sixteen barons who signed the Magna Carta – and his grandfather had died while fighting as a Confederate colonel. Both he and his wife came from wealthy families. Patton never lorded it over Eisenhower. On the contrary, from the start, he treated his younger colleague as a kindred spirit who shared his passion for the future of armored warfare; but these discrepancies in age, military experience, and family background would color their relationship throughout their careers. Patton's many advantages and seniority were always remembered by both men, even after Ike became Patton's commanding officer during the North African and Sicilian campaigns.

During the inter-war years and during the first campaigns of the Second World War Patton experienced a growing reputation as a combat commander. He excelled in the landings and battles of Operation Torch in North Africa in late 1942 and early 1943 and was called on by Ike to replace other officers who proved incapable of leading the relatively untested US troops. The Sicilian campaign further demonstrated Patton's outstanding gifts as a combat commander.

The contrast here with Ike could not be sharper. Ike did not possess a distinguished military pedigree. There was nothing in his heritage that "destined" him either for a military career or for military greatness. Up to that point in the war he had never led a combat unit and, as the Second World War began, he had never even heard a shot fired in anger. Although his administrative abilities had been noticed, on the eve of the US entry into the war he had never held an active command above the level of battalion and was far from being considered as a potential commander of major operations. Ike had risen through the ranks as a result of his managerial and administrative skills, which he demonstrated serving in the late 1920s, in France, as research and writing assistant to a First World War hero: General John J. Pershing, who headed the Battle Monuments Commission. During the 1930s Ike served as chief military aide to General Douglas MacArthur, and at the outset of the Second World War as deputy to Army Chief of Staff General George C. Marshall.

Marshall was responsible for Eisenhower's meteoric rise from little-known staff officer to supreme Allied commander in the North African and Sicilian campaigns. What Marshall saw in his deputy, in addition to a unique aptitude for strategic planning and a talent for logistics, was, as Alan Axelrod writes, "an extraordinary ability to work with others – to get along with them, to persuade them, to mediate among them, to direct them, to encourage them, and to correct them."[6] Ike's ability to manage a coalition of members of military staff of disparate nations was crucial. More than any other war in which the US participated, the Second World War was a multi-national effort. In early 1942, at the time of the US entry into the war, the British, Russians, and free French had been fighting for over two years, and each nation had its roster of brilliant – if prickly – military and political leaders such as Bernard Montgomery or Charles de Gaulle. Although the sheer might of the US effort, its weight in men and machines, strongly counseled a US leadership of the war, the supreme commander had to be able to work with this diverse coalition. Ike put the challenge bluntly when he later described his job as "trying to arrange the blankets smoothly over several prima donnas in the same bed."[7]

Fairness was the key to making this work. The supreme Allied commander could not be perceived as serving his own nation's interests at the expense of those of others in the coalition, or favoring people with whom he had personal relationships. One of Ike's greatest achievements throughout the war was convincing others of his absolute reliability and fairness. The British General Sir Alan Brooke, who sometimes clashed with Ike on particular military decisions and was known to disparage the American general's understanding of strategy, nevertheless observed that Ike "possessed an exceptional ability to handle Allied forces, to treat them all with strict impartiality, and to get the best out of an inter-Allied force."[8] The British general Sir Harold Alexander, who served as Ike's deputy during the North African campaign, seconded this view. Alexander envied the clarity of Ike's mind and his power of accepting responsibility, adding: "He was utterly fair in his dealings."[9]

But the news brought to Eisenhower by the field surgeon and three reporters threatened the very heart of his ability to command. Ike's reputation for fairness was being sorely tried on several counts. First, there was the fact that he was called to issue judgment on the conduct of an officer who was an old friend, a fellow American, and in many ways his senior. Each of these aspects posed possible risks of conflict of interest for Eisenhower. Second, there was Ike's own lack of battlefield experience. How could he, a desk officer who had never really seen battle, call on the carpet a man who had just driven his men into the teeth of formidable German forces? How could he take the side of a perceived coward, when Patton had just watched men fall in battle? Finally, from a military point of view, there was a serious risk to the war effort itself. If being harshly disciplined were to demoralize or embitter Patton (or the men he led), or if a mishandling of the incidents were to unleash a storm of public opinion that forced Patton out, the whole war effort could be damaged. It took little imagination to see that the Nazi propaganda machine would turn to advantage any mistake here on Ike's part, proclaiming that Eisenhower's preference for cowards had driven out his foremost general and doomed the "weak democracies" to defeat.

Ike's Response

Any of us would be pardoned if, faced with the choice that lay before Eisenhower, we wished the problem would just go away. We might be tempted for example to ignore it, although, with the press already involved, that would soon produce catastrophic results. Or we might resort to rationalization. Patton, after all, had just won a magnificent victory. His military value was unparalleled. Furthermore, he had just been through a month of intensely stressful combat. It was completely understandable that he would blow up when confronting a soldier whom he regarded as shirking from his duty. And Patton's misconduct was only a slap. Perhaps a friendly talk with him, man to man, would be enough: a wink and a nod. "I understand your feelings, George, but please don't do it again, at least not in public." From there on, a quiet conversation with the reporters might be in order. "I've spoken to General Patton. I assure you he apologizes for these incidents. It won't happen again." Above all, Ike could stress Patton's accomplishments. "He's our best combat general. How can I damage such an asset? Doesn't high performance sometimes justify breaking or bending the rules?" In the decades since the Second World War we have seen these tendencies to rationalization, excuse, and cover-up repeatedly displayed, in organizational crisis after crisis. Above all, the notion that results justify anything, that success permits us to overlook misconduct reigns supreme.

What did Eisenhower do? How did he handle this challenge to both his and Patton's leadership? The record is clear, because, as in many moments of his life, Eisenhower committed his response to paper. This permits us to arrive at our own conclusions about his performance.

First of all, it is noteworthy that Ike chose to avoid personal contact with Patton. Although managers today frequently believe that any human resources matter can be handled "if I can only meet personally with those involved," Ike recognized that personal engagement – in the form of an order to Patton to come to Ike's headquarters in Algiers, or even in the form of a visit by Ike to Patton in Sicily – had its perils. A meeting would accentuate the personal ties between the two men, point up Patton's age and military seniority, and give the flamboyant general an opportunity to posture, or even to accuse Ike of meddling. A personal meeting could easily end in angry exchanges and undermine the very authority Ike needed in this situation.

To establish that authority, Ike chose the written word. To begin with, he asked Brigadier General Frederick A. Blessé, the theater surgeon general, to conduct an investigation to determine whether the facts reported to Ike about the incidents were accurate. When Blessé confirmed that they were, Ike sent the following letter to Patton, hand-delivered by Blessé:

Letter, Eisenhower to GSP, Jr., August 17, 1943

I am attaching a report which is shocking in its allegations against your personal conduct. I hope you can assure me that none of them is true; but the detailed circumstances communicated to me lead to the belief that some ground for the charges must exist. I am well aware of the necessity for hardness and toughness on the battlefield. I clearly understand that firm and drastic measures are at times necessary in order to secure the desired objectives. But this does not excuse brutality, abuse of the sick, nor exhibition of uncontrollable temper in front of subordinates.

In the two cases cited in the attached report, it is not my present intention to institute any formal investigation. Moreover, it is acutely distressing to me to have such charges as these made against you at the very moment when an American Army under your leadership has attained a success of which I am extremely proud. I feel that the personal services you have rendered the United States and the Allied cause during the past weeks are of incalculable value; but nevertheless, if there is a very considerable element of truth in the allegations accompanying this letter, I must so seriously question your good judgment and your self discipline as to raise serious doubts in my mind as to your future usefulness. I am assuming, for the moment, that the facts in the case are far less serious than appears in this report, and that whatever truth is contained in these allegations reports an act of yours when under the stress and strain of winning a victory, you were thoughtless rather than harsh. Your leadership of the past few weeks has, in my opinion, fully vindicated to the War Department and to all your associates in arms my own persistence in upholding your pre-eminent qualifications for the difficult task to which you were assigned. Nevertheless, you must give to this matter of personal deportment your instant and serious consideration to the end that no incident of this character can be reported to me in the future, and I may continue to count upon your assistance in military tasks.

In Allied Headquarters there is no record of the attached report or of my letter to you, except in my own secret files. I will expect your answer to be sent to me personally and secretly. Moreover, I strongly advise that, provided there is any semblance of truth in the allegations in the accompanying report, you make in the form of apology or other such personal amends to the individuals concerned as may be within your power, and that you do this before submitting your letter to me.

No letter that I have been called upon to write in my military career has caused me the mental anguish of this one, not only because of my long and deep personal friendship for you but because of my admiration for your military qualities, but I assure you that conduct such as described in the accompanying report will not be tolerated in this theater no matter who the offender may be.

We could parse almost every sentence in this letter, which exhibits Eisenhower's keen understanding of human psychology as well as his sense of moral values. Psychologically, the letter communicates a sincere appreciation of Patton's achievements as well as an understanding of the stressful circumstances under which he has been working. However, the letter also notes that none of this excuses poor judgment or emotional outbursts on the part of a field commander. Indeed, just the opposite is true. Patton's loss of control under stress is not an excuse, but must rather lead his superiors to "seriously question" his judgment and self-discipline, qualities essential to command. Implicit here is a powerful threat. If Patton does not cease from such conduct immediately and make amends for what he has done, Ike will pull him out of the line of command. For an officer who believed he had a rendezvous with destiny, as Patton did, no greater threat could be voiced.

Ethically, the letter is equally clear. There will be no arguments about the rightness or wrongness of what Patton did. Brutality, abuse of the sick, or the display of uncontrollable temper in front of subordinates are always wrong, no matter what the reasons for them. Finally, the letter tells us that what Patton did is wrong no matter how highly placed or successful a manager he may be. No one can rise above the law or an organization's values through high performance and by making him-/herself "too valuable" to be disciplined: "conduct such as described in the accompanying report will not be tolerated in this theater no matter who the offender may be."

A leading professor of business ethics once summed up Eisenhower's last point by reporting a conversation he had with a friend. The professor was at a high point in his career and was becoming prone to dealing abruptly with some of his colleagues. Taking him aside, the friend said: "Look, I want you to know that you are special. But you're no damned different." This, in essence, is what Ike was saying to his old friend Patton. "You're special, George, but you're no damned different. Rank and accomplishments do not permit you to act in ways that violate the rules incumbent on everyone else."

Some might argue that Ike's response here was too gentle. The letter and the reprimand it contained, after all, were kept in Ike's secret files. He did not publicly upbraid Patton, not did he initiate proceedings for what was technically a court-martial offense. In addition, by persuading the war correspondents that Patton had been severely reprimanded, Eisenhower was able to prevent the incidents from immediately becoming front-page news.[10] Nevertheless, Patton himself never doubted the seriousness of Ike's reprimand. Responding to Ike's letter, he personally apologized to the two GIs he had slapped, as well as to all the troops under his command. For almost a year, he was also deprived of command, as the allies prepared their forces for D-Day. He would eventually be inserted into combat to facilitate the breakout from the Normandy beachhead; but, for months, Patton remained unsure of whether he would ever be allowed to participate in the great battles ahead. In the end Ike chose to exercise his allowable discretion as to whether to initiate a judicial action in this case, and he also chose not to imperil the Allied cause by removing a vitally useful commander. But, for a general like Patton, who believed he had an "ultimate and eternal destiny of leading a great army in battle,"[11] Ike's interventions were punishment enough.

Carlo D'Este, a leading biographer of both Eisenhower and Patton, describes Ike's letter to Patton as containing "the strongest words of censure written to a senior American officer during World War II."[12] Above all, it serves as a consummate illustration of the meaning of fairness, which Ike embodied throughout his life. In the months following the slapping incidents, Ike would add to his reputation by becoming an active, involved, and successful commander of troops in the field. Nowhere was this better seen than in his personal visits to combat units on the eve of D-Day. These visits, which expressed his abiding and real concern for the millions of ordinary GIs, sent a message to the soldiers, airman, and navy personnel under his command that he was with them in the days ahead, sharing their hopes and their fears. It is commonly said that Ike here proved himself to be the great democratic leader of a democratic army. But Ike already showed the depth of his sense of fairness one year before, in his response to the slapping incidents and in his evident concern for two GIs abused by an arrogant officer.

Patton had many virtues too. But, because he always vaunted himself as special and as an aristocrat of genius, fairness was not among them. As a result, Patton will be remembered as a great combat warrior, while Eisenhower will always be ranked among the greatest leaders of men.

Notes to Chapter Ten

1 Martin Blumenson, *The Patton Papers 1940–1945*. Boston, MA: Da Capo Press, 1996, p. 836.

2 Jean Edward Smith, *Eisenhower in War and Peace*. New York: Random House, 2012, pp. 267, 208.

3 Omar N. Bradley, *A Soldier's Story*. New York: Random House, 1999, p. 160.

4 Rick Atkinson, *The Day of Battle: The War in Sicily and Italy, 1943–1944*. New York: Henry Holt, 2007, p. 147.

5 Carlo D'Este, *Patton: A Genius for War*. New York: Harper Perennial, 1996, pp. 533–534.

6 Alan Axelrod, *Eisenhower on Leadership: Ike's Enduring Lessons in Total Victory Management*. San Francisco, CA: Jossey-Bass, 2006, p. 10.

7 Ibid., p. 16.

8 Smith, *Eisenhower in War and Peace*, p. 257.

9 Ibid., p. 268.

10 In fact the story broke several months later, on November 21, 1943, when Drew Pearson delivered a somewhat inaccurate account of the incidents in his November 21, 1943 radio program. There was a brief flurry of press and political commentary, but the story was by then "old news" and had little effect on Patton's career or on Ike's. See Stanley P. Hirshson, *General Patton: A Soldier's Life*. New York: Harper Perennial, 2003, p. 424.

11 D'Este, *Patton*, p. 322.

12 Ibid., p. 536. See also his *Eisenhower: A Soldier's Life*. New York: Henry Holt, 2002, p. 439.

FDR AND THE A-BOMB
INTELLECTUAL EXCELLENCE

Considering Hitler's goals, the history of the world would have been tragically different had Nazi science realized in 1939 or 1940 (as the reports had so ominously indicated) that a fission bomb was feasible.

Eugene Wigner, a leading nuclear scientist on the Manhattan Project[1]

The illiterate of the future will not be the person who cannot read. It will be the person who does not know how to learn.

Alvin Toffler[2]

We live in an era of rampant populism. In Europe and the United States, there is growing emphasis on the virtues of the "common man" and a rebellion against leadership by elites. In the eyes of many people, an individual's possession of an excellent educational background, advanced degrees, or familiarity with intellectual opinion-makers have all become *disqualifications* for office. Elitism of any type, even the one developed through the hard work of education and personal effort, is disparaged. "Averageness" is lauded for its own sake. In defense of what many regarded as an unqualified nominee to the US Supreme Court, one US Senator asserted that even mediocre people "are entitled to a little representation."[3]

Our stress on the importance of intellectual excellence in leadership tells us otherwise. While an appreciation of the condition of the common man is certainly important – and is signaled by our virtue of caring and compassion – great leaders in any domain cannot be intellectually mediocre. Intellectual curiosity and breadth of knowledge are as important in a political

10 Virtues of Outstanding Leaders: Leadership and Character, First Edition.
Al Gini and Ronald M. Green.
© 2013 John Wiley & Sons, Inc. Published 2013 by John Wiley & Sons, Inc.

leader as tactile skills in a surgeon or strength in an athlete. But so, too, are wide-ranging interests in diverse fields of intellectual inquiry, openness to new developments in science or culture, and a willingness to listen to and learn from others. Great leaders do not dismiss accomplishments in science and technology or disparage intellectual and cultural achievements.

Experience over the past century in the business and political sectors offers countless illustrations of these truths, but one historical episode stands out: the events of the late 1930s and early 1940s surrounding the advent of nuclear energy and the decision to build an atomic bomb. Here we have something analogous to a controlled experiment that illuminates the importance of a leader's intellectual openness. The episode pits two leaders against each other: the US President Franklin Delano Roosevelt and Adolph Hitler, the Führer of the German people. In terms of their basic abilities and context, the two were fairly evenly matched. Both possessed high intelligence and charisma. Both had prodigious material and human resources at their disposal. Both were surrounded by gifted subordinates, including the leading nuclear physicists of their day. Yet Roosevelt, because of his background, education, and temperament, kept an open mind for the new currents in science and culture around him, whereas, Hitler, as a result of his background and ideology, deliberately shut himself off from new and challenging ideas. The result in each case was a fateful decision.

The Scientific Background

As this contest of minds and wills began, Hitler in many ways had the advantage. Nuclear fission was discovered in Germany in 1939. With the occupation of Czechoslovakia in late 1938 and early 1939, Nazi Germany controlled one of the largest sources of uranium ore in the world, a vital requirement for building the bomb. In 1940, following Germany's lightening "blitzkrieg" conquest of Western Europe, the other large source – the mines in the Belgian Congo – potentially came under Hitler's control too. In Werner Heisenberg, winner of the 1932 Nobel Prize in physics, Germany had one of world's leading theoretical physicists. Another leading atomic physicist who worked with Heisenberg, Carl Friedrich von Weizsäcker, was the son of Ernst von Weizsäcker, state secretary at the German Foreign Office from 1938 to 1943. Thus Germany's nuclear research team had powerful political contacts. With scientists like Heisenberg and von Weizsäcker leading its bomb development project, physicists around the world rightly feared that the Nazi regime would easily be the winner of this technological race.

The US, too, had assets. Because of the Nazi regime's virulent anti-Semitism, many of Germany's leading physicists of Jewish background had immigrated to America during the 1930s. These included Albert Einstein, who was visiting the US in 1933 and refused to return to Germany following Hitler's election, and Leo Szilard, who left in 1933 for London and subsequently took a position at Columbia University. Italy's Enrico Fermi was not Jewish, but his wife was, and he feared that it was only a matter of time until she was threatened by Nazi policies. Fermi arrived at Columbia University via Stockholm, following his receipt of the Nobel Prize in 1938. In the forced departure of these scientists, the intellectual closed-mindedness and racial prejudice of the Nazi regime, which ultimately was fostered by Hitler, damaged the German bomb project and strengthened the US effort.

The US also had prodigious material resources at its disposal. The Manhattan project, which led to the development of the bomb, eventually employed more than 130,000 people and cost $2 billion ($24.4 billion in current dollars), an enormous undertaking for a nation at war on two fronts. From 1942 onward a shortage of resources hampered the Nazi program. But we should not exaggerate this difference. At the start of the 1940s Nazi Germany bestrode almost the entire European continent and had hundreds of millions of people at its command. During the war, Germany was able to mount a huge V-1 and V-2 rocket development program under Werner von Braun and to hurl thousands of technologically advanced missiles at Britain. What explains Germany's failure, then, was not a lack of resources as much as the country's being misdirected by a misleader. And that misdirection goes to the heart of the different outcomes in this duel between Roosevelt and Hitler.

Roosevelt's Preparation for Leadership

There is no greater contrast than the one between the backgrounds of these two rival leaders. It is a contrast between wealth and poverty; between opportunity and deprivation. Yet each individual also faced enormous obstacles and overcame them in ways that permanently marked his life and the lives of others.

Born in 1882, Franklin Delano Roosevelt (FDR) descended from two of the oldest and wealthiest American families: the New York Delanos and the Hudson Valley Roosevelts. Probably no president of the United States had a happier and more secure childhood than Franklin Roosevelt. "He was brought up in a beautiful frame," an aunt observed many years later.[4] As an only child, he was doted upon by his mother, Sara, and by his elderly father, James. Once, when Franklin misbehaved and was sent to his father for discipline, the latter smiled and said: "Consider yourself spanked."[5]

Roosevelt's education reflected the privilege of his birth. He was home-schooled for his entire elementary education. In 1888 he began learning German under a tutor: Fräulein Reinsberg. He was soon speaking the language with some facility and wrote to his mother, in German: "I will show you that I can already write in German. But I shall always try to improve it, so that you will really be pleased." French instruction followed under Jeanne Sandoz, a young French-speaking Swiss woman, who proved to be Franklin's favorite teacher. Many years later he wrote to her: "More than anyone you laid the foundations of my education."[6] These language skills were refined during his childhood in the course of many European visits. In 1891, when he was 9, he was enrolled at the local school in Bad Nauheim, Germany, where his father was taking a cure. This was Roosevelt's only experience of ordinary elementary school life. "I go to public school with a lot of little mickies," he wrote a cousin, using an ethnic slur of the period. "We have German reading, German dictation, the history of Siegfried, and arithmetic . . . and I like it very much."[7]

Unfamiliarity with organized schooling probably placed Roosevelt behind other youngsters in terms of social development. In prep school and college, as Roosevelt struggled to fit into his peer group and to develop social and athletic skills, some contemporaries underestimated his intellectual prowess. Some girls of his own set dubbed him a "feather duster," a phrase they used for an intellectual lightweight. But it is clear that from boyhood on Roosevelt evidenced strong intellectual abilities and a variety of interests. Not only was he an omnivorous reader, but he soaked up information easily. He was an enthusiastic stamp collector, a hobby he pursued throughout his life. As one biographer observes, young Roosevelt's "curiosity about foreign lands and geography were well served by this pastime."[8] Another biographer, Nathan Miller, reports the following incident from Roosevelt's youth:

> His mother Sara recalled reading aloud to him one day while Franklin lay sprawled at her feet, seemingly absorbed in his stamp collection. Suddenly, she snapped the book shut. "I don't think there is any point in my reading to you any more," she declared. "You don't hear me anyway." To prove her mistaken, Franklin unhesitatingly repeated word for word the entire last paragraph that his mother had read. When she expressed surprise, he replied: "Why, Mama, I would be ashamed of myself if I couldn't do at least two things at once."[9]

At 14, two years older than most of his classmates, Roosevelt entered Groton, a newly established prep school north of Boston that catered to the sons of affluent families. Under the direction of the Reverend Endicott Peabody, Groton sought to educate boys into social responsibility and leadership. Peabody espoused a "muscular Christianity" and believed that character, which was best developed through the discipline of athletic competition, was more important than intellectual accomplishment. Roosevelt was somewhat short of stature before a later growth spurt and proved unable to compete in football, baseball, or crew, the only sports that mattered. He struggled to fit in. As historian Alan Brinkley observes, Roosevelt "went through his four years at Groton as something of a lonely outsider."[10] Years later, Peabody, who liked the boy but may have underestimated him because of his lack of athletic prowess, remembered Roosevelt as "a quiet, satisfactory boy of more than ordinary intelligence, taking a good position in his form but not brilliant."[11] Nevertheless, Roosevelt's academic achievements were considerable. In a short time after entering Groton he ranked fourth academically in a class of nineteen. Graduating with enough advanced academic credits to skip a year of college later, he was an active debater and won the school's prestigious Latin prize. Throughout his life Roosevelt would remember Groton with affection, saying of Peabody: "I count it among the blessings in my life to have the privilege of [his] guiding hand."[12] But Roosevelt's affection for Groton was not always reciprocated. When he embarked on the course of liberal reforms that marked the New Deal, many of his Groton classmates came to regard him as "a traitor to his class."

Following in the footsteps of his fifth cousin, Theodore Roosevelt, Franklin chose to attend Harvard. The school that he entered in 1900 was in its fourth decade of academic reform, under the presidency of Charles W. Eliot. In contrast to education at Groton, education at Harvard was defined exclusively in intellectual terms and there was little concern for character development. Faculty members were appointed on the basis of their research, and students, after a few required courses in the first year, could take any courses they wanted. Roosevelt and his classmates found this elective system enormously liberating. His course record shows that he may have had presidential aspirations even as an undergraduate – taking classes that included the constitution, public address, and administration of the US government.[13]

Despite his wealth and social background, Roosevelt struggled with the feeling that he was something of an outsider. He tried out for the football team but was cut because of his slender frame (now he was six feet and one and a half inches tall and weighed 146 pounds). He yearned to be admitted to the Porcellian, the most exclusive social club on campus, as his cousin (and then President) Theodore Roosevelt had been before him, but he was not invited. Years later he would describe this failure as "the greatest disappointment" in his life.[14] Yet, as his roommate Lathrop Brown noted:

Franklin was not a typical club man of his generation. He had more on his mind than sitting in the Club's front window, doing nothing but criticizing the passers-by. His not "making" the Porcellian meant only that he was free of any possible restraining influences of a lot of delightful people who thought that the world belonged to them and who did not want to change anything in it.[15]

Admitted to two slightly less prestigious clubs, the Fly and Hasty Pudding, he was appointed librarian of each. In this capacity he indulged a passion for books, buying for the club libraries and for his own collection.

Roosevelt did not excel academically, most of his grades being in the gentlemanly range of low B and C. One biographer notes that he took his studies seriously.

He went to his classes, took copious notes, and once turned down a weekend invitation to a privately owned island in Buzzards Bay because it would have meant taking three cuts.[16]

His less than stellar academic performance may have been due, in part, to his involvement in editorial work on the Harvard's daily student newspaper the *Crimson*. Roosevelt won election to the *Crimson*'s editorial board as a freshman, and, after graduating, he decided to spend a fourth year in Cambridge in order to serve as president and editor-in-chief. Every spare moment was taken up with the paper. In the *Crimson*, Roosevelt found a way of joining campus activism with his own intellectual seriousness. He later declared that "perhaps the most useful preparation I had in college for public service was . . . [on] the Harvard *Crimson*."[17] When he became president, FDR took pleasure in telling journalists that he had once been a newsman, just like them.

In 1904, following graduation from Harvard, Roosevelt entered Columbia Law School. He chose Columbia in order to be near Eleanor Roosevelt, a distant cousin and the niece of President Theodore Roosevelt. In the same year, despite the protestations of his mother, who felt he was too young to marry, Franklin and Eleanor became engaged. Although at the age of 19 Eleanor was not as vivacious as many of the young women in Franklin's circle, he was smitten. The fact that she was the niece of President Theodore Roosevelt may have appealed to the ambitious young man. But biographers also stress Eleanor's seriousness and qualities of mind. A biographer writes: "She was very intelligent, a refreshing departure from the usual vacuous social flibbertigibits who abounded in debutante circles in and near New York, Boston, and Washington."[18] Although the pair would eventually experience serious marital difficulties because of their different temperaments and needs, it is generally agreed that they formed a life-long intellectual partnership, Eleanor furnishing many of the ideas and some of the motivation for Franklin's reformist social agenda.

Roosevelt did not enjoy his legal studies, and he dropped out of Columbia. After passing the New York bar in 1907, he took a job with a prestigious Wall Street firm. But corporate law did not appeal to him either. Instead politics and public service were for him. When the opportunity arose in 1910, he chose to run as a Democrat for a seat in the New York state senate representing Duchess County, where his family's Hyde Park home was located. From that moment on, Roosevelt never looked back. His life became dedicated to reformist politics and public service. A commitment to social justice and to improving the plight of the ordinary man was already part of Roosevelt's Democratic Party political heritage, and it was influenced by the sense of *noblesse oblige* he had inherited from his patrician family and by his education at Groton and Harvard. This commitment was intensified following a bout with polio in August 1921 that left him permanently paralyzed and unable to walk without assistance. Although many people might have been embittered by this sharp reversal of fortune, with Roosevelt it seems instead to have deepened and matured his personality and to have inspired empathy with others' suffering.

In 1932, following service as assistant secretary to the navy, a failed candidacy for the vice presidency, and two terms as governor of New York, Roosevelt was elected president of the United States. During an unprecedented chain of four terms in office, he struggled to pull the country out of the depths of the Great Depression and to carry it to victory in the Second World War. In this role as a charismatic and revered leader, the somewhat shy and intellectually inclined young man finally achieved the public recognition that he had sought – but never quite attained – at Groton and Harvard. At the same time, Roosevelt's sharp intellect and inquiring mind, developed by years of academic effort and excellent educational preparation, would serve him well in the challenges that lay ahead.

Hitler's Ascent to Leadership

If Roosevelt was brought up in "a beautiful frame," Adolph Hitler's childhood situation can only be called ugly. Born in 1889 in a village in the town of Braunau am Inn, Austria, he was the fourth of six children of Alois Hitler and Klara Pölzl. All of Adolf's older siblings died before reaching 3 years of age. Another brother died when Hitler was 1 year old. Hitler's mother was especially protective of Adolph, her only surviving son, and he was extremely attached to her.

The opposite was true of Hitler's relationship to his father. Alois Hitler was the illegitimate child of Maria Anna Schicklgruber. Maria later married Johann Georg Hiedler (the name morphed into Hitler), whom Alois' uncle formally attested to be Alois' father, but the young boy's true paternity always remained in doubt.[19] After trying and failing at farming, Alois secured a position as a minor Austrian customs official and wanted his son to follow in his footsteps, which caused much conflict between them. According to family sources, Alois frequently beat Adolph.[20]

Hitler wanted to attend a classical high school and to become an artist, but in September 1900 his father sent him to a technical high school in Linz. Hitler rebelled against this decision and failed his first year, hoping that once his father saw "what little progress I was making at the technical school he would let me devote myself to the happiness I dreamed of."[21] But his father was unrelenting.

Alois died on January 3, 1903. Hitler's behavior at the technical school became more disruptive, and in 1904 he was asked to leave. He enrolled at another technical school in September of that year; but, two years later, following a drunken episode in which Hitler tore up his school certificate and used it as toilet paper, he was expelled from school.[22]

In 1905 Hitler drifted to Vienna, living a bohemian life with financial support from orphan's benefits and from his mother, who died of breast cancer in 1907. During this period he applied to the Academy of Fine Arts Vienna for a degree in painting but was twice rejected because of his "unfitness for painting." He was recommended to study architecture, though he lacked the academic credentials required for admission to architecture school.[23]

This marked the end of Hitler's formal education. From this time on he lived hand to mouth, earning some income by painting tourist postcards and living in homeless or workingmen's shelters. His intellectual life was guided by his own interest and passions. As a child he was passionate about the cowboy and Indian stories of the popular novelist Karl May, which offered a purely imaginative and racist view of life on the American continent.[24] Contemporaries report that he later gathered books from wherever he could find them, often from public libraries, and read voraciously. Over the course of his life he received books as gifts and assembled an enormous collection; many of them bear marginal notations indicating his reading and interests.[25] But Hitler was an autodidact in the full sense of this term: a self-taught individual. His reading was extremely eclectic and erratic, comprising historical and military treatises, occult religious speculation, and a variety of anti-Semitic treatises that were popular during those years of turmoil in Germany and Austria. He read and absorbed what interested him and rejected or ignored what didn't fit his background, tastes, or prejudices.

Hitler's career took many sharp turns from those bohemian years in Vienna until his ascendency to the post of chancellor of Germany in 1933. After receiving the balance of a small inheritance from his father in 1913, he moved to Munich, wishing to live in a "real" German city. At the outbreak of war in 1914 he eagerly joined the Bavarian army, serving with distinction as a corporal on the Western front. Returning to Munich after the war, he became involved in nationalist political agitation and rose to prominence in a small national socialist workers' group: the Nationalsozialistische Deutsche Arbeiterpartei, later known as the Nazi Party. A failed putsch against the Bavarian government in 1923 led to Hitler's arrest and imprisonment. Hitler used his year in Landsberg prison to write a long and rambling statement of his nationalist and anti-Semitic philosophy, *Mein Kampf* (*My Struggle*). From this point onward, Hitler and his party committed themselves to the legal seizure of power. Unemployment and inflation in Weimar Germany in the decade following the war fed the party's growth, which was accelerated in 1929 with the onset of the global world depression. In parliamentary elections in 1932 the Nazi Party achieved a plurality of votes, and in January 1933 Hitler became chancellor in a coalition government. Within a matter of months, following turmoil that included the fiery destruction of the Reichstag (German parliament) under questionable circumstances, the Nazis were able to persuade and intimidate legislators to pass an enabling act that put an end to German democracy. Hitler became undisputed dictator – a post he would occupy until his death by suicide, as Russian troops advanced on his bunker in Berlin in April 1945.

Few people who ever met or worked with Hitler doubted his intelligence. He had a quick grasp of concepts and a prodigious memory for things that interested him. This especially included details about weapons. Wilhelm Keitel, who served under Hitler as head of supreme command of the German armed forces, testified at the Nuremberg trials that,

> To a degree which is almost incomprehensible . . . Hitler had studied general staff publications, military literature, essays on tactics, operations and . . . he had a knowledge in the military fields which can only be called amazing . . .[26]

It was a matter of pride in the inner Nazi military circle that Hitler could recite the details of almost any capital ship in the world's navies.

At the same time, those who worked closely with Hitler observed that his mind was closed to anything that contradicted his preconceived opinions. No one, even at the highest levels, dared to oppose or correct him on matters in which Hitler's stand was firm. Admiral Karl Dönitz, commander-in-chief of the German navy, asserted in his Nuremberg testimony that, "[a]s a matter of principle, there can be no question of a general consultation with the Fuehrer."[27] Hermann Göring, chief of the Luftwaffe, who probably worked longer and more closely with Hitler than any Nazi leader and who prided himself on the extent of his influence, stated at Nuremberg:

> Foreign policy on the one hand and the leadership of the Armed Forces on the other hand enlisted the Führer's greatest interest and were his main activity . . . He busied himself exceptionally with these details . . . In certain cases he would ask for data to be submitted to him without the experts knowing the exact reason. In other cases he would explain to his advisors what he intended to do and get from them the data or their opinion. Final decisions he took himself . . .[28]

Göring concluded his Nuremberg testimony by observing that Hitler's own strong views could never be contradicted: "Suggestions and advice were curtly brushed aside whenever he had once made his decisions."[29]

This closedness of mind and intolerance of views that challenged his own were certainly reflected in the authoritarian and totalitarian regime that Hitler created around him. Convinced of his own absolute authority and wisdom, Hitler could not permit anything that questioned or undermined his power. But these mental traits also deeply reflected Hitler's intellectual upbringing. An autodidact, he had created his own thought world and had never been challenged to defend his views by a thorough education or through systematic exposure to alternative viewpoints. Although Hitler's authoritarianism and untested intellectual self-confidence would serve him very well in his rise to power and during the initial years of his political and military leadership, his closed mind and limited intellectual outreach would ultimately be his undoing.

The A-Bomb Decision: The United States

What makes the respective responses of the German and American leaders to the possibility of building atomic weapons so remarkable, and such a telling illustration of the importance of a leader's mental acuity and breadth of intellect, is that the circumstances surrounding the decisions were so similar. Roosevelt and Hitler were both informed by leading scientific advisors. Both were presented with a project that would require the enormous diversion of manpower and resources and that was far from certain of success within the timeframe of the war. And both were also informed of the project's incredible potential: it was a new source of energy, which could power industry, ships, and submarines endlessly and could finally lead to the development of a bomb that could level whole cities.

Roosevelt learned of these possibilities in mid-October 1939, only months after American researchers confirmed the discovery of nuclear fission in Germany and two years before the attack on Pearl Harbor brought the US into the war. He received word of the developments in the form of a letter signed by Albert Einstein, which was hand-delivered to him by Alexander Sachs, vice-president of Lehman Brothers investment company. In the early 1930s Sachs had served as chief of the economic research division of the National Recovery Administration (NRA), one of Roosevelt's favorite New Deal programs. Over the years, the two men had become friends.

The letter that Sachs delivered by hand was written by Leo Szilard, one of the leading Jewish émigré scientists. Recognizing that he needed more clout to get the president's attention, in late July 1939 Szilard and another leading émigré scientist, Eugene Wigner, drove to eastern Long Island, to find Einstein at his remote summer place and to ask him to sign the letter. Although Einstein was a pacifist, he understood the threat represented by a Nazi bomb and agreed to sign the letter drafted by Szilard. The two-page document was completed and signed on August 2. It highlighted developments in atomic fission and said it was "almost certain" that a nuclear chain reaction in a large mass of uranium could be achieved in the immediate future. It then added:

> This new phenomenon would also lead to the construction of bombs, and it is conceivable – though much less certain – that extremely powerful bombs of a new type may thus be constructed. A single bomb of this type, carried by boat and exploded in a port, might very well destroy the whole port together with some of the surrounding territory.[30]

Szilard approached Sachs, whom he had previously met and who had assured him that Franklin Roosevelt was committed to "experiment" in all areas of policy and was open to new ideas.[31] Recognizing the gravity of the issue, Sachs agreed to carry the letter to Roosevelt. The start of war in Europe and other events prevented Sachs from doing so for two months; but, late on the afternoon on October 11, Sachs finally met with the president in the Oval Office.

Sachs was ushered into the Oval Office by presidential secretary Pa Watson. He was warmly greeted by a president who was in a relaxing mood, as the cocktail hour approached. Knowing that Roosevelt could deflect serious issues with his joviality, Sachs responded to the president's greeting with a plaintive plea.

"Mr. President," he said with a grin, "I want you to know I paid for my trip to Washington. I can't deduct it from my income tax. So won't you please pay attention?" Roosevelt laughed and ruefully nodded his assent.

There are varying reports of what followed – all derived from Sachs, since Roosevelt left no record.[32] One account has Sachs reading aloud three documents he had come to deliver personally: Einstein's letter, a longer memo on atomic energy by Leo Szilard, and an explanatory letter by Sachs himself. Following this, Sachs handed the documents to Roosevelt, who perused the Einstein letter carefully. Other accounts have Sachs reading memoranda of his own that summarize the Einstein letter and re-emphasize the potential of atomic energy.

Roosevelt had good reason to pay attention to Einstein's warning. It was not just that the Nobel Prize-winning physicist was the most famous scientist in the world. Roosevelt also knew Einstein personally. In January 1934, shortly after Einstein had refused to return to Germany, he and his wife Elsa were invited by FDR to the White House. They dined with the Roosevelts, conversed at length in German, and stayed the night. Einstein later recalled that FDR spoke German very well.[33]

All accounts of the Sachs–Roosevelt meeting agree on what happened next. "What you are after," the president said to Sachs, "is to see that the Nazis don't blow us up."

"Precisely," Sachs replied.

Roosevelt then pressed a button, summoning his secretary.

"Pa," said Roosevelt, handing over the two letters and Szilard's memorandum, "this requires action!"

As historians note, it was a long way from this order to the reality of the bombs dropped over Japan in August 1945. It would take six more years and a vast Manhattan project to develop a useable weapon. In 1939 America was not yet at war. During the next two years isolationism and a military establishment that could not think beyond familiar weapons slowed progress. Indeed, months after Sachs' meeting, on March 17, 1940, the same day that Hitler invaded Czechoslovakia with its deposits of uranium, Enrico Fermi visited Admiral S. C. Hooper at the office of the chief of naval operations in Washington. Hoping to accelerate Washington's efforts, he carried a letter by George Pegram, physics professor and graduate dean at Columbia. Instead of the admiral, Fermi saw two youthful lieutenant commanders. He strained in his imperfect English to explain the importance of the new discoveries. The officers listened politely and sent Fermi off, telling him to keep them informed. This detail may be apocryphal, but the story of the visit concludes with one of the officers turning to the other and saying, "That wop is crazy!"[34] Fermi was so annoyed by his reception that that he vowed never again to deal with army or navy officers.

We laugh at such ignorance today; but it was a natural response, given the novelty of the information and the questionable background of the émigré scientists. Following the development of the atom bomb, physicists became cultural heroes. But in 1939–1940 they were easily seen as crackpots. What is remarkable is that FDR took the same information seriously and spurred its implementation. This is partly due to the efforts of the scientists. But no one can ignore the role played by the president's openness of mind and by his solid educational background. To Roosevelt, Einstein, whom the Nazi leadership had driven from their country, was a welcome house guest and conversation partner. Their mutual trust was greatly aided by Roosevelt's good background in German and by his ability to speak to Einstein in his mother tongue.

The A-Bomb Decision: Germany

The picture in Germany around the same time is both similar and different. As in the United States, scientists recognized the importance of the discovery of fission. In April 1939, just four months after the discovery, leading German scientists alerted the army ordnance office, the Reich ministry of war, and the Reich research council of the developments. To organize research, an informal group of leading scientists was assembled, calling itself the Uranium Club (*Uranverein*). When the approach of war in August caused some of its members to be called up for military service, the group was reformed under the military auspices of the army ordnance office. New members included some of the leading German physicists, among them Friedrich von Weizsäcker and Werner Heisenberg.

As in the United States, progress up to 1942 was slow; much basic research on nuclear constants was needed in order to determine whether it was possible to create a nuclear reactor capable of sustaining a chain reaction, and, beyond that, an atomic bomb. In February 1942, when it was clear that development of reactors or a bomb would require a major commitment of resources, scientists decided to appeal for support directly to the highest level of the government. A conference was organized to which were invited dignitaries such as Hermann Göring, Martin Bormann, Heinrich Himmler, Navy Commander-in-Chief Admiral Erich Raeder, Field Marshal Wilhelm Keitel, and Albert Speer, Hitler's admired architectural protégé, who was now serving as minister of armaments and war production. Heisenberg and other leading nuclear scientists were scheduled to speak. Unfortunately, a mistake in the printed invitation made it appear as though this was a tedious conference on esoteric research, and none of the dignitaries showed up.

Speer would obviously be vital to the support needed to build a bomb. He was very close to Hitler and controlled the resources needed for a bomb project. In his memoirs he reported that atomic energy first came to his attention at the end of April 1942, in a private luncheon with General Friedrich Fromm, the commander of the Home Army. Fromm told Speer that Germany's only chance of winning the war lay in developing a weapon with totally new effects. Fromm said he had contact with a group of scientists who were on the track of a weapon that could annihilate whole cities, and he proposed that the two of them meet with these men.[35] This conference took place on June 4, 1942, when Heisenberg and other atomic scientists met at Kaiser Wilhelm Society's Harnack House, to brief Speer and the three military heads of weapons production on their work.

In the course of the conference, Field Marshal Erhard Milch of the Luftwaffe asked how large a bomb would be that could destroy a large city such as London. To the astonishment of those present, Heisenberg, perhaps referring only to the fissile uranium component, replied: "About the size of a pineapple." Heisenberg, by his own account, hastened to add that a bomb could not be produced within a matter of months. If the Americans were working flat out, they might have a uranium pile very soon, and a bomb in no earlier than two years. A similar economic effort for Germany, he indicated, might be impossible. However, he stressed the importance of trying to build a reactor.

Later that month, Speer met with Hitler to offer an account of the conference. Speer probably suspected that Hitler would be resistant. The Führer had been influenced by the view, prevalent among ardent Nazis, that all modern physics influenced by Einstein was worthless. To table companions, Hitler sometimes referred to nuclear physics as "Jewish physics."[36] In general, says Speer, Hitler's whole approach to atomic energy reflected his "amateurishness and his lack of understanding of fundamental scientific research." In his memoirs, Speer describes his June 23 meeting with Hitler:

> Hitler had sometimes spoken to me about the possibility of an atom bomb, but the idea quite obviously strained his intellectual capacity. He was also unable to grasp the revolutionary nature of nuclear physics. In the twenty-two hundred recorded points of my conferences with Hitler, nuclear fission comes up only once, and then is mentioned with extreme brevity. Hitler did sometimes comment on its prospects, but what I told him of my conferences with the physicists confirmed his view that there was not much profit in the matter. Actually, Professor Heisenberg had not given any final answer to my question

whether a successful nuclear fission could be kept under control with absolute certainty or might continue as a chain reaction. Hitler was plainly not delighted with the possibility that the earth under his rule might be transformed into a glowing star. Occasionally, however, he joked that the scientists in their unworldly urge to lay bare all the secrets under heaven might some day set the globe on fire. But undoubtedly a good deal of time would pass before that came about, Hitler said; he would certainly not live to see it.[37]

Following these meetings, Speer scaled down the Reich's commitment to atomic research. Heavy uranium metal was diverted to use in anti-tank shells. Research by Heisenberg and others would continue, but without the intensity that the Führer's wholehearted support would have given to it. By the end of the war, Germany's scientists had not even developed a working atomic reactor.

Ever since the Second World War, scholars and historians have tried to understand why Nazi Germany, with its obvious head start in scientific resources and manpower, never developed the atom bomb. One theory holds that the German scientists themselves deliberately dragged their feet, being unwilling to give a world-dominating weapon to this terrible tyrant. Although this theory was actively promoted after the war by some of the German scientists themselves, notably by Heisenberg, there is little evidence for it. Recent research based on secretly recorded conversations among the captured German scientists after the war does not support it.[38] Others point to a variety of factors that clearly impeded the German effort, from theoretical mistakes made by the scientists to Allied attacks on Norway's vital heavy water supplies and to military reverses from 1943 onward that strained German resources and caused Germany to halt most long-term weapons projects.

All these factors surely played a role. But one cannot overlook the decisive part played by Hitler himself. In mid-1942 the Führer was at the apogee of his power. German forces seemed to be on the verge of a victory in Russia that would guarantee Germany control of the entire European continent and millions of skilled workers. Hitler maintained his acute interest in weaponry, closely following every new development in tanks or artillery. Under his direction, Germany would apply huge sums of money and armies of slave laborers to the development of a new rocket technology that Hitler hoped would allow him to turn the air war back against Britain. With atomic warheads, these rockets could have leveled Britain and destroyed the D-Day invasion forces on the beaches. Without them, the rocket program was a terrifying but militarily useless waste of time.

It was not stupidity, then, and not lack of will that prevented Germany from getting the bomb. It was Hitler's narrowness of mind, poor educational background, and lack of a broader perspective that included science or learning. Over the course of his life, as is reflected in his Nazi ideology, he had developed little respect for the role that intellectuals or scientists could play. His regime, after all, had ordered the burning of books and the expulsion of leading physicists. As a passionate militarist, Hitler could not envision a role for science in war beyond the perfecting of the traditional weapons he had encountered as a trench soldier in the First World War. If Hitler did not support his atomic scientists, it was not because they failed to reach him, but because he did not respect them. Unlike Roosevelt, who personally honored the aging, wooly-haired émigré Einstein, Hitler regarded his best scientists as crackpot tinkerers who might set the earth on fire.

Individual human beings can shape the course of history, and individual moments of decision can do so as well. The differing fates of the American and German bomb projects reveal how important curiosity, education, and the virtue of intellectual excellence are to outstanding leadership.

Notes to Chapter Eleven

1   Leona Marshall, *The Uranium People*. New York: Crane, Russak, 1979, p. 126.
2   Alvin Toffler, Famous-Quotes.com. At http://www.1-famous-quotes.com/quote/99850 (last accessed November 26, 2012).
3   William H. Honan, "Roman L. Hruska Dies at 94; Leading Senate Conservative." *New York Times*, April 27, 1999.
4   Nathan Miller, *FDR: An Intimate History*. Garden City, NY: Doubleday & Company, 1983, p. 15.
5   Ted Morgan: *FDR: A Biography*. New York: Simon & Schuster, 1985, p. 52.
6   Ibid., p. 20.
7   Miller, *FDR: An Intimate History*, p. 21.
8   Conrad Black, *Franklin Delano Roosevelt: Champion of Freedom*. New York: Perseus, 2003, p. 20.
9   Ibid.
10   Alan Brinkley, *Franklin Delano Roosevelt*. New York: Oxford University Press, 2010, p. 5.
11   Miller, *FDR: An Intimate History*, p. 27.
12   James MacGregor Burns, *Roosevelt: The Lion and the Fox*. New York: Harcourt, Brace & World, 1956, p. 16.
13   Bita M. Assad, "The Legacy of Franklin Delano Roosevelt: Restoration Project in Adams House Aims to Open Doors to FDR's Life." *The Harvard Crimson*, February 24, 2009. At http://www.thecrimson.com/article/2009/2/24/the-legacy-of-franklin-delano-roosevelt/ (last accessed November 25, 2012).
14   Frances Richardson Keller, *Fictions of US History: A Theory and Four Illustrations*. Bloomington, IN: Indiana University Press, 2002, p. 116.

15   Quoted in Jean Edward Smith, *FDR*. New York: Random House, 2007, p. 33.

16   Morgan, *FDR: A Biography*, p. 73.

17   Miller, *FDR: An Intimate History*, p. 39.

18   Black, *Franklin Delano Roosevelt*, p. 40.

19   Alan Bullock, *Hitler: A Study in Tyranny*. London: Penguin Books, 1962, p. 24.

20   Although Hitler, in *Mein Kampf*, claims to have had a good relationship with his father, he reported on these beatings to Hans Frank, to his lawyer, to one of his secretaries, and to various family members. See Sherree Owens Zalampas, *Adolf Hitler: A Psychological Interpretation of His Views on Architecture, Art, and Music*. Bowling Green, OH: Bowling Green State University Press, 1990, p. 8. Also Anton Neumayr, *Dictators in the Mirror of Medicine: Napoleon, Hitler, Stalin*. Lansing, MI: Medi-Ed Press, 1995, p. 162. That Hitler was thrashed by his father is attested to by Hitler's sister Paula. See John Toland, *Adolph Hitler*. Garden City, NY: Doubleday, 1954, vol. 1, p. 13.

21   From article "Adolf Hitler" in Wikipedia. At http://en.wikipedia.org/wiki/Adolf_Hitler#cite_note-Payne-16 (last accessed November 25, 2012).

22   Robert Payne, *The Life and Death of Adolf Hitler*. New York: Hippocrene Books, 1990, p. 41.

23   Bullock, *Hitler*, pp. 30–31.

24   Payne, *The Life and Death of Adolf Hitler*, pp. 27–28.

25   Timothy W. Ryback, "Hitler's Forgotten Library." *The Atlantic Monthly*, 291(4), 2003. Also available online at http://www.theatlantic.com/past/docs/issues/2003/05/ryback.htm.

26   *Nuremberg Trial Proceedings*, vol. 10: One Hundredth Day, Friday, 5 April 1946, Morning Session. At http://avalon.law.yale.edu/imt/04-05-46.asp#keitel3 (last accessed November 25, 2012).

27   *Nuremberg Trial Proceedings*, vol. 13: One Hundred and Twenty-Fifth Day, Thursday, 9 May 1946, Morning Session. At http://avalon.law.yale.edu/imt/05-09-46.asp (last accessed November 25, 2012).

28   *Nuremberg Trial Proceedings*, vol. 9: Eighty-Fourth Day, Monday, 18 March 1946, Morning Session. At http://avalon.law.yale.edu/imt/03-18-46.asp; and *Nuremberg Trial Proceedings*, vol. 9: Eighty-Seventh Day, Thursday, 21 March 1946, Morning Session. At http://avalon.law.yale.edu/imt/03-21-46.asp#Goering8 (last accessed November 25, 2012, both).

29   *Nuremberg Trial Proceedings*, vol. 9: Eighty-Third Day, Saturday, 16 March 1946, Morning Session. At http://avalon.law.yale.edu/imt/03-16-46.asp#Goering4 (last accessed November 25, 2012).

30   A photocopy and text of this letter are available online at the Franklin Delano Roosevelt Presidential Library site (http://docs.fdrlibrary.marist.edu/psf/box5/a64a01.html).

31   Kenneth S. Davis, *FDR: Into the Storm, 1937–1940: A History*. New York: Random House, 1993, p. 483.

32   For a discussion of these, see ibid., pp. 509–510.

33   Smith, *FDR*, p. 578.

34   Ibid., pp. 482–483.
35   Albert Speer, *Inside the Third Reich*. New York: Macmillan, 1970, p. 225.
36   Ibid., p. 228.
37   Ibid., p. 227.
38   Jeremy Bernstein, *Hitler's Uranium Club: The Secret Recordings at Farm Hall*. Woodbury, NY: American Institute of Physics, 1996.

HERB KELLEHER AND THE PEOPLE OF SOUTHWEST AIRLINES

CREATIVE THINKING

> We've never tried to be like other airlines ... From the very beginning we told our people, "Question it. Challenge it. Remember, decades of conventional wisdom has sometimes led the airline industry into huge losses."
>
> Herb Kelleher[1]

Southwest Airlines' record of success is astonishing. What began as a small, intra-state Texas airline in 1971 with just three planes is now the largest single carrier in the US, with over 3,500 flights a day, more than 550 aircraft, and 88 million passengers each year. Despite enormous upheaval in the airline industry, which has seen numerous carriers come and go, Southwest has experienced forty straight years of profitability, and it managed to do this without ever laying off employees. Year after year, Southwest has led the industry in terms of employee productivity, the lowest rate of employee turnover, fewest customer complaints, smallest number of mishandled bags, and best on-time performance. Despite intensive use of airplanes for many short-haul flights in ways that place extra stress on the aircraft and people, Southwest has maintained the best safety record in the industry, with no in-flight passenger fatalities in its history.[2]

How did Southwest do all this? Part of the answer lies in the energy and imagination of Herb Kelleher, one of the airline's founders, its CEO from 1982 to 2001, and its executive chairman from 1978 to 2008. Born in New Jersey and having completed an English major and a philosophy minor at Wesleyan University, this adoptive Texan, chain-smoking and bourbon-sipping, helped create the "maverick spirit" that launched and sustained Southwest. But Kelleher

10 Virtues of Outstanding Leaders: Leadership and Character, First Edition.
Al Gini and Ronald M. Green.
© 2013 John Wiley & Sons, Inc. Published 2013 by John Wiley & Sons, Inc.

would be among the first to reject the "lone ranger" view that traces corporate success to one man. Southwest's success is a result of the maverick culture that Herb and others helped shape and of the people at Southwest who carry that spirit on. That culture itself is a vivid illustration of the importance of the virtue of creativity and independent thinking, since almost everything about Southwest is innovative.

Southwest's Start

Southwest's maverick culture had its beginning in the events of the company's formation. Legend has it that in 1971 Kelleher and one of his law clients, Texas businessman Rollin King, created the concept that later became Southwest Airlines on a cocktail napkin in a San Antonio restaurant in Texas. The two men recognized the need for improved low-cost air service between Texas's three largest cities, San Antonio, Dallas, and Houston. In those days air travel was mostly confined to businessmen willing to pay hefty fares. Kelleher's and King's vision was not just to serve those travelers, but also to make air travel available to ordinary people by offering few amenities but low fares. To implement this maverick idea, they planned to use Houston's Hobby Airport. Abandoned by the larger carriers, who preferred the Houston Intercontinental Airport further out of town, Hobby was close to the city center and promised the fast turnarounds needed to fully utilize Southwest's small fleet. Here, in a nutshell, was the set of creative new ideas that would foster Southwest's success: the lowest fares for the short-haul, frequently flying, point-to-point traveler; and, to sustain those low prices, the most efficient use of aircraft through rapid turnarounds at non-congested airports, bypassed by the larger carriers. "Nutshell" is an appropriate word. To free its in-flight and lean ground staff from the burden of food provisioning and service, Southwest served only peanuts.

Instead of trying to learn from and compete with this innovative model, Southwest's leading competitors – Braniff and Texas International Airlines – tried to stifle Southwest at its birth by using powerful legal and regulatory tools, already at their disposal. They argued before the Texas Civil Aeronautics Board that Southwest's entry into local markets would disadvantage them as inter-state carriers. Braniff also put pressure on investors to withdraw from Southwest's initial public stock offering. Postponing payment of his own legal fees, paying costs out of his own pocket, and sometimes showing up in court disheveled from a night of work, Kelleher fought these efforts from court to court, finally prevailing only at the Texas Supreme Court level. This fight to get started helped create what Southwest's people call the company's

"Warrior Spirit." As Colleen Barrett, Kelleher's executive secretary at the time and later president of the company, put it, the Warrior Spirit is not just about having a fighting attitude. It means, she says,

> you want to be the best, work hard, be courageous, display a sense of urgency, persevere, and innovate. You want to be a winner. People don't want to work for a loser. You want to win at what you set out to do.[3]

Southwest's Service Innovations

Perhaps because he never worked in the airline industry, perhaps just because he's a maverick, Herb Kelleher never thought like an airline executive. He and his colleagues at Southwest took their own path, applying common sense and solid values to their decisions. One of those colleagues, Howard Putnam, a former vice president at United Airlines who served as Southwest's CEO from 1978 to 1981, once got a big laugh out of Kelleher when someone asked, "What was the greatest thing you ever did for Southwest Airlines?" and Putnam replied, "I didn't implement anything I learned at United."[4] By thinking "out of the box," Putnam, Kelleher, and their people changed the airline industry and fostered Southwest's success. Although innovative ideas, approaches, and attitudes marked the airline from its start, they have been honed to a fine pitch and adapted as was needed for coping with new circumstances. Almost every aspect of the Southwest way, from its utilization of equipment to its treatment of its people and its philosophy of business – its business ethic – was novel at its introduction and, in many ways, still remains an exception to standard airline and American business practice.

Pricing

From the start, Southwest set out to "democratize the skies." This meant low fares – all the time. Behind this idea lay a radically new philosophy of business: that the primary purpose of a business organization is to create and provide desired products or services at the best price. It may seem absurd to call this idea new. Doesn't free enterprise exist in order to provide good products and services efficiently? Yet, surprisingly, if you ask many American business people – and business theorists – what the purpose of business is, you'll get a host of other answers. "Maximize shareholder return," is a leading one.[5] "Grow in size and increase market share" is another. These answers assume the need to provide goods and services to people, but that aim is usually instrumental to these other "more important" financial and organizational goals. Not so at

Southwest. From the beginning, creating and providing low-cost airline service has been the primary purpose, almost everything else, from profitability to market share, being directed at serving this goal.

A story told by Kevin and Jackie Freiberg in their still relevant and informative 1996 book about Southwest illustrates this difference in thinking. Once, when Braniff's coach price between Dallas and San Antonio was $62 and Southwest's fare was just $15, one of Southwest's shareholders asked Kelleher: "Don't you think we could raise our prices just two or three dollars?" "You don't understand," Kelleher replied. "We're not competing with other airlines, we're competing with ground transportation."[6] Southwest's aim was to open up air travel for the vast number of people who previously could not afford to fly.

Because of this approach to business, which puts service and price first, Southwest has made it possible for people in commuter marriages to see one another more often and for divorced parents to see their children. Grandparents and the elderly can fly and families are able to take vacations because of Southwest's low "Wanna Get Away" fares. A Dallas mother was able to fulfill her dream of becoming a lawyer by commuting 200 miles daily from her home to the University of Texas Law School in Austin. Southwest even made it possible for medical students living in Detroit to fly to Chicago once a week for a class. When the students wrote to Kelleher explaining that the airline's schedule made them fifteen minutes late, he changed the flight schedule to accommodate them.

Novel tactics

Achieving the lowest price led Southwest to a host of other innovations for the airline industry. One was reliance on point-to-point travel from non-congested and often underserved airports and cities: Chicago's Midway instead of O'Hare, Baltimore–Washington instead of Reagan or Dulles. The prevailing practice was the "hub-and-spoke" system, which fed passengers from smaller outlying cities into large, centralized airports like Atlanta's Hartsfield International Airport. Although justified in terms in terms of efficiency, in practice this approach resulted in higher costs and poor service because of frequent flight and scheduling delays. By flying point to point from smaller, less congested airports, Southwest was able to insure on-time arrivals and departures and to employ its aircraft better. In 1986 Southwest learned this the hard way, when air traffic delays at Denver's Stapleton Airport caused backups across its entire system. The company decided to terminate service to the mile-high city. It returned in force to Denver in 2006 with the opening of Denver International Airport, and it now rivals United and Frontier as the largest airline at that airport.

A further consequence of this approach was the ability to serve previously unrecognized and undervalued markets. For example, when Southwest chose to utilize Providence's Francis Green Airport, it significantly contributed to the rebirth of this fading industrial city. Small wonder that, if Southwest chooses a new destination, it receives enthusiastic cooperation from local politicians and officials. When Southwest selects a new city for its route, everyone benefits: travelers, communities, and Southwest. This is consistent with its core business philosophy of creating value by providing better service at lower cost.

Key to making its point-to-point service work is Southwest's rapid turn-around of its aircraft. During the Texas start-up days, when it had only a handful of planes, the goal was to turn around a plane in 10–15 minutes. Forty years later, that interval has been stretched to twenty minutes, still half the time of other airlines. A Southwest plane's landing is treated like an Indiana-polis 500 pit stop. Ramp and gate personnel pitch in, and pilots can be seen helping passengers who need assistance. Without obvious commotion, up to 180 passengers exit and are replaced by newcomers. To speed boarding, South-west introduced open seating, with passengers queuing up and entering on a first-come, first-seated basis. (Recently this unique system was improved, to permit flyers to secure their queue number in advance at the ticket counter or online.) As one of Southwest's famously humorous advertisements put it: "Your seat is reserved; you just don't know which one it is." But Southwest's turnaround process is no joke. Twenty-minute turnarounds permitted South-west to use considerably fewer airplanes than an airline performing at the industry's average. With the cost of a new 737 at nearly $70 million, Southwest saves billions of dollars in capital investments, which help sustain both lower fares and higher profits.

Greatly easing the pace of these fast turnaround efforts for both passengers and staff is the humor that accompanies Southwest's service. Southwest hires with an eye to a sense of humor, asking applicants: "Tell me how you recently used your sense of humor in a work environment to defuse a difficult situation."[7] Every Southwest passenger has his or her favorite Southwest joke. One example is the flight attendant who announced:

Okay. It's been a really long day for us. To tell you the truth, we're tired. Ordi-narily, this is the part of the flight when we announce we're going to be passing out peanuts and crackers, but as I said, we're tired. So instead of passing the peanuts out, we're going to put them in a big pile up here at the front of the plane. When the plane takes off, the peanuts are going to slide down the center aisle.[8]

And then, to everyone's surprise, he did just that. Another example is the attendant who performed the entire pre-flight routine in rap, earning You Tube immortality.[9] And then there is the pilot who, as people delayed putting up their carry-on bags, announced from the cockpit that his wife had just called him to say that her mother was on her way to catch the plane. "Now, if you put your bags up real quick and get seated," he drawled, "we can get away from here without her." Humor renews passengers' attention to overly familiar safety announcements and makes the quick turnarounds less stressful for everyone.

Southwest and Its People

The importance of humor to Southwest culture is not just a tactic to expedite service. It deeply reflects the airline's commitment to its people, both staff and passengers. Perhaps influenced by the personality of Kelleher himself, who once showed up at a corporate event dressed as Elvis Presley, it testifies to Southwest's belief that, as a central part of people's lives, work should be fun. A business exists not just to make money for abstract investors, but also to provide meaning, fulfillment, and enjoyment to all those who work there. No wonder that so many people want to do that. In 2010 Southwest received over 143 thousand résumés for just over 2,000 positions.[10]

Employees come first

An almost heretical idea is a fixed part of Southwest's culture: employees come first. One might ask: "How can this be? Isn't Southwest a service company?" Yes, it is, and it sees itself as such. One of the company's mantras is that Southwest is a service organization that happens to be in the airline business. "But doesn't service mean that the customer comes first, and is always right?" No. Southwest's primary loyalty, above passengers, above investors, is to its own people. Employees are number one at Southwest as a result of the belief, deeply embedded in the company's culture, that the way you treat your employees is the way they will treat your customers.[11]

Once again we can look to Herb Kelleher as a model of this cultural value. Organizational cultures are nourished by stories, and the stories of Kelleher's attention to Southwest's people abound. Kelleher receives many requests to give speeches or to attend executive round tables, but he sends his regrets if he is scheduled to be with Southwest employees. The Freibergs report that, during filming for a video with Tom Peters, the business guru asked Kelleher if he had any advice for other CEOs. Kelleher's reply? "Spend more time with your people and less time with other CEOs." During the course of his tenure as CEO, leading by example, Kelleher would routinely show up on Thanksgiving at Dallas's Love Field, to help staff load planes on the industry's busiest day of the year. The Freibergs continue with this story:

> Kathy Pettit, director of customers and a former Braniff flight attendant, remembers the first day she met Kelleher. She was working the ticket counter and Kelleher appeared from out of nowhere, kissed her on the cheek, and told her that Southwest was really lucky to have her. He welcomed her aboard and then went on his way. She turned to her training agent and said, "Who was that guy?" "Oh, that's Herb," she said. "Isn't he just the neatest thing?" When Pettit found out who "Herb" was, she was stunned.[12]

As for the slogan "the customer is always right," Southwest doesn't agree. Because it believes that employees come first, the airline will not tolerate passengers who are abusive or act in ways that injure or demean responsible Southwest employees. One other Herb Kelleher story reported by the Freibergs illustrates this contrarian philosophy.

> Jim Ruppel, director of customer relations, and Sherry Phelps, director of corporate employment, tell the story of a woman who frequently flew on Southwest, but was disappointed with every aspect of the company's operation. In fact, she became known as the "Pen Pal" because after every flight she wrote in with a complaint. She didn't like the fact that the company didn't assign seats; she didn't like the absence of a first-class section; she didn't like not having a meal in flight; she didn't like Southwest's boarding procedure; she didn't like the color of the planes; she didn't like the flight attendants' sporty uniforms and the casual atmosphere. And she hated peanuts! Her last letter, reciting a litany of complaints, momentarily stumped Southwest's customer relations people. Phelps explains, "Southwest prides itself on answering every letter that comes to the company and several employees tried to respond to this customer, patiently explaining why we do things the way we do them. It was quickly becoming a volume until they bumped it up to Herb's desk, with a note: 'This one's yours.' In sixty seconds, Kelleher wrote back and said, 'Dear Mrs. Crabapple, We will miss you. Love, Herb.'"[13]

No layoffs

It would be a mistake to take Southwest's "our people first" policy and the warmth, fun, and mutual respect that permeates the company's culture and separate this from the hard facts of business practice through which this value system is expressed. One of these facts is Southwest's commitment to not furloughing or dismissing employees during financial hard times or industry downturns, treating staff like a spigot that can be turned on or off in good times or bad. This attitude is especially prevalent in the airline industry, which has met bouts of competition through layoffs and has seen downsizing as the key to low-cost service.

Not at Southwest. When Southwest hires someone, the expectation is that it is for life. During the jet fuel crisis of the late 1970s, the recession of 1990–1994, the catastrophic reduction of passenger traffic in the wake of 9/11, and the recent economic downturn, Southwest has never laid off employees. Prudent management contributes to this. Southwest hires leanly, adding employees only when it has developed confidence in the need for expansion. It also manages its money conservatively. When other airlines over-expanded during boom times, in the quest for increased market share, Southwest held back, recognizing that market share does not always equate with profitability and acting on the premise that you "manage in the good times for the bad times." Kelleher regarded laying off people as contrary to the kind of organization and culture that Southwest strives to develop. "It never entered our minds," he said.

> Our philosophy very simply is that it is a very short-term thing to do. If your focus is on the long term, the well-being of your business and its people, you don't do it.[14]

Southwest's total value system further supports this approach. The absence of rigid hierarchies, the fluidity of staff positions, workers' broad familiarity with others' job areas (reinforced by formal programs of job exchange), and the willingness of staff to pitch in to help others out make it possible for Southwest to weather downturns without laying off people. One consequence of this "no layoff" policy is incredible employee loyalty. During the first Iraq War the price of fuel skyrocketed. Southwest employees came up with a program called Fuel from the Heart, designating a certain amount of money from their salary to help pay for the costs of fuel.

Profit sharing

In 1973 Southwest became the first airline to introduce a profit-sharing plan for its employees. It did so not under pressure and without asking for wage concessions, because the board of directors thought it was the right thing to do. Over the years, the company has invested around 15 percent of its pre-tax operating earnings in the plan, about 25 percent of which goes to the purchase of stock. Employees now own about 5 percent of the company. Stories abound of long-term Southwest employees who have become millionaires as a result of profit sharing and stock ownership. From the company's side, profit sharing and stock ownership give employees a stake in Southwest's economic performance. When a ticket agent from another carrier was loaned a stapler by a Southwest agent, she found herself being followed back to her counter. "I want to make sure we get our stapler back, the Southwest agent explained. "It's a part of my profitsharing."[15]

Unionization

Employee involvement in the financial wellbeing of a company, willingness to cooperate with the company in hard times, and flexibility in job performance are not things you associate with unionization. Indeed most people, if asked, would say that Southwest owes its success to the absence of unions. Nothing could be further from the truth. Eighty-two percent of Southwest's employees are union members, and over the years the airline has had the highest levels of unionization in the industry.

Here again, Southwest approaches its business in innovative and creative ways that distinguish it not only from other airlines, but from many other American companies generally. The much more prevalent attitude and approach is epitomized by the behavior of Robert Crandall, president and chairman of American Airlines. During the early 1990s, as recession, deregulation, and the entry of low-cost airlines jeopardized American's leadership position, Crandall announced that he was going to downsize the airline and end the jobs of many employees. He proposed a "transition plan" according to which American would continue to fly only in those markets where it could still compete, would exit the markets where American could no longer do so, and would grow its more profitable back-office non-airline businesses.[16] Among other things, this plan was intended to put pressure on American's unions to make further concessions so as to enhance competitiveness with new low-cost entrants like Southwest, but its impact was largely adverse: a legacy of embittered management–union relationships and strikes, including a 1993 strike by flight attendants. In 1995, because of this grim history of labor relations, the board of directors removed Crandall from leadership of the airline, although he continued to serve as CEO of AMR Corporation, American's parent company. Adversarial relationships with employees and unions slowed American's ability to adapt to the new competitive environment.

In contrast to this, from its inception, Southwest welcomed a union presence. Instead of viewing unions as adversaries, Kelleher and others saw them as a way for employees to express and protect their vital interests. Colleen Barrett reveals this attitude when she states, "our union folks participate in everything we do; their Leaders are involved in all major decision making."[17] She reports that,

> when the first group of Employees had an opportunity to vote on whether they wanted to be part of a union, Herb told them, "I think unions are great, as long as we still sit on the same side of the table. I don't want, and I don't think you would want, a union whose leaders want to sit on the other side of the table."[18]

Another Kelleher story illustrates how well he put this attitude into practice. According to the Freibergs,

> A Wall Street analyst recalls having lunch one day in the company cafeteria when Kelleher, seated at a table across the room with several female employees, suddenly leapt to his feet, kissed one of the women with gusto, and began leading the entire crowd in a series of cheers. When the analyst asked what was going on, one of the executives at his table explained that Kelleher had, at that moment, negotiated a new contract with Southwest's flight attendants.

The primacy of relationships and maintaining trust

The respect for employees embodied in all of Southwest's policies and practices directly underlies its consistent and continuing economic performance. By putting its people first, Southwest has engendered an attitude of trust and cooperation that gives it the flexibility to respond to challenging new situations. Jody Hoffer Gittell argues that the primacy that Southwest places on fostering good relationships among all its stakeholders is the key to its business success: The "secret ingredient," she says, that makes Southwest so distinctive "is its ability to build and sustain high performance relationships among managers, employees, unions, and suppliers. These relationships are characterized by shared goals, shared knowledge, and mutual respect."[19]

Close cooperation between ramp personnel and Boeing, for example, led to the redesign of a lavatory service panel. This expedited cleaning during turnarounds. The aircraft maker's strong relationship with the airline – to simplify maintenance and training, Southwest flies only Boeing 737s – makes Boeing more than willing to provide the kind of aircraft Southwest needs at attractive prices. By taking the time and resources to foster relationships and mutual trust, Southwest builds for the long term. In one instance, a new manager in the properties department made a $400,000 verbal commitment to the City of Austin, in a deal that ended up being a mistake. When Kelleher learned about it, he insisted that the deal be honored.[20] Maintaining relationships with the leaders of a destination city and keeping faith in Southwest's word was more important than a short-term loss.

The emphasis on relationships explains another seemingly puzzling feature of Southwest's business practice: the high degree of managerial presence in Southwest's operations. Here again, Southwest opposes the prevailing wisdom of the airline industry and of many other American business firms. To reduce low costs and meet cheaper competition, standard thinking says: flatten organizations and eliminate "unproductive" managerial staff. Although this way of thinking is sometimes justified in terms of "returning responsibility" to the lower ranks, in practice it is often as a way of downsizing and forcing employees to work harder.

But Jody Hoffer Gittell observes that Southwest takes just the opposite tack: the company has "more supervisors per frontline employee than any other airline in the industry."[21] For example, there is a single operations agent for every Southwest flight. This contrasts with the situation in other airlines, which have one operations agent for anywhere from three to fifteen flights. The operations agent is a supervisor who oversees the coordination of gate, ramp, and cabin staff that makes fast turnarounds possible. The agent often steps in to help with frontline work, even demanding physical tasks like baggage handling. Remarkably, discipline plays little role in the agent's function. As a Los Angeles supervisor explained: "If there is a problem like one person taking a three-hour lunch, they take care of that themselves for the most part. Peer pressure works well."[22] Instead these supervisors tend to view those who report to them as their internal customers, and they see themselves as being there to help them do their jobs. As Gittell notes: "Higher levels of supervisory staffing at Southwest gave supervisors fewer direct reports, enabling them to engage in more frequent and intensive interaction with their direct reports."[23] This supervisory presence facilitates training, helps communicate company values and attitudes, and builds the strong team spirit that makes everything at Southwest work smoothly and efficiently. Not surprisingly, at Southwest the job of operations agent is an important stepping stone for career advancement. Precisely because they have been intimately involved with every facet of frontline work, operations agents are well prepared for higher managerial roles.

Closely bound to this ability to work well in relationships with others is the egalitarian spirit that pervades Southwest. We saw that the airline's earliest ambition was to "democratize" the skies. But the same sense of equality and mutual respect also characterizes the company and builds relationships within it. It is what makes Southwest employees willing to assume responsibility for their part in the organization's work. As Dallas-based flight attendant Candace Boyd puts it:

> We're all in it together. No one's job is too important that they can't pick up trash on the airplane. The Pilots come back and help us pick up trash during our quick turns. Everyone's pitching in and helping each other.[24]

This egalitarian spirit also applies to Southwest's pay scales. While the airline pays employees above-average salaries, it pays its officers less than their counterparts at competing carriers. Kelleher explains:

> Our officers (whom I consider the best in the business) are paid 30 percent less, on average, than their counterparts . . . On the other hand, most of our employees are at or above average pay levels in our industry. We try to make up that difference to our officers with stock options, but of course that depends on how well the company does.[25]

Commenting on this egalitarian spirit, Colleen Barrett, who herself rose from the job of executive secretary to president, expresses her discomfort with the term "manager":

> as someone said years ago, "You can't manage a horse to water." So, at Southwest Airlines, although we have Manager titles, we prefer to use the word Leader because we want all our People to realize they have the potential to be a Leader; they can make a positive difference in anyone's work and life, regardless of whether they are in a management position. So we try to hire Leaders, no matter what role we want them to fill.[26]

Leadership is a good word on which to conclude, because Southwest is a lesson in leadership. Great Southwest figures like Herb Kelleher, Colleen Barrett, and others exemplify many of the virtues that go into outstanding leadership. Deep honesty, compassion, care, and fairness have all played a role in Southwest's phenomenal success. We have emphasized the airline's constant creative thinking, its people's ability to "think out of the box" and develop new ways of approaching work. In many ways, Southwest has said "Nuts" to a lot of conventional wisdom, even as it has recovered the wisdom in many older values. Southwest's creativity includes new procedures and new ways of doing business that have lowered the cost of flying and made air travel available to millions of new passengers. It has also introduced attitudes that challenge the "profit first" mentality of so much American business. By prioritizing employees and building relationships with internal and external customers on the basis of trust and mutual respect, Southwest has shown that moral excellence fosters long-term business success.

Notes to Chapter Twelve

1   Quoted in Kevin Freiberg and Jackie Freiberg, *Nuts! Southwest Airlines Crazy Recipe for Personal and Business Success*. Austin, TX: Bard Press, 1996, p. 130.

2   On December 8, 2005, while landing during a snowstorm, Southwest flight 1248 slid off the end of the runway at Midway Airport, Chicago, killing a 6-year-old boy in a car with his parents outside the airport and injuring others. On April 1, 2011 the fuselage of a Southwest Boeing 737–300 ruptured at 36,000 feet en route to Sacramento. The accident was traced to metal fatigue in the older model plane. No one was injured in the event.

3   Colleen Barrett and Ken Blanchard, *Lead with LUV: A Different Way to Create Real Success*. Saddle River, NJ: FT Press, 2010, p. 72.

4   Freiberg and Freiberg, *Nuts!* p. 44.

5   For a recently expressed opposite view, see Michael Useem, "On Leadership: The Business of Employment: Time to Revise Investor Capitalism's Mantra." *Washington Post*, August 9, 2011. At http://www.washingtonpost.com/national/on-leadership/the-business-of-employment-time-to-revise-investor-capitalisms-mantra/2011/08/09/gIQAh8rs4I_story.html.

6   Freiberg and Freiberg, *Nuts!* p. 44.

7   Ibid., p. 67.

8   Barrett and Blanchard, *Lead with LUV*, pp. 44–45.

9   This story can be found at http://www.youtube.com/watch?v=G9lZV_828OA.

10 "Look Who's 40." *Spirit*, June 2011, p. 245. *Spirit* is Southwest's in-flight magazine.

11 Freiberg and Freiberg, *Nuts!* p. 151.

12 Ibid., p. 274.

13 Ibid., pp. 269–270.

14 Ibid., p. 7.

15 Ibid., p. 101.

16 Jody Hoffer Gittell, *The Southwest Airlines Way: Using the Power of Relationships to Achieve High Performance*. New York: McGraw Hill, 2003.

17 Barrett and Blanchard, *Lead with LUV*, p. 58.

18 Freiberg and Freiberg, *Nuts!* p. 83.

19 Gittell, *The Southwest Airlines Way*.

20 Freiberg and Freiberg, *Nuts!* p. 134.

21 Gittell, *The Southwest Airlines Way*, p. 73.

22 Ibid., p. 75.

23 Ibid., p. 81.

24 Barrett and Blanchard, *Lead with LUV*, p. 79.

25 Quoted in Jeffrey A. Krames, *What the Best CEOs Know*. New York: McGraw-Hill, 2003, p. 184.

26 Barrett and Blanchard, *Lead with LUV*, p. 79.

STEVE JOBS AND APPLE
AESTHETIC SENSITIVITY

I want to put a ding in the universe.

Steve Jobs[1]

Few major business leaders exhibit the contradictions in character of Steven Paul Jobs. For many, he was a genius innovator of the computer industry, held in awe by those inside and outside the firms he headed. But he is also widely portrayed as the "boss from hell" who fired people in elevators, manipulated partners, and took credit for others' achievements. If charisma can have its dark and light sides, Jobs had both in abundance. Followers and acquaintances still speak of the "the bad Steve" and "the good Steve." The bad Steve could be a loathsome tyrant and intimidator, while the good Steve was one of the most creative, inspiring, and charismatic of figures.

Jobs's record of leadership illustrates what we described as the "fragmentary" nature of virtue. Outstanding excellence often comes in bits and pieces. A leader can possess numerous character flaws and yet show absolute brilliance with regard to one or more individual virtues. Fragmentary excellence can make a career. Whatever Steve Jobs's other failings, one virtue permitted him to overcome numerous reverses and emerge as a global leader: his outstanding sensitivity to aesthetics and design.

Beginnings

Jobs's passion for design emerges as one of the earliest themes in his biography. In a now famous commencement address delivered at Stanford University in

10 Virtues of Outstanding Leaders: Leadership and Character, First Edition.
Al Gini and Ronald M. Green.
© 2013 John Wiley & Sons, Inc. Published 2013 by John Wiley & Sons, Inc.

2005, Jobs highlights this theme. After being given up for adoption by his unwed biological mother, Jobs was raised by devoted, working-class parents in Cupertino, California. His adoptive parents had promised his biological mother to send him to college, and when that time came, Jobs chose Reed, one of the most prestigious – and expensive – private schools. He was attracted by its artistic reputation.[2] As his parents struggled to support him, Jobs underperformed and felt that he was wasting their money.

> After six months, I couldn't see the value in it. I had no idea what I wanted to do with my life and no idea how college was going to help me figure it out. And here I was spending all of the money my parents had saved their entire life. So I decided to drop out and trust that it would all work out OK. It was pretty scary at the time, but looking back it was one of the best decisions I ever made. The minute I dropped out I could stop taking the required classes that didn't interest me, and begin dropping in on the ones that looked interesting.[3]

Living on money he earned by returning Coke bottles and sleeping in empty dorm rooms, Jobs took one class that changed his life:

> Reed College at that time offered perhaps the best calligraphy instruction in the country. Throughout the campus every poster, every label on every drawer, was beautifully hand calligraphed. Because I had dropped out and didn't have to take the normal classes, I decided to take a calligraphy class to learn how to do this. I learned about serif and san serif typefaces, about varying the amount of space between different letter combinations, about what makes great typography great. It was beautiful, historical, artistically subtle in a way that science can't capture, and I found it fascinating. None of this had even a hope of any practical application in my life. But ten years later, when we were designing the first Macintosh computer, it all came back to me. And we designed it all into the Mac. It was the first computer with beautiful typography . . . If I had never dropped out, I would have never dropped in on this calligraphy class, and personal computers might not have the wonderful typography that they do.[4]

The impact on Jobs of that first exposure to design went far beyond typefaces. It kindled a fire in him that burned from the start of his career.

In 1974, after definitively dropping out of Reed, Jobs returned to Cupertino and became involved in the budding hobbyist electronics culture. He teamed up with Steve Wozniak, a young electronics wizard, and the pair worked to develop the Apple I and II, which were among the first consumer-oriented computers. After modest success among hobbyists with the Apple I, the two turned their attention to the Apple II. Because Wozniak brought to the projects an expertise in circuitry that Jobs lacked, Jobs focused on developing the computer's case. Hobbyists had been content to stuff the electronics in old boxes built from wood, but for this new project Jobs wanted the finish and appearance of a fine stereo unit. With little money at their disposal, the team nevertheless offered $1,500 to Jerry Manock, a Hewlett Packard designer who had become a freelance consultant. Manock's wedge-shaped design molded in quality beige plastic was just what Jobs had in mind; but, when the first units emerged from the mold, they were marked by pits and bubbles, and Jobs was dismayed. Facing the deadline of an impending 1977 West Coast Computer Faire, Jobs set the small crew of Apple employees to work sanding, scraping, and spray-painting. The result was a computer that walked away with the show and founded an industrial empire. Between its introduction and the end of production in 1993, Apple sold somewhere between five and six million Apple II series computers.

The Apple II effort reveals many of the leadership traits that were to distinguish Jobs in the years ahead. One was the willingness to drive everyone, including himself, to the limits of endurance in order to get an exciting new product out the door. Behind this was a passion for the product itself. In the Apple II Jobs saw a machine for the masses: a device that could revolutionize the way people lived their lives. His aim, as he said just a few years later, was to make a product "so important that it will make a dent in the universe."[5] Integral to this was the product's design. Job realized that, if the computer was to go beyond the small circle of wireheads that were happy to cobble together their own machines, it had to be attractive and easy to use by the average consumer. The Apple II's case was one of the first expressions of this business philosophy.

The Macintosh

The same traits emerged even more strikingly a few years later with the development and introduction of the first Macintosh computer. By 1980 Apple was on top of the computer world. An IPO (initial public offering) had made Jobs rich, and the company itself now had tens of millions of dollars available to implement his ideas. Investors were lined up to buy stock even before the public offering. One of these was the giant copier manufacturer Xerox. Jobs allowed Xerox to buy 100,000 Apple shares on the condition that he and a handful of Apple employees be allowed to tour Xerox's Palo Alto Research Center (known as PARC), where many of Xerox's future products were being developed.

Jobs recalled that visit: "I remember they showed me three things. But I was so blinded by the first one, I didn't really see the other two." That "thing" was the graphical user interface (GUI), a method of arranging information on the screen that replaced complex commands with visual metaphors that ordinary people could understand and manipulate. In place of a black screen with blinking letters, Job saw a paper-white virtual desktop. To move or delete a file, one simply dragged it to a destination icon. Jobs was astonished: "I thought it was the best thing I'd ever seen in my life," he said. "It was obvious to me that all computers would work like this some day."[6]

A graphical interface soon made its appearance on the Macintosh. Jobs's goal was what he called "elegant simplicity." User-friendliness and attractiveness of design would work together to invite the consumer to the machine and to encourage its use. To this end, designers gave the Mac a host of other user-friendly features. Susan Kare, a PhD design professional, developed the distinctive icons that symbolized the machine's functions. In the years ahead, her work – the smiling Mac face that welcomed you when the computer booted, the tiny wristwatch that appeared when the Mac was performing a heavy-duty task, or the dreaded system bomb – became cultural icons.

Jobs himself concentrated on the case. Unlike the flat consoles of most existing computers, the Mac would be vertical, with the central processing unit at the bottom, topped by a CRT (cathode ray tube) display. According to Jerry Manock, "Steve had been looking at mass-market consumer products, such as coffeemakers, which occupied very little counter space, and decided that the Mac should have a small footprint as well." Jobs imagined it sitting on an executive's desk, says Manock.

> It had to be small enough so that someone sitting on the other side of the desk could see around it. Because the Mac would be viewed from both sides of the desk, it had to be pleasing from the back as well as the front.[7]

Many other features of the Mac revealed this commitment to design perfection. For example, to prevent the user from accidentally turning the unit off, the power switch was placed at the back. But this required the user to reach around and hunt for it. To make the task easier, the otherwise textured case had a smooth area along the back corner to guide the user's hand. "That's the kind of detail that turns an ordinary product into an artifact," Manock said.[8] The circuitry itself also had to be perfect. For Jobs, "elegant simplicity" was just as important inside as outside. When he saw an initial design for the circuit board, he rejected it on aesthetic grounds, in the belief that circuits and components should be as balanced and harmonious as a fine painting. He explained his reasoning this way:

When you're a carpenter making a beautiful chest of drawers, you're not going to use a piece of plywood on the back. Even though it faces the wall . . . the aesthetic has to be carried all the way through.[9]

Job's aesthetic perfectionism even carried through to packaging design. Toward the end of the program, designer Ben Pang worked with Apple's marketing, manufacturing and creative services to design the Mac's cardboard and Styrofoam packaging and to make it as unique as the product it contained. The Mac came wrapped in bleached white cardboard, with a simple black-and-white photo of the Mac. "Like everything else. Steve wanted the packaging to be elegant," says Pang. "As you open the box, the computer should be presented to you immediately. So it sits right on top."[10] All the remaining parts of the product – the keyboard, mouse, software disks, cords, and manuals – were packaged in separate compartments. This forced the user to remove, unwrap and discover each component in a specific sequence. Jobs and the Apple team believed that this ritual helped establish a personal relationship between owner and machine. In the years ahead, these ideas shaped the packaging of all Apple products.

The Whole Widget

In the course of this design phase, Jobs made one other decision that, in its broad implications, would have fateful consequences for Apple. This was his commitment to what some have called "controlling the whole widget." In those early days, hobbyists reveled in tinkering with their machines: adding circuit boards or modifying the wiring. Even competing computer makers like IBM, Compaq, and Dell were introducing models with expansion boards that would allow the user to increase memory or processing power. One consequence of these practices was that computers were notoriously unreliable, prone to constant crashes, freezes, and reboots, as the software failed to keep up. To prevent this, Jobs ordered that the Mac not have expansion slots; and, to enforce this decision, the case was locked shut, with screws that could only be loosened with a proprietary screwdriver not available to users.

"Controlling the whole widget" also meant that the Mac would be sold as an integral system: hardware and software united in a single functioning machine. During these years, manufacturers often approached Jobs and Apple wanting to buy their innovative software to distribute it in cheaper "cloned" machines. This was the approach soon adopted by Microsoft, but Jobs was adamant: software and hardware had to go together, to provide a reliable and satisfying user experience.

But this vision of "controlling the whole widget" was years ahead of its time. Apple and Jobs would eventually return to it with renewed success. In the shorter run, the decision proved destructive. Within a few years, following great initial success with the Mac, cheap PC clones using the Microsoft operating system and software flooded the market and almost drove Apple to extinction. Looking back, analysts have tried to understand why Apple's strategy of total control was temporarily defeated. Andy Hertzfeld, a whiz kid programmer on the original Mac development team, explained that Mac had erred in trying to impose simplicity at a moment when rapid technological change favored innovation:

> The biggest problem with the Macintosh hardware was pretty obvious, which was its limited expandability. But the problem wasn't really technical as much as philosophical, which was that we wanted to eliminate the inevitable complexity that was a consequence of hardware expandability, both for the user and the developer, by having every Macintosh be identical. It was a valid point of view, even somewhat courageous, but not very practical, because things were still changing too fast in the computer industry for it to work.[11]

To celebrate the completion of the Mac's design, Jobs held a "signing party." Champagne was served, and key members of the team signed the inside of the case. Jobs explained: "Artists sign their work."[12] The Mac's development culminated with a dramatic product introduction ceremony that would also become part of Jobs's legacy. At the annual shareholders meeting, Jobs took the stage, recited a few lines from the Bob Dylan ballad "The Times They Are A-Changin'," then reached into a canvas bag to pull out a Macintosh. As he did so, the machine's synthesized voice said, "Hello . . . I am Macintosh . . . It sure is great to get out of that bag."[13]

Although the Mac itself was an enormous success and solidified the loyalty of millions of Mac users, its introduction was also the beginning of the end for Jobs at Apple. Recognizing the importance of marketing, in 1983 Jobs brought on board John Sculley, president of PepsiCo, to head up Apple's marketing efforts. It wasn't an easy sell. Scully would have to give up a powerful and profitable leadership position in one of America's most successful companies to accept a position in a new organization where he would share power with a demanding and mercurial founder-figure. Jobs turned his prodigious salesmanship skills to the task, asking Sculley at a New York meeting: "Do you want to sell sugar water for the rest of your life, or do you want to change the world?"

But Sculley's ascent at Apple soon led to Jobs's descent. Apple's loss of market share to the clone makers and discontent with what many in the company and on the board regarded as Jobs's authoritarian management style led to his progressive marginalization within the firm. By 1985 he was out. Sculley was named CEO. Jobs, rich by any standard with well over $100 million in Apple stock, found himself sidelined in an industry that had become his life's passion. He looked for his next opportunity.

Learning from Failure

Almost every feature of Steve Jobs's life is not what it seems to be. At the pinnacle of his success, having pioneered and introduced the Mac, he appeared to be a failure. In the next phase of his life – the NeXT and Pixar phase – seeming failure would become amazing success.

This phase was also marked by Jobs's obsession with design. Before leaving Apple and following a competition, Jobs had brought in as design consultants employees of an outstanding European firm, headed by Hartmut Esslinger, that called itself "frogdesign." Under Esslinger and frogdesign, Apple embarked on the "SnowWhite" project, which would introduce a unified, clean, and modern look to the whole line of Apple products and would help sustain the brand's reputation for design over the years ahead. One feature of the Snow-White "language" was a manufacturing technique known as "zero-draft" molding. This allowed Apple to produce extremely refined plastic cases with precise lines and details. From a business standpoint, the technique made counterfeiting very difficult. A Macintosh copy made without the more costly zero-draft technique announced its cheapness. Years down the line, Jobs would bring this union of design and competitive advantage to a whole new line of Apple products.

But, in 1985, Jobs's challenge was to outdo Apple. The vehicle for this would be the NeXT computer, which Jobs envisioned as a powerful new workstation for the education market. For the heart of the machine, Jobs and his engineers chose a version of Unix, an operating system that was recognized for its stability. If one program crashes, the machine itself keeps going.

In the fall of 1985 Jobs decided that he needed to communicate his passion for aesthetics to the NeXT team. He and some of his top people flew to Pittsburgh to spend a few days at Carnegie Mellon University, a distinguished center for computer science research. At the close of the visit, Jobs took the group on a day trip into the Pennsylvania countryside for a special private tour of Fallingwater, Frank Lloyd Wright's landmark modernistic house of concrete, glass, and steel, cantilevered over a waterfall. As Alan Deutschman observes: "He wanted them to understand the nature of good design by studying a creation that was both beautiful and functional."[14]

As before, Jobs focused much of his energy on the NeXT's case. Working once more with frogdesign, NeXT developed a die-cast magnesium cube-shaped case that gave the machine its name: NeXTcube. But not even outstanding design could save NeXT. Jobs soon learned that the education market was not ready for an expensive machine. Over its eight-year life, NeXT sold only 50,000 units, and the company hemorrhaged money. Despite major infusions of cash from Canon and from millionaire Ross Perot, Jobs saw his fortune dwindling. In 1993 NeXT shut down its hardware business and remaindered large parts of its manufacturing and office operations. It was the lowest point of Jobs's career.

It is said that if you have to choose between having a leader who's smart and one who's lucky, you should choose the one who's lucky. In retrospect, we can see that Jobs was among the lucky. But some people make their own luck. In Jobs's case this was accomplished through the decision, which he took on leaving Apple in 1985, to spend $10 million to buy a computer animation company in northern California; the company had been put up for sale by George Lucas after a messy divorce. During the NeXT years Jobs paid little attention to the business, leaving it in the hands of a skilled group of engineers, software designers, and artists. By 1990 Jobs's small company had won several Oscars and Oscar nominations for animated short subjects. At Jobs's urging and with his help, it embarked on a feature-length movie in cooperation with Disney. The movie turned out to be the 1995 blockbuster feature-length "Toy Story." The company was Pixar. With a multiple film commitment from Disney, Pixar went public in late 1995. Jobs was now a billionaire.

Apple, meanwhile, was floundering. Although the company had some good years under Sculley's leadership, the late 1980s and early 1990s saw it overwhelmed by competitors that had turned to the Microsoft standard. Once Jobs was gone, Apple drifted away from its obsession with design. As one member of the frogdesign team put it. "Suddenly, our role was to do the work and keep our heads down."[15] With profits dropping, Apple reached out to clone makers; but the sales of Apple software did little to buttress its core business. Its stock price had fallen from $60 a share in 1992 to $17 a share at the end of 1996. Market share fell from 12 percent to 4 percent. In 1993 Sculley was out. During this period, Sculley, followed by his successor, Michael Spindler, tried to sell the company to big players in the global electronics field – Philips, Siemens, Kodak, AT&T, IBM, Toshiba, Compaq, and Sony – but nobody wanted to buy a firm they saw as a loser.

By 1995 Apple had a new CEO, Gilbert Amelio. He began the search for a new operating system to replace Apple's aging software. By happenstance, and without the authorization of the CEO of either company, someone at Apple phoned engineers at NeXT to inquire about the NeXT OS. Events moved quickly. Jobs soon found himself back at Apple, pitching the NeXT system. In 1996 Apple agreed to buy it for $429 million and 1.5 million shares of Apple stock. Jobs had turned a sow's ear into a silk purse. The negotiations also brought Jobs back into conversations with Apple's board. To the industry's surprise, in 1996, eleven years after he left, Jobs was back at Apple. The following year he replaced Gil Amelio and assumed the position of interim CEO.

Stories abound about Jobs's behavior in his first years back at Apple. Leander Kahney describes a key meeting in July 1997:

> Apple's top staff were summoned to an early-morning meeting at company HQ. In shuffled the then-current CEO, Gilbert Amelio, who'd been in charge for about eighteen months. He had patched up the company but had failed to reignite its inventive soul. "It's time for me to go," he said, and quietly left the room. Before anyone could react, Steve Jobs entered the room, looking like a bum. He was wearing shorts and sneakers and several days' worth of stubble. He plonked himself into a chair and slowly started to spin. "Tell me what's wrong with this place," he said. Before anyone could reply, he burst out: "It's the products. The products SUCK! There's no sex in them anymore."[16]

It became routine for Jobs to convene a series of meetings in the Apple boardroom with its panoramic view of the Cupertino campus. One by one he would call in the head of a product team and all of its key players. Engineers and managers had to show Jobs their existing products, from monitors to software, and to explain their future plans. With an undercurrent of tension, Jobs would occasionally upbraid people. Looking them in the eye, he asked what they would cut if they could only keep a quarter of their product line. He insisted that he would only keep great and profitable products.

Jobs killed the clone business. Recognizing that Apple had always been pressured to sell dirt-cheap computers, he insisted that Apple should never compete in a race to the bottom in the commodity computer market. Instead of going head to head with Dell and others to make the cheapest possible computer, Apple should make quality products and enough money to develop even more of them. Jobs believed that the market was ready for new ideas and design innovation. "Computers are still awful," he complained.

> They're too complicated and don't do what you really want them to do – or do those things as well as they could . . . My purpose in coming back to Apple was that our industry was in a coma. It reminded me of Detroit in the '70s, when American cars were boats on wheels.[17]

Apple was not without assets. Jobs streamlined the company's management structure, reducing it to five key managers who reported to him. One of these was Jonathan Ive, who headed the in-house Apple Industrial Design Group (IDg). Born in London, with a father who was a silversmith and a woodworker, Ive was an award-winning designer whose special interest was in the innovative materials that went into industrial products. Shortly after his return to Apple, Jobs commented that, in Ive and the IDg, "I found . . . the best industrial design team I've ever seen in my life."[18]

Even before Jobs came back on board, Apple had introduced the very successful fruit-colored, teardrop-shaped iMac desktop computer line. These units lacked a disk drive, on the assumption that future communications between computers would take place via the Internet. By adopting this strategy, Jobs was showing that he perceived the future. As Jeffrey S. Young and William L. Simon observe:

> He was sure that Apple had a good chance to be a serious player again if only he could graft the ease of use and the elegance of the Macintosh to the freedom of the Internet.[19]

Apple Reborn

Under Jobs's direction and with his usual meticulous attention to detail, usability, and beauty, Apple engineers and designers set to work adapting the NeXT operating system. In 2000, after two and a half years of work by nearly one thousand programmers, the powerful new Mac OS X operating system was ready for release. It remains one of the most sophisticated personal computer operating systems ever developed, with complex, real-time graphics effects like transparency, shadowing, and animation. Jobs was actively involved in every phase of its development, often intervening to insist on elegant simplicity and user-friendliness. In the upper left corner of each window, for example, there were three buttons. One would close the window, another would store it away, and the third toggled to reduce or expand its size. The original buttons were all gray, but Jobs insisted that they be given colors (red, yellow and green) to indicate their different functions. Describing the OS to a *Fortune* reporter, Jobs remarked: "We made the buttons on the screen look so good you'll want to lick them."[20]

Jobs introduced the new operating system at the January 2000 Macworld exposition in San Francisco, which, with Jobs back, vibrated with the energy and excitement that marked Apple's earliest product introductions.[21] After finishing his presentation of OS X, Jobs, almost as an aside, said he had "one last thought." He thanked all the Apple people who had made these new products possible and, to enormous applause of the audience, announced that he was dropping the word "interim" from his title. He would become Apple's permanent CEO. Cordell Ratzlaff, an Apple manager who had been brought over from frogdesign and who was charged with overseeing development of OS X, remarked that Jobs's announcement was carefully timed. "He was waiting for the last big parts of the company to be running to his standards before he took on the role of Apple CEO."[22]

Beyond OS X, one of the first fruits of the collaboration between Ive and Jobs was the iPod music player, introduced in November 2001. Digitized music was not new. Young people had learned that they could convert CDs to the digital MP3 format and share songs or albums across the Internet. Sean Parker had given impetus to the pirated music business when he co-founded Napster, a free file-sharing service for music that drew the wrath of both music industry executives and recording artists. But the Napster/MP3 approach had many problems. Foremost was the illegality of this activity, which invited lawsuits and eventually shut Napster down. But MP3 players and the software were also problems. The players were clunky and hard to use. To load songs, one had to find tunes, drag them to just the right place in one's files, and hope that they were in the right format. Music often failed to download or upload properly.

The iPod solved these problems. Under Ive's and Jobs's direction, the Apple Design Group came up with a thin portable player able to hold up to a thousand songs, whose distinctive scroll wheel controller allowed the user to get to any song in three steps. Purchased songs downloaded seamlessly, and CDs could easily be uploaded into the user's own device. iPod sales boomed from the day of its introduction, eventually reaching nearly 300 million by the end of 2010. Smash Mouth front man Steve Harwell spoke for many other later iPod owners: "I'll take two of 'em! One for me and one for my girlfriend, 'cuz I'm not sharin' this with nobody!" He also expressed a sentiment that Steve Jobs must have enjoyed: "This kicks every other product's ass right here."[23]

Once again, using his astonishing powers of salesmanship, Jobs persuaded most of the leading labels in the recording industry to make their music available via Apple's iTunes website store. Jobs understood what made this unprecedented deal possible. The industry faced potential collapse at the hands of pirates, whereas, for a fee represented by Apple's percentage of each sale, Jobs offered to give everyone a chance for continued profitability. As journalist Peter Lewis put it, Jobs was "almost single-handedly dragging the music industry, kicking and screaming, toward a better future."[24] Jobs also perceived that most people, if given a reasonably priced and efficient choice, would choose to do the right thing. "Stealing music," he said, "is a behavioral problem more than a technological problem. We believe most people are honest and want to pay for their music." He was only partly right. As Jobs recognized, Apple's technology *was* important. It gave substance to the efficiency and reliability that users wanted as their part of the deal. "We don't see how you convince people to stop being thieves, unless you can offer them a carrot – not just a stick," Jobs said. "And the carrot is: We're gonna offer you a better experience . . . and it's only gonna cost you a dollar a song."[25]

Behind this offer was the understanding that the iPod was more than a clever electronic device. It was an integral part of the whole music system. Equally important were the free, downloadable iTunes software, soon made available for non-Mac platforms, and the iTunes store. Like the Mac before them, the iPod, the iTunes, and the iTunes store were sealed units. To the chagrin of some users, not even the iPod's battery could be changed outside of an Apple repair facility. The same was true of the Apple store. Music purchased there was downloaded in a proprietary format that could not be shared with others' iPods or MP3 players. In a new way, Apple had returned to "controlling the whole widget."

To some critics, this level of control – which they claim to reflect Jobs's personality – is a fault. Since Apple demanded a percentage of each Apple store transaction, they also see it as unvarnished greed. But, while Jobs and Apple were certainly interested in profit, this criticism misses the point. Apple's control of the iPod system was the way the company could guarantee the reliability, ease of use, security, and profitability that were essential to digital music's availability. Jobs summed up the iPod's ease of operation to *Fortune* in five words: "Plug it in. Whirrrrrr. Done."[26] The user-friendly approach to industrial design that had inspired the Apple II and the Mac achieved their fullest realization in the iPod system.

In the process, Apple not only reinvented itself as a music company, but created a previously non-existent business sector. Increasingly in the years ahead, Apple's profits would come not from sales of its computers, but from its iTunes store. With the later introduction of the brilliantly conceived and beautifully designed iPhone and iPad, Apple would repeat these successes. iPhone and iPad "apps," developed for its integral systems and vetted for their ability to work with those systems, became major product lines. Striking new computers – such as the solid aluminum block Macbook portables designed by Ives and running Mac's formidable OS X operating system – added to the momentum and made Apple computers once again competitive and profitable in an industry that had almost left them behind. In 2011 Apple, with over $300 billion of market value as compared to Microsoft's $200 billion, had became the world's most valuable technology company.

The Centrality of Design

What are the leadership lessons of Steve Jobs's career? While Jobs has both strengths and weaknesses as a business manager and both admirable and questionable character traits, his commitment to the aesthetic quality of his companies' products and of their design has never wavered. He epitomizes the value of this commitment, and his success illustrates its importance.

For many American business managers design is an afterthought. You try to offer a useful product and a service, price it right, organize its distribution – and your job is done. Aesthetics, the thought that the product is attractive, that it beautifies the world in which its users live, that it impressively integrates its component parts and is easy to use – these are afterthoughts. One consequence of this mentality is the shrinking share of American industrial products in the global marketplace. Although many factors contributed to the near destruction of the American automotive industry, the "boats" of the 1970s that Jobs decried helped make "made in America" a phrase of derision.

For Jobs, in contrast, design isn't just decoration, or a veneer added onto a product. It is, most fundamentally, about how a product works. As Jobs explained in a 1996 interview with *Wired*:

> Design is a funny word. Some people think design means how it looks. But of course, if you dig deeper, it's really how it works. The design of the Mac wasn't what it looked like, although that was part of it. Primarily, it was how it worked. To design something really well, you have to get it . . . It takes a passionate commitment to really thoroughly understand something, chew it up, not just quickly swallow it. Most people don't take the time to do that.[27]

Jobs's and Apple's experiences also reveal that excellence in design, or the beauty and functionality of products (and services) can be a key factor to business survival and flourishing. Jobs realized that, in a world of global competition, advanced nations cannot succeed as industrial centers by trying to be commodity producers. In such a world there are always countries whose low-cost workers can produce cheaper steel, electronic chips, and even cloned music players and computers. Market leaders must provide innovative technology and products, from the best personal computers or cell phones to aircraft or entertainment products. Design, in Jobs's full sense, is integral to all these endeavors. Ugly and hard-to-use products will not succeed in a global marketplace. Only products with value-added allure will do so.

The best of these products have a further value: they create their own market. By identifying and satisfying new needs and wants, these products create business sectors that never existed before. Think for a moment of Coca-

Cola. This worldwide product, with its flavor, trademark, and distinctive bottles, didn't emerge in response to an existing need: it created that need. In many ways, the same is true of the iPod, iPhone, and iPad. None of these products filled an existing market niche. Their innovativeness and design created one. Out of nowhere, through the creativity and full aesthetic sense of Steve Jobs and others, a new business came into being.

This insight is supported by accounts of Steve Jobs's approach to the design of a new product. As Leander Kahney notes, in designing the iPod and other products, Jobs strenuously rejected using focus groups. This doesn't mean that he didn't pay attention to customers' needs. "We have a lot of customers, and we have a lot of research into our installed base," Jobs told *Business Week*.

> We also watch industry trends pretty carefully. But in the end, for something this complicated, it's really hard to design products by focus groups. A lot of times, people don't know what they want until you show it to them.[28]

In a conversation with John Sculley he amplified this point: "How can I possibly ask someone what a graphics-based computer ought to be when they have no idea what a graphics-based computer is? No one has ever seen one before."[29]

In the last analysis, Steve Jobs has been his own best one-man focus group. Dag Spicer, a senior curator at the Computer History Museum in Mountain View, California, notes that, although Jobs had no formal technical training, "he's followed technology since a teenager. He's technically aware enough to follow trends, like a good stock analyst. He has a layman's view. It's a great asset."[30] Guy Kawasaki, who worked at Apple during the 1980s as chief promoter of the Macintosh, put it succinctly: "Steve Jobs doesn't do market research. Market research for Steve Jobs is the right hemisphere talks to the left hemisphere."[31]

Throughout his business career Steve Jobs brought to his work, and to the companies he led, an acute sense of the importance of industrial design in all its meanings. This aesthetic sensitivity (plus a lot of luck and brilliance) saved his career and added immeasurably to our society's richness. The result has been just what Steve Jobs hoped for: a dent in the universe. Now, the question for Apple is: Can they survive without Steve Jobs?

Notes to Chapter Thirteen

1   Quoted in Leander Kahney, *Inside Steve's Brain*. New York: Penguin Group, 2008, p. 150.

2   Walter Isaacson, *Steve Jobs*. New York: Simon & Schuster, 2011, p. 33.
3   " 'You've got to find what you love,' Jobs says." Stanford Report, June 14, 2005. (Available online at http://news.stanford.edu/news/2005/june15/jobs-061505.html.)
4   Ibid.
5   Jeffrey S. Young and William L. Simon, *Icon: Steve Jobs: The Greatest Second Act in the History of Business*. Hoboken, NJ: John Wiley and Sons, 2008, p. 261.
6   Paul Kunkel, *Apple Design: The Work of the Apple Industrial Design Group*. New York: Graphics Inc., 1997, 1:8.
7   Kunkel, *Apple Design*, 2:2.
8   Kahney, *Inside Steve's Brain*, p. 82.
9   Ibid.
10   Kunkel, *Apple Design*, 2:6.
11   Kahney, *Inside Steve's Brain*, p. 250.
12   Ibid., p. 83.
13   Ibid., p. 151.
14   Alan Deutschman, *The Second Coming of Steve Jobs*. New York: Broadway Books, 2000, p. 43.
15   Kunkel, *Apple Design*, 5:2.
16   Kahney, *Inside Steve's Brain*, p. 16.
17   Ibid., p. 31.
18   Ibid., p. 34.
19   Young and Simon, *Icon: Steve Jobs*, p. 261.
20   Kahney, *Inside Steve's Brain*, p. 56.
21   The announcement – "Macworld San Francisco 2000-Steve Jobs Becomes iCEO of Apple" – can be viewed at http://www.youtube.com/watch?v=JgHtKFuY3bE.
22   Kahney, *Inside Steve's Brain*, p. 57.
23   Ibid., p. 282.
24   Ibid., p. 293.
25   Ibid., pp. 60–61.
26   Ibid., p. 233.
27   Ibid., p. 71.
28   Ibid., p. 65.
29   Ibid., p. 64.
30   Ibid.
31   Ibid., p. 67.

CHARLES DE GAULLE AND EXITING ALGERIA

GOOD TIMING

No modern military commander has been so disparaged in British and US government, military, and media circles as Charles de Gaulle. Derided as arrogant, pompous, disdainful, and uncooperative, de Gaulle has been the butt of criticism in the West for 60 years. He was selfish, and difficult for Eisenhower and Churchill to deal with in World War II, threw NATO out of France in the mid-sixties, and seemed to go out of his way – as perceived by many Americans – to tweak America at every opportunity. But this is a wholly one-sided impression. The truth is different. De Gaulle was in fact a great leader who played *the* critical role in shaping modern France. He is worthy of study, respect, and admiration.

Michael E. Haskew[1]

Many different words have been used to describe Charles de Gaulle's virtues and vices. Among them are "resolute," "principled," "progressive," "visionary," "reactionary," "stubborn," "haughty," and "arrogant." To some extent, despite their seeming contradiction, all these descriptions are accurate. De Gaulle was an extraordinarily complex individual, who combined in himself the best and worst of the French spirit. Yet rarely invoked in the list of de Gaulle's virtues is that of "good timing." This is a blend of political insight, patience, and courage that allows a leader to defer action and to resist criticism until just the right moment for action, when success can best be achieved. Whatever other virtues or vices Charles de Gaulle displayed, his life is a study in good timing.

10 Virtues of Outstanding Leaders: Leadership and Character, First Edition.
Al Gini and Ronald M. Green.
© 2013 John Wiley & Sons, Inc. Published 2013 by John Wiley & Sons, Inc.

Youth and the First World War

Charles André Joseph Marie de Gaulle was born in the industrial northern French city of Lille on November 22, 1890. His father was a professor of philosophy and literature. His family – one of devout Roman Catholics – was both nationalist and traditionalist. Growing up in this environment, the young de Gaulle became intensely interested in the fate of his nation. Writing in his memoirs many years later, de Gaulle expressed his passionate attachment to his country:

> All my life I have had a certain idea of France. This is inspired by sentiment as much as by reason. The emotional side of me tends to imagine France, like the princess in the fairy stories or the Madonna in the frescoes, as dedicated to an exalted and exceptional destiny. Instinctively, I have the feeling that Providence has created her either for complete successes or for exemplary misfortunes. If, in spite of this, mediocrity shows in her acts and deeds, it strikes me as an absurd anomaly, to be imputed to the faults of Frenchmen, not to the genius of the land. But the positive side of my mind assures me that France is not really herself unless in the front rank; that only vast enterprises are capable of counterbalancing the ferments of dispersal which are inherent in her people; that our country, as it is, surrounded by the others, as they are, must aim high and hold itself straight, on pain of mortal danger. In short, to my mind, France cannot be France without greatness.[2]

After a solid start in life as a student of the *lycée* (French high school) and a preparatory year as an infantry soldier in the ranks of the army, in 1910 de Gaulle entered St. Cyr, France's elite military academy. Although other students derided his great height and his large nose – they dubbed the 6-foot 5-inch tall de Gaulle "the Big Asparagus" – he did well academically, graduating 13th in a class of 211. He was commissioned as a second lieutenant and, with the First World War looming, he joined an infantry regiment commanded by Colonel Henri-Philippe Pétain. De Gaulle was wounded twice in the first few months of the conflict, then he was promoted to the rank of captain in February 1915 and assigned to Verdun, the epicenter of the French defense. After leading patrols into German lines and suffering further injuries, the young officer was captured by the German army and spent the next 32 months in prisoner-of-war camps. De Gaulle made five heroic but unsuccessful attempts to escape; he always considered his imprisonment a terrible misfortune, because it prevented him from fighting for France during the remainder of the war.

After the Armistice, de Gaulle served with a Polish army unit formed in France. Fighting against the Red Army, he won Poland's highest military decoration. In April 1921 he wed Yvonne Vendroux, the daughter of a well-respected family from Calais. A son, Philippe, was born, somewhat prematurely, in December of that year, and two daughters arrived later: Elizabeth in 1924 and Anne, born with Down syndrome, in 1928. Throughout his life de Gaulle drew strength from his family's love. He was especially devoted to Anne, of whom he remarked that she had not chosen to come into the world and that the family would do all it could to make her happy.[3]

Up to the Battle of France

If the inter-war years were personally satisfying for de Gaulle the young officer, they also proved difficult for him. Regarded as arrogant and a loner, he was never popular with other officers, or with the high command. Nevertheless his relationship with Pétain, now lauded as "the hero of Verdun" and promoted to the exalted rank of marshal of France, eased his way. During this period de Gaulle lectured frequently at the French War College and at his alma mater, St. Cyr. He became convinced that the only way to avoid the stalemate and butchery of trench warfare, which had just taken millions of lives, was to develop new mobile armored forces with tanks at the forefront. He developed these ideas and lectures into a book, *The Army of the Future* (1934). Similar ideas were being developed in Britain and in Nazi Germany; but de Gaulle's warnings went largely unheeded in France, where millions of francs were instead being spent on the static defense of the Maginot Line. During this period de Gaulle collaborated in writing with his former commander, Pétain, but disagreement about authorship credit led to a breach that the outbreak of war would vastly widen.

Theory became practice on May 10, 1940, when German Panzer tanks broke out of the Ardennes forest, charged around the end of the unfinished Maginot line, and threatened to cut France into two. On the eve of the attack, de Gaulle had taken command of the French Fourth Armored Division and could now apply his ideas under fire. Coordinating his tankers' movements, de Gaulle charged into the flank of the German armored column. In one attack, on May 28, he became the only French commander to force the Germans to retreat. But it was too little, too late. Within days, German forces had reached the English Channel and French leaders were either fleeing or thinking of suing for peace.

In early June, French Prime Minister Paul Reynaud called de Gaulle to Paris. Leapfrogging him over many senior officers, he appointed de Gaulle minister of war. Vigorously taking on this role, de Gaulle visited London to confer with Churchill and other British leaders; but on return to France on

16 June he learned that Pétain had ousted Reynaud as premier and was forming a government that would seek an armistice with Germany.

De Gaulle now faced a moment of truth. Should he remain in France and serve, under his old commander, a puppet regime that was prepared to strike a humiliating truce with Hitler? Or should he defy orders and seek to preserve France's honor by forming or joining a still non-existent government in exile in London? De Gaulle chose the latter course. After taking steps to ensure that his wife and family would follow him to safety, he flew back to London on June 17. Five days later an armistice was declared, and the Vichy regime – a collaborationist government under Pétain – was installed. Declared a traitor by the regime, de Gaulle was sentenced to death in absentia.

The situation that awaited de Gaulle in London was bleak. He had no recognized authority and carried only $500 in francs; this was the total sum remaining in the government's reserve, and it had been given to him by Reynaud. The British were still uncertain about the fate of France and about their relationship to its new regime. Refugee Frenchmen were undecided in their loyalties. Describing this moment in his memoirs, de Gaulle said: "I seemed to myself, alone as I was and deprived of everything, like a man on the shore of an ocean, proposing to swim across it."[4]

And yet de Gaulle moved fast to fill this vacuum with decisive and independent action. Asserting his leadership of the Free French movement, over the objections of others in the British Cabinet he secured permission from Churchill to broadcast a message to the French people. This famous radio address, known as the Appeal of June 18, was heard by few, but its gist was later widely circulated through leaflets dropped over France: "France has lost a battle, but France has not lost the war." He concluded his radio address by inviting all Frenchman who could help to join him in London.

The next four years were a series of battles not only against France's Nazi occupiers, but also against British and American Allies, who often denigrated France's contributions to the war and wanted only a compliant figurehead representing France. What they could not see was that de Gaulle remained true to the cause that had animated him from his youth: the honor and destiny of France. Fighting for a role and for independent recognition in every Allied collaboration and meeting, he finally prevailed as both the symbol and the leader of his country. On August 25, 1944 the Free French forces marched triumphantly through the streets of liberated Paris, with de Gaulle as their rightful leader. He would soon be elected head of France's first post-war government.

De Gaulle's rise to national leadership can be traced back to those events of June 1940. His actions evidence his decisiveness and moral courage. In choosing to defy the Nazis and the defeatist Vichy regime, de Gaulle put his own life on the line, and even risked the lives of his family members. But de Gaulle's actions also provide a vivid illustration of his keen sense of timing. Having decided to relinquish his army command and to fly to London, de Gaulle quickly recognized the power vacuum he faced. He realized that at that moment his countrymen needed above all the assurance that *someone* would champion their cause before their allies and the world. True, de Gaulle had few credentials. A relatively little-known army officer with almost no political experience, he was hardly the person most Frenchmen would think of as the voice of their nation. But by identifying the need, *at that moment,* for such a voice and by realizing that there was no time for delay to buttress his authority de Gaulle made that voice his own. His astonishingly rapid rise from the relative obscurity of military command to international statesmanship was the result of his keen sense of how and when to act.

Postwar Retreat amidst Political and Military Turmoil

The end of the war brought a return to democratic rule in the form of the French Fourth Republic. In many ways this was a revival of the Third Republic that had been in place before the war, and it suffered from many of the same problems of intense partisan politics, a revolving door of governments, and practical paralysis. In November 1945 a Constituent Assembly unanimously elected de Gaulle as head of the government; but, fed up with partisan bickering, he abruptly resigned office a few months later, blaming the party system. After an unsuccessful effort to foster a non-partisan conservative movement, Rally of the French People (RPF), de Gaulle retreated to his home in Colombey-les-Deux-Églises, a village about 250 kilometers southeast of Paris, where he would spend much of the next decade writing his memoirs. Some of de Gaulle's biographers have described the years following the Second World War as his "wandering in the desert," a time during which the man of destiny waited to complete his mission.

It proved to be a tumultuous period. At home, frequent changes of government and waves of strikes and inflation slowed recovery. Abroad, in Africa and Asia, rising independence movements, some nourished by Communist ideology, challenged France's control of its colonial possessions. The first of these to precipitate military action was the national liberation movement under Ho Chi Minh in Vietnam. The French Indochina War, as it was called, lasted from 1945 to 1954, when it culminated in a humiliating defeat of the French forces in the battle of Dien Bien Phu. France left Indochina, but its army smarted from another reversal on the field of battle, and at home the political climate was as toxic as ever.

Indochina had barely faded from the scene when the conflict in Algeria erupted. France had been in Algeria since the 1830s. Over the years, many citizens of France and other European countries had emigrated there and established a flourishing national culture and economy. Named possibly after their role in the wine industry, these "Black Feet" (Pieds-Noirs) were a shrinking Algerian minority in a rapidly growing indigenous Muslim population, and, while there were many poor laborers among the Pieds-Noirs, the group as a whole was economically, legally, and socially dominant, controlling most aspects of Algerian life. France regarded Algeria, unlike her other possessions, not as a colony but as an integral part of the French nation. Its abandonment was as unthinkable to most Frenchman as the US's giving up of Alaska or Hawaii.

Over the years, various attempts had been made to expand participation by the Muslim population in the political and economic life of the country, but most had failed in the face of strong opposition from Pied-Noir leaders. Harsh repression of nationalist stirrings only fanned discontent in the Muslim majority. In early May 1945, local authorities in Sétif, a market town in northeastern Algeria, used force against Muslim demonstrators, who then went on a rampage, killing 103 non-Muslims. In the days that followed the French army and Pied-Noir mobs killed about 6,000 Muslim Algerians.

Long-simmering discontent in the indigenous population exploded into full-scale war on November 1, 1954 when, under the leadership of the newly formed National Liberation Front (FLN), guerrillas launched attacks in various parts of Algeria against military and civilian targets in what became known as "La Toussaint Sanglante" (Bloody All-Saints' Day). France soon countered by escalating its involvement: the troop presence raised to more than 400,000 soldiers, including many conscripts, whose rising death toll made the war a source of growing controversy back in France. Frequent acts of terrorism against civilians, reprisals on all sides, and massive movements of population for security purposes soon made this what one writer has described as "a savage war of peace."[5]

Controversy intensified in the wake of the Battle of Algiers, which commenced on September 30, 1956, when three Muslim women simultaneously placed bombs at three civilian sites in downtown Algiers, including a milk bar frequented by Pied-Noir young people. Reprisals and civilian casualties mounted on both sides. After months of struggle, the French army, under the leadership of a tough general, Jacques Massu, subdued the outbreak. But, in order to achieve this and to break up the secretive FLN cells, Massu used torture to extract information from captured militants. Although the Battle of Algiers was technically a victory for French forces, memories of Gestapo torture were still close to the surface in France. These reports from Algeria greatly increased internal French divisions about the wisdom of the country's involvement in the war.

By early 1958 dissent was nearing crescendo, with many French intellectuals and leftists protesting in the streets and calling for a pullout. Although the army had made great strides in defeating the FLN insurgency in cities and in the countryside, the conflict was unending and FLN prestige was on the rise; anti-colonialist countries like Russia, China, and the United States were voicing criticisms of the war. Still sensitive about their loss in Vietnam and fearing that Paris politicians would squander their hard-won achievements on the battlefield, a number of army leaders took matters in their own hands.

On the night of May 13, 1958 an army junta under General Massu seized power in Algiers. Another general, Raoul Salan, assumed leadership of a Committee of Public Safety formed to replace the civil authority there. On May 24 French paratroopers from the Algerian corps landed on the French island of Corsica, taking the island in a bloodless action. Simultaneously, preparations were being made in Algeria for Operation Resurrection, which was aimed at the seizure of Paris by paratroop forces and at the removal of the French government.

During this turmoil de Gaulle was widely regarded as sympathetic to the army and opposed to the weak leadership of the Fourth Republic. Shortly before midnight on May 13, Massu had stated:

> We appeal to General de Gaulle, the only man who is capable of heading a Government of Public Safety, above all the parties, in order to ensure the perpetuation of French Algeria as an integral part of France.[6]

De Gaulle distanced himself from the acts of the rebels in Algiers; but, under pressure from various factions and assured by the politicians that real political reform would follow, he decided to accept the post of prime minister. On June 1, just hours before the projected launch of Operation Resurrection, his appointment was overwhelmingly approved by the French parliament.

Taking Command

De Gaulle faced an unenviable situation. France teetered on the verge of civil war. Nothing short of a perpetuation of "French Algeria," the Pieds-Noirs' term for their continued control and dominance, would satisfy them. With its pride at stake, the army would not be easily pacified. Yet the FLN uprising, if momentarily under control, would not go away and was gaining momentum through international support.

If the conspirators thought they had a friend in de Gaulle, they were badly mistaken. De Gaulle had little affection for the Pied-Noir settlers or "colons," whose intransigence and placement of their own interests above those of France he despised. Furthermore, de Gaulle could not forget that the Pieds-Noirs had once been fervent supporters of the Vichy regime.

In a deeper sense, de Gaulle had the breadth of vision to see that France's continued control of Algeria was impossible. He realized three things. First, that France's burden of modernizing Algeria and of quelling the discontent of its indigenous population had become unsupportable. The country, which had once been a source of wealth, had now become an ever-expanding liability. Second, he recognized that, all over the world, colonial peoples were demanding independence and were willing to accept enormous sacrifices to achieve it. Writing in his memoir he noted the force of both these developments:

> While progress, there as elsewhere, multiplied needs, we were obliged to bear the increasing costs of administration, public works, education, social services, health and security over vast areas while at the same time we witnessed a growing desire for emancipation which made our yoke seem heavy if not intolerable to our subjects.[7]

Finally, he took note of the demographics. In 1958 Algeria's indigenous population numbered over 10 million people, alongside a Pied-Noir population of barely one million. More importantly, with families of six, seven, or eight children, the growth rate of the Muslim population was much higher than that of Europeans. De Gaulle realized that these facts rendered any effort to maintain a French Algeria impossible: continued political control by the "colons" had become impossible. They also ruled out any attempt to pacify all factions by increasing Muslim sovereignty within a French framework; for, in time, a growing Muslim Algeria (within decades, its population would expand to nearly 40 million) would become the tail that wagged the dog of the home country. Although de Gaulle hoped to establish some kind of continued "association" between the French and their former colony – something on the lines of Britain's strongest commonwealth relationships – he realized almost from the outset that the only long-term solution was to cut the tie.

Nevertheless, with civil war impending, this was not the time to announce such a policy. De Gaulle knew that he had to proceed deliberately – and cautiously. He needed time to apprise himself of the options, and, even more importantly, to prepare the country for the difficult decisions ahead. With good timing and political sensitivity, he decided that the first thing to do was to calm things down. In his memoir he describes his thinking at this moment:

As for my tactics, I should have to proceed cautiously from one stage to the next. Only gradually, using each crisis as a springboard, for further advance, could I hope to create a current of consent powerful enough to carry all before it. Were I to announce my intentions point-blank, there was no doubt that the sea of ignorant fear, of shocked surprise, of concerted malevolence through which I was navigating would cause such a tidal wave of alarms and passions in every walk of life that the ship would capsize. I must, therefore, maneuver without ever changing course until such time as, unmistakably, common sense broke through the mists.[8]

After taking power, on June 4, 1958 de Gaulle flew to Algiers. Speaking from a balcony of the general government building before a vast crowd of Pieds-Noirs and many Muslims, de Gaulle delivered a short speech in which he declared: "I have understood you!" ("*Je vous ai compris*"). He would later describe these words as "seemingly spontaneous but in reality carefully calculated" and aimed at establishing "emotional contact."[9] This ambiguous proclamation soothed Pied-Noir feelings and eased the immediate threat of civil war. It also committed de Gaulle to no set policy.

During the months that followed, de Gaulle turned much of his attention to political renewal in France. In a September referendum nearly 80 per cent of voters approved the constitution of the Fifth Republic, which would greatly strengthen the position of the president above party politics. In December de Gaulle became the first president of the new Republic. In 1958 and 1959 he also made repeated visits to Algeria, often touring frontline military outposts in what came to be known as "the tour of the mess halls." Each of these visits gave him a chance to advance the idea of an end to the war on the basis of initiatives that would grant some kind of independence to the entire Algerian population. With his profound knowledge of the army, de Gaulle sought to balance two seemingly conflicting imperatives. On the one hand, he applauded the army's progress in pacifying the country and in suppressing the rebellion. Behind this was his conviction that, for the sake of both the army and the nation, France's disengagement from Algeria could not be seen as compelled by military setbacks. In de Gaulle's words, "I . . . wanted our forces to remain masters of the territory until such time as I deemed it advisable to withdraw them."[10]

On the other hand, de Gaulle also had to convey to the army and others the message that France's hegemony in Algeria must come to an end, that democratic self-determination for the entire Algerian population was the only alternative. In a meeting with leading military officers in Algiers, he delivered praise along with a stern warning:

Having expressed lively satisfaction at what my inspection had revealed to me as regards the military situation, I went on to say that "although the success of the operations in progress was essential whatever happened, the Algerian problem would not be solved thereby . . . that it could not be solved until we eventually reached an understanding with the Algerians . . . As for yourselves, mark my words! You are not an Army for its own sake. You are the Army of France. You exist only through her, for her and in her service. It is I who, in view of my position and my responsibilities, must be obeyed by the Army in order that France should survive. I am confident of your obedience and I thank you for it in the name of France."[11]

Day by day and step by step, de Gaulle was leading both his French country-men and the Algerians to some form of independence that he knew was inevitable. In September 1959, in a broadcast, he laid out three options for Algeria: total independence; total integration with metropolitan France; or association, "government of Algerians by Algerians, supported by French aid in close union with France."[12] Although de Gaulle favored the third, it was clear that he would not oppose a complete separation from France if the majority of the Algerian population demanded it.

By now the most intransigent elements of the Pied-Noir population real-ized that de Gaulle, whom they thought they had brought to power to support their cause, was not their friend. Anger erupted in January 1960, when Pied-Noir militants staged a revolt in Algiers, occupying public places in what came to be known as "the week of the barricades." From Paris, de Gaulle, appearing in his military uniform, broadcast an address in which he called on the army to remain loyal and rallied popular support for his Algerian policy. Within days the revolt collapsed.

French fatigue with the war and growing anger at the Pieds-Noirs' intran-sigence were accelerating an acceptance of the idea of Algerian independence. In January 1961 de Gaulle placed a referendum before the entire French and Algerian populations, asking whether independence should be granted to Algeria once peace had been restored. Of French voters, 75 percent said yes; and 70 percent of Algerians did so as well.[13] In late April another coup erupted, as rebels and troops supporting them seized control of Algiers and arrested representatives of the government. De Gaulle's response was swift. Acting on a provision of the constitution that granted the president emergency powers, he broadcast to the nation and ordered all troops to remain loyal and to oppose the generals leading the insurrection. The attempted coup ground to a halt.

Now Algerian independence was inevitable. In May 1961, in Evian, Geneva, de Gaulle's government opened negotiations with the GPRA (the Provisional

Government of the Republic of Algeria), the political arm of the Algerian liberation movement. Talks would drag on for a year, and most of de Gaulle's own demands, including enhanced security for the European population and a continued foothold for France in Algeria, would be abandoned. But on March 19, 1962, more than four years after de Gaulle took power, the Evian accords went into effect, following two referenda that received wide support. Algeria was now an independent country and France was freed from responsibility for its future.

For some, the immediate consequences of these events were tragic. In May 1961, at the onset of the Evian negotiations, a cabal of disenchanted army officers led by General Salan formed the Secret Army Organization (OAS). Declaring a no holds barred war on the Muslim population and on the French supporters of independence, they had the aim to impose their will on the indigenous Algerians and to create an independent Algeria under Pied-Noir control. The result was a bloody campaign killing thousands, which reached into France itself. In August 1962, months after the Evian accords went into effect, OAS agents ambushed de Gaulle's car as he drove with his wife and family to the airport. Out of the 150-odd bullets aimed at them, fourteen hit the car, but the General and his family members were unhurt.

In Algeria, Pied-Noir residents, members of the Jewish community, and Muslims who had supported the French presence found themselves under assault. Turning to a vengeful policy of destroying every asset of the French colonial presence, the OAS embarked on waves of property destruction and killings. On its side, the FLN, in an effort to eliminate the European presence, announced a policy of "the suitcase or the coffin." As a result, between May and June 1962 an average of seven thousand people a day crowded desperately onto boats and airplanes to Marseilles. There had been a million Europeans in Algeria, but fewer than a hundred thousand remained. For many of the refugees, years of hardship lay ahead as they struggled to re-start their lives in what was to them a foreign country.

Aftermath

Although there was a great human and financial toll to France's disengagement from Algeria, it soon dwindled next to the enormous boost in self-confidence and energy produced by releasing the country from the burden of the Algerian conflict. De Gaulle was now free to pursue his goal of restoring France's global prestige, which included extricating it from dependence on Anglo-American military support through the development of France's own atomic strike force, and promoting its pivotal role in the European community. Under his leadership, France made significant progress toward realizing his childhood dream: "France cannot be France without greatness."

De Gaulle arrived in London in June 1940 with little more than his personal baggage and a resolve to save his country from defeat. With scant support and in the face of outright opposition, he nevertheless realized that someone had to act, and act immediately. Within days, his voice stirred his nation's rebirth and his own rise to eminence. In May 1958 it was not immediate action that was called for but slow advance against a formidable array of obstacles. Although de Gaulle was committed from the start to some form of Algerian independence, he realized that France was not yet ready, that the army was not ready, and that he had to educate his countrymen into the reality of independence. This included allowing events themselves to render the costs of continued involvement clearer. He also sensed that, if he proceeded cautiously, his opponents' fanaticism would lead to their marginalization.

Separated by eighteen years, these two episodes in de Gaulle's life illustrate his understanding that as important as the act itself is the choice of *when* to act. Whatever else they exemplify, these moments in his career testify to the virtue of good timing.

Notes to Chapter Fourteen

1   Michael E. Haskew, *De Gaulle: Lessons in Leadership from the Defiant General*. Palgrave Macmillan, 2011, p. vii.
2   Ibid., p. 17–18.
3   Ibid., p. 75.
4   Don Cook, *Charles De Gaulle: A Biography*. New York: G. P. Putnam's, 1983, p. 72.
5   See Alistair Horne's history *A Savage War of Peace: Algeria 1954–1962*. New York: New York Review of Books, 1977, 1987, 1996, 2006.
6   Andrew Shennan, *De Gaulle*. London and New York: Longman, 1993, p. 79.
7   Charles de Gaulle, *Memoirs of Hope: Renewal and Endeavor*. New York: Simon & Schuster, 1970, p. 38.
8   Ibid., pp. 46–47.
9   Ibid., p. 47.
10 Ibid., p. 86.
11 Ibid., p. 75.
12 Shennan, *De Gaulle*, p. 97.
13 Edward A. Kolodziej, *French International Policy under de Gaulle and Pompidou: The Politics of Grandeur*. Ithaca, NY: Cornell University Press, 1974, p. 460.

MARTIN LUTHER KING, JR.
DEEP SELFLESSNESS

If a man hasn't discovered something that he will die for, he isn't fit to live.
Martin Luther King, Jr., June 23, 1963[1]

Genuine leaders display deep selflessness. They put their cause, their purpose, their calling before themselves. They live, as Ignatius of Loyola suggested, "a life for others." However, this does not mean that they are saints. Their lives, like those of all of us, display flaws, momentary lapses, and episodes of self-indulgence. Despite this, however, their focus remains fixed on concepts, issues, or communities beyond themselves. Nowhere is this truer than in the life of Martin Luther King, Jr.

Centuries before King lived, Marcus Tullius Cicero, Roman statesman, orator, and philosopher, distrusted and disliked the young and ambitious Julius Caesar because he thought that Caesar's desire for power was purely personal. Cicero believed that Caesar did not just wish to rule Rome; he believed that Caesar wanted to be Rome.

Ambition can be a virtue or a vice, a driving force or a destructive preoccupation. It can result in energy, enthusiasm, and efficiency. Or it can result in self-indulgence, self-gratification, and selfishness. Cicero thought that Caesar was a *misleader* whose vision was solely focused on the acquisition of power for the purposes of self-aggrandizement. For him, Caesar was a slave to his vanity and covetousness.

From a larger historical perspective, it can be argued that perhaps the core failures and vices of all overly ambitious misleaders are the two deadliest among Pope Gregory the Great's "seven deadly sins" – pride and envy.

10 Virtues of Outstanding Leaders: Leadership and Character, First Edition.
Al Gini and Ronald M. Green.
© 2013 John Wiley & Sons, Inc. Published 2013 by John Wiley & Sons, Inc.

Spinoza claims that pride is a "species of madness" because it leads us to think that we can accomplish all things. The fundamental psychology of pride is that it produces a distorted view of self and the world. Pride is about self-absorption, excessive self-esteem, inordinate self-love, and egregious self-evaluation. The *Oxford English Dictionary* defines pride as "an unreasonable conceit of superiority . . . and overweening opinion of one's qualities, talents, and abilities."[2]

In effect, what pride does is to strip the ability of a person to be objective, to make sound judgments, to be critical. Pride is an excuse for excess, a roadblock to moderation, and a stairway to arrogance. Pride, says poet and Trappist monk Thomas Menton, robs us of our humility and our basic concern for objectivity, because we are constantly focused on self.[3] For Thomas Aquinas, pride is more than narcissism; it is the "distorted desire to be exalted." This desire, suggests Aquinas, leads to an exaggeration of our ability and rights and contempt for the ability and rights of others. For Aquinas, pride is the beginning of every sin and, by his reckoning, the "queen of them all."[4] Pride leads to complete "selfishness" and to the total abandonment of the concept of "selflessness."

If pride is the queen of the seven deadly sins, clearly envy is her lady in waiting. Envy may be the most pervasive of all the sins. Envy is both a positive and a negative part of the human condition. It figures in all of our interactions with others. It is a part of our competitive nature as well as of our contemptuous feelings toward those who seem to be or to do better than us.[5]

Envy is not just about wanting, desiring what others have. Envy is about resenting the good things others have, be they status, talents, abilities, or possessions. Envy is not just desire. It is the inordinate desire for that which belongs to another – whatever that might be.[6] To be envious is to covet, to be deeply angry, and to harbor hostility, malice, and hatred. In effect, when the envious person sees someone of greater good fortune, his or her response is: "Why not me? Why this person instead?" To deeply envy another means "I want your life!" and "I hate you for having it." Immanuel Kant argues that envy is an "abominable vice, a passion not only distressing and tormenting to the subject, but intent on the destruction of the happiness of others."[7] Building on Kant, philosopher John Rawls argues that envy is an antirational sentiment that is socially dangerous because it diminishes the possibility of achieving fairness and justice between individuals. Envy, says Rawls, "is a form of rancor that tends to harm both its object and its subject."[8]

Given the crippling effects of pride and envy, what Cicero was suggesting is that misleaders see leadership as their right, not as a responsibility to others. Misleaders seek subordinates and sycophants, not associates and partners. Misleaders are unnecessarily self-absorbed and suffer from the delusion of omniscience. They seek their own agenda and actively deny the concept that "the ultimate task of leadership is to create human energies and human vision."[9] Misleaders subscribe to Louis XIV of France's famous statement *l'état, c'est moi* ("I am the state").

Perhaps the single, overarching problem regarding all forms of leadership is the need for "impartiality" and the ability to overcome our natural tendency to be self-absorbed. Leaders need to focus on those they lead. Misleaders find it hard to do this because they find it hard to stand outside the shadow of self. Ethical leadership is possible only when leaders are able to step away from themselves – or, to borrow a phrase, "forget themselves on purpose." Leaders must be able to see beyond their own self-contained universe of personal concerns.[10] They must be able to become more selfless than selfish. Martin Luther King, Jr. was such a leader.

His Calling

Martin Luther King, Jr., in his life and in his death, has been loved and worshipped, hated and feared by millions. Born on January 1, 1929 and assassinated on April 4, 1968, he had a public career that only lasted 13 years (1956 to 1968), and yet his ministry, his mission, his leadership irrevocably altered the course of civil rights in America.

Martin Luther King, Jr. was not a saint, not even a perfect husband. As an ordained Baptist minister who publicly preached the virtue of temperance, he nevertheless liked to drink, he regularly smoked, and he enjoyed expensive restaurants. He was also very conscious of clothes, style, and fashion and took great pride and pleasure in the cut and fit of his suits. Although he had always been a good student and a solid scholar, after his death it was revealed that he plagiarized large portions of his doctoral dissertation. A number of his biographers have pointed out that King had numerous extra-marital liaisons. To draw on former Democratic Senator Gary Hart's comment about his own indiscretions, King was not always "perfectly faithful" to his marital vows. Moreover, King's attitude toward women in general would probably be deemed sexist today. He, like so many men of his era, thought that women's role and status in society was secondary to that of men. Although he was an apostle of racial equality, King believed that a woman's proper place was at home, in the role of wife and mother. Great moral leaders are not always perfectly moral in their private lives. Like any human being, leaders are fallible, and their private behavior often does not mirror their public persona. Yet, even when a leader is flawed, he or she can still remain committed, focused, and faithful to a cause larger than him- or herself. Only when these flaws compromise that larger commitment should we question both his/her character and his/her efficacy as a leader.

Martin Luther King, Jr. never thought of himself as a revolutionary fire-brand or a social activist. Raised in segregated Atlanta, he nevertheless had the privilege of growing up in the "cradle of a black bourgeois lifestyle" where his father, Martin Luther King, Sr., was a community leader and a pastor of Eben-ezer Baptist Church. A loving son, a solid student and a Christian believer, King, Jr. dutifully followed in the footsteps of both his father and grandfather and entered the seminary.

When the newly ordained King, Jr. accepted the pastorate of the Dexter Avenue Baptist church in Montgomery, Alabama, he was not yet a man on a mission or driven to be an agent of change. He thought he would serve the community for a few years, and then perhaps pursue an academic career. But, when Rosa Parks refused to surrender her bus seat to a white man on the afternoon of December 1, 1955, King became the champion of her cause. Suddenly and without anticipating or seeking it, King, at 26 years of age, became the leader of a 386-day-long bus boycott that proved to be the first event in the modern American civil rights movement.

His leadership in Montgomery immediately thrust him into the national limelight.

> This is not the life I expected to lead. But gradually you take some responsibility, then a little more . . . You have to give yourself entirely. Then once you make up your mind that you are giving yourself, you are prepared to do anything that serves that Cause and advances the Movement. I have reached that point. I have given myself fully.[11]

By his own admission, King both lost and found himself when he gave himself over to a cause larger than himself.[12] He had not sought leadership, but, once it was given to him, he embraced it and accepted the fact that leaders are necessary and that leaders must necessarily lead. From the very first meeting to organize the bus boycott in Montgomery, King's life was forever changed and no longer his own. He became more and more the face and the heart and soul of a movement.

As King's involvement grew, his schedule became increasingly hectic. He desperately tried to wrestle with the demands of writing, speechmaking, lob-bying, fundraising, administering, pastoring, planning, and campaigning. According to one estimate, he delivered 350 speeches during 1963, traveled over 275,000 miles, and spent nine days in ten away from home. In King's own words, "I . . . find myself so involved I hardly have time to breathe."[13] And yet he persisted, because he was convinced that people are often led to a cause and often become committed to great ideas through persons who personify those ideas. They have to find the embodiment of the idea in flesh and blood in order to commit themselves to it.[14]

King wanted to be a leader, a witness for others. His own needs, including those of his family, took second place to the cause.

His Gift

Robert Bly, poet and leader of the Men's Movement, called Martin Luther King, Jr. the quintessential charismatic leader.[15] To begin with, said Bly, King was a gifted and compelling speaker. He had extraordinary ability to orchestrate his words, tone, timing, and timbre into a message that riveted an audience's attention. Bly said that King had the ability to hook an audience with his voice, and that he used his voice as a tool, a vocal instrument, to capture the attention of his listeners. The rhythm of his voice, his phrasing, his ability to dramatically control and project the volume of his voice drew audiences in and invited them to pay attention to what was being said.

But, said Bly, as any musician will tell you, technique is never enough. The perfect instrument and the most solid technique are nothing without a good score to play – or, in an orator's case, something worthwhile to say. King was an *auteur*, an original creator of his own material. King, said Bly, was not only a messenger (a magnificent speaker); he also had a message. A message he believed in. A message he felt compelled to share with others. A message he dedicated his life to.

Among the best examples of King's mission and message are his "Letter from a Birmingham Jail," April 16, 1963, and his speech "I've Been to the Mountaintop," April 3, 1968. While other cities in the South were making some progress in dismantling segregation, Birmingham, Alabama remained firmly entrenched in a system of racial separation and open hostility to any form of racial equality. In the spring of 1963, King was invited to Birmingham to spearhead a series of demonstrations against racial bullying and segregation. On April 12, 1963, which was Good Friday, King and a group of other protesters were arrested. While in jail, King wrote a letter to a group of eight white clergymen who had already published an open letter entitled "An Appeal for Law and Order and Common Sense." This previous letter implied that the protesters were anarchists, extremists, and law breakers. It also asked King and the other leaders of the protest to be more moderate and patient in their demands.

King's response was sincere, conciliatory, and compelling. He told them he was in Birmingham because "injustice is in Birmingham," and "injustice anywhere is a threat to justice everywhere." He wrote that, as a minister and as one who loved the church, he felt compelled to disobey any unjust law, because according to Christian teaching "an unjust law is no law at all." He told them he was there as a man of the Gospel doing the work of the Lord.

> Just as the prophets of the eighth century BC left their villages and carried their "thus saith the Lord" far beyond the boundaries of their hometowns, and just as the Apostle Paul left his village of Tarsus and carried the gospel of Jesus Christ to the far corners of the Greco-Roman world, so am I compelled to carry the gospel of freedom beyond my own hometown. Like Paul, I must constantly respond to the Macedonian call for aid.[16]

"I am here," he continued, because

> We have waited for more than 340 years for our constitutional and God-given rights . . . Perhaps it is easy for those who have never felt the stinging darts of segregation to say, "Wait." . . . [But] when you are harried by day and haunted by night by the fact that you are a Negro, living constantly at tiptoe stance, never quite knowing what to expect next, and are plagued with inner fears and outer resentments; when you are forever fighting a degenerating sense of "nobodiness" – then you will understand why we find it difficult to wait. There comes a time when the cup of endurance runs over, and men are no longer willing to be plunged into the abyss of despair. I hope, sirs, you can understand our legitimate and unavoidable impatience.[17]

He wrote that he was saddened that his fellow clergymen were seemingly more "devoted to order than to justice." He was saddened that they found his method of "nonviolent direct action" dangerous and extremist.

> Was not Jesus an extremist for love: "Love your enemies, bless them that curse you, do good to them that hate you, and pray for them which despitefully use you, and persecute you." Was not Amos an extremist for justice: "Let justice roll like waters and righteousness like an ever-flowing stream." Was not Paul an extremist for the Christian gospel: "I bear in my body the marks of the Lord Jesus." Was not Martin Luther an extremist: "Here I stand; I cannot do otherwise, so help me God."[18]

Finally, he wrote, that except for a few notable exceptions, he was "disappointed with the Church."

> I have traveled the length and breadth of Alabama, Mississippi, and all the other Southern states. On sweltering summer days and crisp autumn mornings I have

looked at the South's beautiful churches with their lofty spires pointing heav-
enward. I have beheld the impressive outlines of her massive religious-education
buildings. Over and over I have found myself asking: "What kind of people
worship here? Who is their God? Where were their voices of support when
bruised and weary Negro men and women decided to rise from the dark dun-
geons of complacency to the bright hills of creative protest?"[19]

King concluded by saying that he loved the church and saw it as the body of
Christ. But he warned that we have, through social neglect and fear, scarred
the body of Christ and blemished his mission. We have forgotten, he said, a
basic fact of social justice: "Oppressed people cannot and will not remain
repressed forever."

King's words to his fellow clergymen were carefully chosen. He wanted
them to know that he and his people were growing impatient. He wanted them
to be fully aware of the injustice he and his people had borne. But his words
were not full of rage and hatred. He wanted to be passionate, but not hostile.
His point was to apprise them of "the Negro's plight" and to remind them of
their Christian duty to offer help and assistance.

Perhaps the clearest statement of King's deep selflessness can be found in
the speech he delivered the night before he died in Memphis, Tennessee. He
spoke that night as a pastor and as a person. He spoke as a leader and as a
fellow follower. He spoke as someone determined to be free, committed to
nonviolence, and fully aware of the risks that he knew were endemic to his
role in the Civil Rights Movement.

In March 1968 King agreed to go to Memphis to support 1,300 black sani-
tation workers who were on strike for higher wages and with whom the all-
white city administration refused to negotiate. On March 28 King led a
demonstration that went terribly wrong. Windows were broken, stores were
looted, police attacked the crowd in full riot gear, and a young black boy was
shot and killed. King was horrified and distressed by the violence and pledged
to organize a "massive disciplined nonviolent demonstration on April 5," to
protest both the injustice of the police's violence and the refusal of the city
to enter into fair and honest negotiations with its public servants.

On the night of April 3, 1968 King addressed a rally at the Masonic Temple,
in support of the scheduled demonstration on April 5. He had been sick and
he was tired, so he considered not going. But he had made a promise, and he
kept his word.

I'm just happy that God has allowed me to live in this period, to see what is
unfolding . . . And I'm happy that he's allowed me to be in Memphis . . . I can
remember when Negroes were just going around . . . scratching where they

didn't itch and laughing when they were not tickled. But that day is all over. We mean business now, and we are determined to be people . . .

We don't have to argue with anybody . . . We don't have to curse and go around acting bad with our words. We don't need any bricks and bottles, we don't need any Molotov cocktails, we just need to go around and say, "God sent us by here, to say to you that you're not treating his children right. And we've come by here to ask you to make the first item on your agenda – fair treatment."

Now, let me say as I move to my conclusion that we've got to give ourselves to this struggle until the end . . . Be concerned about your brother . . . either we go up together, or we go down together. Let us develop a dangerous unselfishness . . . [Jesus once] talked about a certain man, who fell among thieves . . . a Levite and a priest passed by on the other side. They didn't stop to help him. And finally a man of another race came by. He got down from his beast, decided not to be compassionate by proxy. But he got down with him, administered first aid, and helped the man in need. Jesus ended up saying, this was the good man, this was the great man, because he had the capacity to project the "I" into "thou," and to be concerned about his brother . . . And so the first question that the priest asked – the first question the Levite asked was, "If I stop to help this man, what will happen to me?" But then the Good Samaritan came by. And he reversed the question: "If I do not stop to help this man, what will happen to him?"

Well, I don't know what will happen now . . . We've got some difficult days ahead. But it doesn't matter with me now. Because I've been to the mountaintop. And I don't mind. Like anybody, I would like to live a long life. Longevity has its place. But I'm not concerned about that now. I just want to do God's will. And He's allowed me to go up the mountain. And I've looked over. And I've seen the promised land. I may not get there with you. But I want you to know tonight, that we, as a people will get to the promised land. And I'm happy, tonight. I'm not worried about anything. I'm not fearing any man. Mine eyes have seen the glory of the coming of the Lord.[20]

The next day, April 4, 1968, King and his staff met to work out the details of the upcoming march. Around 6 p.m. he left his room at the Lorraine Motel for a dinner engagement. While talking with some colleagues on the balcony that overlooked the parking lot of the hotel, a single shot rang out. The bullet struck him in the head. One hour later, 39-year-old Martin Luther King, Jr. was dead.

In his last speech King drew on a biblical tradition he knew extremely well. In the last paragraphs of that speech he evoked the imagery and reminded the audience of Moses. Although Moses led his people out of slavery, he never saw the promised land. Like Moses, King helped his people out of bondage, but he did not live long enough to share in the final victory. Martin Luther King,

Jr. did not seek out death. He did not invite martyrdom. Nor did he ever present himself as a sacrificial offering. But he fully knew the risks he was taking. He was always aware of the animosity and dangers he faced. He understood the dark side of racial conflict. He was aware that his words and his actions were perceived as a threat and a danger by others. From his earliest involvement in the bus boycott in Montgomery, Alabama, he accepted the fact that he was in harm's way. At the personal level, although King relished life, his deep selflessness readied him for the worst.

His Legacy

Martin Luther King, Jr. had a cause and a dream. But it was not just his cause or his dream. It was about his people, all people, God's people. It was his job to be the messenger and the interpreter, both of the dream and of the cause. It was his job to exhort others to pursue that dream and cause. It was his job to live a life dedicated to that dream and cause – a life for others.

The biblical text on which King's last sermon drew suggests the powerful truth that the greatest leaders may never witness the personal fulfillment of their dreams. They always risk looking on from the distant mountaintop. That image symbolizes the deep selflessness that great leadership requires.

Notes to Chapter Fifteen

1 Quoted in Roy B. Zuck, *The Speaker's Quote Book: Over 5,000 Illustrations and Quotations for All Occasions*. Grand Rapids, MI: Kregel Academic, 2009, p. 140.

2 Henry Fairlie, *The Seven Deadly Sins Today*. Notre Dame, IN: Notre Dame Press, 1979, p. 39.

3 Solomon Schimmel, *The Seven Deadly Sins*. New York: Oxford University Press, 1997, p. 40.

4 Thomas Aquinas, *Summa theologica I–II*, translated by Fathers of the English Dominican Province. New York: Benziger Brothers, 1947, Question 84, Art. 2, at p. 863.

5 Joseph Epstein, *Envy*. New York: Oxford University Press, 2003, p. xvi.

6 Ibid., pp. 18, 19, 21, 53.

7 Ibid., p. xx.

8 J. Rawls, *A Theory of Justice*. Cambridge, MA: Harvard University Press, 1971, p. 533.

9 Peter F. Drucker, "Leadership: More Doing Than Dash." *The Wall Street Journal*, January 6, 1988.

10 Brian J. Mahan, *Forgetting Ourselves on Purpose*. San Francisco, CA: Jossey-Bass, 2002.

11   Donald T. Phillips, *Martin Luther King, Jr. on Leadership*. New York: Warner Books, 1999, p. 42.

12   Martin Luther King, Jr., *The Autobiography of Martin Luther King, Jr.*, edited by C. Carson. New York: Warner Books, 1998, p. 1.

13   Ibid., pp. 48, 91.

14   Phillips, *Martin Luther King, Jr. on Leadership*, p. 42.

15   Robert Bly, "Message or Messenger?" WBEZ-FM, Chicago Public Radio: Interview with Al Gini, October 25, 1991.

16   Adam Fairclough, *Martin Luther King, Jr.* Athens, GA: University of Georgia Press, 1995, p. 189.

17   Ibid., p. 192.

18   Ibid., p. 198.

19   Ibid., p. 200.

20   Phillips, *Martin Luther King, Jr. on Leadership*, pp. 326, 328.

CONCLUSION

Skillful pilots gain their reputation from storms and tempests.

Attributed to Epicurus[1]

No one book can do complete justice to a topic as complex as leadership by covering every facet of it. Leadership is more than a set of facts or theories; it is a lived process. Time, place, issues, problems, circumstances, and the particular individuals involved shape the outcomes and play a crucial role in achieving success or failure. The leadership equation is never set or fixed. There is no one prescription for leadership. And there is no one model leader, who embodies a perfect temperament and has all the tools and talents necessary for being successful in any and every arena – be it politics, war, religion, or business. In an article entitled "In Praise of the Incomplete Leader," Deborah Ancona and her colleagues claim that no leader is perfect. In fact the best ones don't even try. Rather they concentrate on honing their own strengths and skills while at the same time searching for others who can make up for their limitations.[2]

Just as there is no one perfect leader, there is no one perfect set of leadership virtues. Nor can any one text delineate and develop all of the technical competencies and talents needed for successful leadership. Having said that, we feel remiss, in regard to this text, because we have not developed more fully at least one other key factor in the leadership equation: the fundamental role of experience and pain, trial and failure in the development of individual leaders.

Warren Bennis and Robert Thomas have argued that "the ability to learn is a defining characteristic of being human; and the ability to continue

10 Virtues of Outstanding Leaders: Leadership and Character, First Edition.
Al Gini and Ronald M. Green.

learning is an essential skill of leaders."[3] For Bennis and Thomas, real learning is the result of time, experience, effort, education, involvement, achieving success, and, most importantly, experiencing setbacks and real failure. As in the detailed curriculum laid out by Plato in the *Republic* for the training of the rulers of the state, Bennis and Thomas argue that the ability to be a leader is the result of training, time on the job, the capacity to survive the test of both minor and major failures, and the talent to extract both wisdom and skills from these experiences.

Bennis and Thomas are convinced that

> one of the most reliable indicators and predictors of true leadership is an individual's ability to find meaning in negative events and to learn from even the most trying of circumstances.[4]

In other words, they believe that the skills required to conquer adversity and to emerge stronger from that experience are the same ones that make an extraordinary leader. They call these experiences that come to shape leaders "crucibles: a place, a time, or a situation characterized by the confluence of powerful, intellectual, social, economic or political forces; a severe test of patience or belief . . ."[5] They argue that this crucible is a trial, a test, a point of deep reflection that forces individuals to question who they are and what matters to them. "It requires them to examine their values, to question their assumptions, and to hone their judgments."[6] A "crucible," they argue, is a transformative experience in which the very basis of a person's identity and individual perspectives is challenged to the core.

According to Nelson Mandela, "[i]f I had not been in prison [for 27 years], I would not have been able to achieve the most difficult task in life, and that is changing yourself."[7] Mandela referred to his Robben Island cell, located just off of the coast of South Africa, as "the University." "The University of Prison," he argued, taught him to be a full human being. Moreover, it taught him self-control, discipline, and focus – things essential to leadership.[8] In the words of Aldous Huxley: "Experience is not what happens to a man. It is what a man does with what happens to him."[9]

Pain, suffering, illness can also be looked upon as a test, a crucible, that can lead to a transformative experience in a person's life. In his recent book, *A First-Rate Madness: Uncovering the Links between Leadership and Mental Illness*, psychiatrist Nassir Ghaemi argues that the trials of physical illness, of struggling with melancholy, of dealing with mood disorders, and/or of serious mental depression can result in a more objective and realistic perspective on reality, in hightened resilience, and in greater empathy for the shortcomings and sufferings of others. He argues, for example, that Abraham Lincoln's bouts with melancholy made him more empathetic to the plight of African American slaves. Ghaemi contends that Winston Churchill's episodes of the "black dog" (acute and often suicidal depression) heightened his ability to recognize the dark side of others, as well as the tenacity to prevail against foes. Finally, Ghaemi is convinced that Franklin D. Roosevelt's losing battle with polio totally changed his attitude toward life and others. In Eleanor Roosevelt's own words: "Anyone who has gone through great suffering is bound to have greater sympathy and understanding of the problems of mankind."[10] Polio, suggests Ghaemi, transformed FDR from being a politician who simply sought office into a reformer who rather sought office to serve the common good.[11]

At the core of Bennis's, Thomas's, and Ghaemi's argument regarding the challenge of crucibles and of difficult situations in general is the idea that crisis can produce in an individual what they consider to be the *sine qua non* capacity of successful leadership: adaptability. They argue that adaptive capacity – the ability to transcend the limits of a particular moment in time – is much more important than intelligence, talent, or specific skill sets, and that it is the defining competence required for leaders to do well despite life's inevitable changes and losses. Every national leader winds up governing a country and dealing with problems that they never expected to have to handle. This places a premium on the ability to adapt and change.

Continuing this line of thought, political journalist James Fallows argues that no leader or president is perfect and that every president or leader is bound to fail in various crucial aspects of his/her job. The reason for this is simple, says Fallows. Political leaders, especially a president, regularly fail (or are less than perfectly successful) because not to fail would require a perfect temperament and a range of native talents and learned skills that no real person can reasonably be expected to possess.

Fallows believes that leaders need the analytic ability to cope with a stream of short- and long-term decisions that come at them nonstop. They must be sufficiently self-aware to recognize their own defects and to try to offset them. They need to be well informed, omni-prepared, confident in their decision-making. They need to have a mission and a vision and yet to remain practical. They need to be physically fit, disease-resistant, and capable of being fully alert at a moment's notice. And they need to be political chess-masters, always able to see several moves ahead of their supporters and opponents.[12]

In the end, adaptability – the ability to deal with chaos, change, and constant turmoil – is the product of experience, patience, and practice. What Bennis, Thomas, Ghaemi, and Fallows are all suggesting is that ultimately leadership is a practical art form, and, as in all forms of art, proficiency is the product of experience, trial, and error.

Our attempt, in this text, has been modest. Our central thesis is that true leadership is based on character, ethics, and service to others. We do not deny that there are many non-ethical skills needed by a successful leader, not the least of which would be relevant competency. But we insist that, without a larger ethical commitment to guide leaders' and followers' purposes, even brilliant technical competence will end in organizational failure and destruction.

Certainly there have been many noted examples of unethical people at the top of major organizations, countries, and communities. Like comets across the sky, these are able to show flashes of brilliance, and they are sometimes called "great leaders." We have identified some of these people and called them "misleaders." In almost every case, such leaders have undermined their own personal flourishing and have pulled their followers down with them into the abyss.

We agree with Bennis that "the process of becoming a leader is much the same as the process of becoming a fully integrated human being."[13] We believe that this statement has a number of important implications. First, no leader – not even the best – is perfect or godlike. Each has his/her own share of human weaknesses and human strengths. Second, the opportunity to become a leader potentially stands before each of us. Given the right set of circumstances and personal strength of character, any one of us can poten- tially be of service as a leader in the various communities and organizations to which we belong. Third, all leadership virtues are acquired skills that grow with exercise and repetition. They are good habits, but they must be developed through practice in order to overtake the bad habits that always threaten us. As Aristotle has been interpreted to say:

> Excellence is an art won by training and habituation. We do not act rightly because we have virtue or excellence, but we rather have those because we have acted rightly. We are what we repeatedly do. Excellence, then, is not an act but a habit.[14]

Without embracing or endorsing any of the religious overtones of Robert K. Greenleaf's notion of "servant leadership," we find ourselves in full agreement with his basic thesis. For Greenleaf, the key ethical imperative of leadership comes from the fact that leadership is not about the leader. Greenleaf believes that the essence of leadership and of all forms of authority is the subordina- tion of one's self or one's ego to the needs and desires of a community of others.

> The servant–leader *is* servant first . . . It begins with the natural feelings that one wants to serve, to serve *first*. Then conscious choice brings one to aspire to

lead. That person is sharply different from one who is *leader* first, perhaps because of the need to assuage an unusual power drive or to acquire material possessions. For such, it will be a later choice to serve – after leadership is established. The leader-first and the servant-first are two extreme types. Between them are the shadings and blends that are part of the infinite variety of human nature. The difference manifests itself in the care taken by the servant-first to make sure that other people's highest priority needs are being served. The best test, and difficult to administer, is this: Do those served grow as persons? Do they, *while being served*, become healthier, wiser, freer, more autonomous, more likely themselves to become servants? And what is the effect on the least privileged in society? Will they benefit or at least not be further deprived?[15]

In a very real sense, Greenleaf's views on leadership mime and mirror psychologist Mihaly Csikszentmihalyi's meditation on the art of living with others. "One cannot lead a life that is truly excellent without feeling that one belongs to something greater and more permanent than oneself."[16] More bluntly, Steve Jobs called it "making a dent in the universe."

In the "Afterword" of the 25th anniversary edition of the publication of *Servant Leadership*, theorist Peter Senge argues that servant leadership does not only refer to servant leaders at the top. The concept of servant leadership must be applied at every level throughout organizational life. Anything less, says Senge, would deny the profound paradox that is the essence of servant leadership. Genuine leadership is both deeply personal and always inherently collective.[17]

Arguably one of the most obvious twentieth-century examples of what Greenleaf means by servant leadership is Nelson Mandela. Like Washington and Lincoln, of course, Mandela's true character and legacy is clouded by popular mythology and by the almost cult-like worship of a man who is revered by millions around the world.

We believe that one reason why Nelson Mandela is an undisputed icon of leadership excellence in our day is that he exemplifies so well many of our key leadership virtues. Exhibiting deep honesty, he refused ever to lie, to himself or to others. His word was his bond. Faced repeatedly with physical threats and death, he carried on, never relinquishing his core values. When others around him called for revenge and bloodshed, he had the moral judgment and vision to see that what was needed in order to build a nation was not hatred, not "our time has come," but reconciliation and forgiveness. He showed compassion even for those who would kill and torture him, and he earned their respect. His legendary fairness and sense of justice is captured in his remark: "Equal rights for all, regardless of race, class or gender, pretty much everything else is tactics."[18] Even while he was in prison, he read, he studied and developed his intellectual excellence, and he encouraged its development in those around him. Although life dictated Mandela's timing, he patiently used the years of confinement in such way that he could act decisively when his moment came. As far as deep selflessness is concerned, nothing captures his possession of this final key virtue more vividly than his closing words at the Rivonia trial in 1963–1964, where he was condemned to a life in prison:

> During my lifetime I have dedicated my self to [the] struggle of the African people. I have fought against white domination, and I have fought against black domination. I have cherished the idea of a democratic and free society in which all persons live together in harmony with equal opportunities. It is an ideal which I hope to live for and to achieve. But if need be, it is an ideal for which I am prepared to die.[19]

Unlike Mandela, outstanding leaders do not always possess the full roster of our virtues. Steve Jobs remains in some ways a blemished leader. He was a virtuoso of aesthetic sensitivity, good timing, creative thinking, and intellectual excellence. But, as his most recent biographer, Walter Isaacson, has observed, Jobs was often abusive with colleagues and subordinates. "Cruel and harmful," "cold and brutal," "petulant," "harsh," "rude," and "tyrannical" are among the adjectives that pepper Jobs's colleagues' descriptions of him in Isaacson's biography.[20] Nevertheless, Jobs grew as a person and manager. It may well be that his failures, the abrupt firing from Apple, the business reversals at NeXT, even his final encounter with cancer served to mature the brash young man and, in the end, produced one of the most outstanding business leaders in American history.

Then, of course, there is always the example of some great leader whom all of us admire and revere and whose conformity to our list of virtues seems almost complete. But then, suddenly, tragically, we see that a key virtue is not just unfulfilled in him, but seriously lacking. When this occurs, virtue becomes vice. Sadly for all of us, Penn State football coach Joe Paterno illustrates this phenomenon. For years, Paterno was a living hero of the gridiron. He was the coaches' coach, a model and a mentor to young men. The winningest coach in the history of college football, Paterno was also a major benefactor to the university and a national spokesman for numerous philanthropic causes. He was the individual whom every parent wanted their football-playing son to play for.

Paterno had many of the virtues on our list. But events revealed that he lacked at least two: moral judgment and compassion and care. When confronted with almost a decade of sordid and sexually predatory behavior by one of his leading staff members, the evidence suggests that Paterno turned his back.[21] It seems that the reputation of the football program and the university were more important to him than the emotional health of young boys. With this seeming neglect, Paterno abdicated his status as teacher, coach, and role model.

On Sunday, July 22, 2012, Joseph Vincent Paterno's statue was removed from its pedestal outside Penn State's Beaver Stadium and placed in storage. Nothing more clearly symbolizes his fall from grace. We saw that, in discussing virtue, Aristotle emphasized two things. First, that one should never count someone happy (or virtuous) until that person is dead. Sadly, Joe Paterno's fate tells us that failures can reach even *beyond* a person's lifetime. Aristotle's second point was that character is a construct. Virtue is habit; it requires ongoing, constant, and repetitive exercise. Each of the genuine paragons of virtue we have showcased in this book had his/her moral and personal failures, but each learned from these failures and increased his/her adherence to integrity and moral excellence. This lesson applies not just to presidents, generals, or CEOs. It is applicable to all of us as we strive to become outstanding leaders in our families, schools, workplaces, and communities.

Notes to Chapter Sixteen

1   See the collection edited by John Digby and published in London by S. Briscoe in 1712 under the title *Epicurus' Morals*, at p. 175 ("Vindication of Epicurus").

2   Deborah Ancona, Thomas W. Malone, Wanda J. Orlikowski, and Peter M. Singer, "In Praise of the Incomplete Leader." *Harvard Business Review*, February 2007, pp. 92–100.

3   Warren G. Bennis and Robert J. Thomas, *Geeks and Geezers*. Boston, MA: Harvard Business School Press, 2002, p. 1.

4   Warren G. Bennis and Robert J. Thomas, "Crucibles of Leadership." *Harvard Business Review*, 2004, p. 152.

5   Bennis and Thomas, *Geeks and Geezers*, p. 14.

6   Bennis and Thomas, "Crucibles of Leadership," p. 155.

7   Bennis and Thomas, *Geeks and Geezers*, pp. 17, 18.

8   Richard Stengel, *Nelson Mandela*. New York: Random House, 2010, p. 14.

9   Bennis and Thomas, *Geeks and Geezers*, p. 94.

10 Dorris Kearns Goodwin, *No Ordinary Time*. New York: Simon & Schuster, 1994, p. 17.

11 Nassir Ghaemi, *A First-Rate Madness: Uncovering the Links between Leadership and Mental Illness*. New York: Penguin Press, 2011.

12 James Fallows, "Obama, Explained." *The Atlantic*, March 2012. At www.theatlantic. com/magazine/print/2012/03/obama_explained/8874/.

13 Warren Bennis, *On Becoming a Leader*. New York: Basic Books, 2009, p. xxxii.

14　Will Durant, *The Story of Philosophy*. New York: Simon & Schuster, 1991, p. 76.
15　Robert K. Greenleaf, *Servant Leadership*. Mahwah, NJ: Paulist Press, 2002, p. 27.
16　Mihaly Csikszentmihalyi. *Finding Flow*. New York: Basic Books, 1997, p. 131.
17　Greenleaf, *Servant Leadership*, p. 359.
18　Stengel, *Nelson Mandela*, p. 8.
19　Ibid., p. 103.
20　Walter Isaacson, *Steve Jobs*. New York: Simon & Schuster, 2011.
21　Freeh Sporkin and Sullivan, LLP, "Report of the Special Investigative Counsel Regarding the Pennsylvania State University Related to the Child Sexual Abuse Committed by Gerald A. Sandusky," July 12, 2012. At http://thefreehreportonpsu. com/.

INDEX

10 Virtues of Outstanding Leaders: Leadership and Character, First Edition.
Al Gini and Ronald M. Green.
© 2013 John Wiley & Sons, Inc. Published 2013 by John Wiley & Sons, Inc.